# LISTENING TO
# SILENCE

PHILIP MARKS

ISBN 978-1-64003-050-3 (Paperback)
ISBN 978-1-64003-051-0 (Digital)

Covenant Books, Inc.
11661 Hwy 707
Murrells Inlet, SC 29576
www.covenantbooks.com

Dedication - *For my parents*

# Acknowledgements

The author offers his heartfelt appreciation and gratitude to Rachael Zorn Mitchell. Thank you for your meticulous attention to detail and unfeigned encouragement. You are the embodiment of true grace.

To Jeffrey Edmund Heath, Danny Lee Litowitz, Roy Willis McLean, James Edward Ripple and Mr. Mark C. Ulrich: Our friendship will endure forever.

And to Suzanne, Jeffrey, Nadia, Laura, Sean and a player to be named later. I shall love you with an everlasting love.

# Listening to Silence: Synopsis

Born with the gift of voice, Ginny Simmons is convinced by her lifelong friend Lorry Cullen to pursue a career as a professional singer. While attending the obscure Northern State University in the late '60s, Ginny discovers she suffers from massive stage fright with no confidence of ever fulfilling their shared dream. She overcomes her phobia with the help and guidance of freshman Matthew Jensen, Mattie, an astonishingly talented musician who is totally without guile and unfazed by Ginny's beauty. He mystically appears just before Lorry and Ginny decide to quit and kindly offers his extraordinary musical aptitude and skills to help Ginny truly discover and nurture her remarkable talent. Ginny's new confidence and unique gift ultimately send her on a breakneck rise from the obscurity of an isolated, small, backwater college town of Three Forks to performing at the Kennedy Center.

During their college years as performers, a tender yet platonic bond forms between Ginny and Mattie and peaks when Ginny realizes that she has fallen hopelessly in love with him. To her dismay, to her talented but bashful accompanist, it is a love of which he is unaware. Ginny is crushed when Mattie reveals that he has fallen in love with someone else, and she struggles for years with the need for forgiveness when her attempt to ruin the wedding of Matthew Jensen and Carrie Hardesty fails.

After college, their lives proceed on different pathways. With Lorry Cullen's shrewd and careful management, Ginny, with her extraordinary voice, becomes a worldwide phenomenon.

But Matthew Jensen's life is shattered by the death of his young wife, leaving him emotionally empty and totally inept to be both father and mother to his two young daughters. As a result, he helplessly descends into major depression disorder, an illness he recognizes has haunted him throughout his life. During his years of therapy, he frantically tries to understand the insidious nature of his mental illness, which has isolated him from his family, friends, and all things familiar. His children detest him for his absence in their lives. Those who have always been close to him neither accept nor comprehend that the once-cheerful and dauntless Matthew Jensen could so easily succumb to the abyss of despair.

After ten exhausting years of performing throughout the world, Ginny abruptly ends her career. She retires in exile to a life of solitude and loneliness until the indomitable and pugnacious Lorry Cullen reappears to hatch a meticulous plan to reunite Ginny and Matthew in an evening of intervention. Lorry also hopes that Matthew will find reconciliation with his now-grown daughters, who have disowned him, and with his old college friends from Northern State University. Hesitant at first, Matthew surrenders to Lorry's scheme, and it is with both great apprehension and, finally, relief that an evening of healing with his children, Shelly and Claire, results with the possibility of healing. The evening's affair rises to a crescendo when Ginny appears onstage, overwhelming one and all, but especially Matthew's daughters, who have no knowledge of their dad's previous relationship with the world-famous singer Virginia Simmons.

Ginny concludes this intervention by performing "Listening to Silence," a melody written years ago by Matthew but the lyrics recently written by Ginny. She desperately hopes the music and lyrics will have a magical and powerful impact on Matthew. Ginny Simmons hopes that the music he has abandoned long ago to grief may once again pulse through his veins, freeing him from his entangled restraints. She hopes that his capacity to give love and, most importantly, receive love will be restored. She hopes he has forgiven her.

Before the song begins, Ginny, whose love for Matthew has grown through the years, reaches out to him to join her onstage to perform "Listening to Silence," together, as it should be. The intention to reinforce the magic of a love that has never ended for Ginny is at first frightening for Matthew. Ginny's plan works, their song, the lyrics recently written by Ginny and the music written years before by Matthew, revives feelings he has thought lost forever and builds a fragile foundation with his children and reestablishes his cherished lifelong friends.

# PART ONE

Hide not your talents,
they for uses were made.
What's a sun-dial in the shade?

—Benjamin Franklin

# Three Forks

Even when wearing high heels, Lorry Cullen barely reached a height of five feet. She seemed to be the same height whether standing or seated, as she was now, wearing a flawless yet conservative dark-blue pin-striped Evan Picone suit. Lorry was presenting a new business proposition to the three very conservative members of the Three Forks Downtown Merchants Association. It was Lorry Cullen's intention to show the proper respect to the hierarchies of the Downtown Merchants Association regardless if she needed their approval to open a business or not. She was primly sitting with her knees pressed firmly together on a chair directly across the three cheerless men precariously perched upon rickety folding metal chairs behind a folding metal table that looked like it had been pilfered from the grade school cafeteria. The association had been established in the late 1940s with the sole intent of protecting their own interests by making swift and mocking denials to any notions of entrepreneurial spirit or the pursuit of new ideas. They had succeeded in denying any plans for enterprises that might compete for the dollars brought into the isolated college town of Three Forks, where the students and faculty stayed for nine months and then hastily fled like migratory birds. The empty town and allied businesses struggled to keep the doors open until their return. This predictable and notable flight enticed local merchants into gouging the captive and confined students and faculty with relentless and extortionate prices on even the simplest of goods and services and felt quite justified in so doing. It was beyond the simple practice of flagrant and impenitent greed; it was avaricious conquest. At times, Lorry Cullen facetiously wondered if Three Forks deliberately showcased itself to the rest of the world simply to prove how wretched and insignificant a town could become. Their prohibitive traditions and staunch refusals to budge had caused the decay and slow death of Three Forks, which now, as the opening of fall semester 1968 approached, had as many unoccupied crumbling buildings as there were occupied. Having already spent three years here at Northern State University as an undergraduate, Lorry knew that any new venture would be met with conservative skepticism. And although it was not Lorry's intent to push on any of the association's traditional boundaries, she would go from soup to nuts to persuade this obscure provincial community to accept her vision and would not leave the room until successful. Lorry Cullen had an indomitable spirit to achieve and was quite stubborn that, once her plans were set in motion, she would see them through to completion.

The Downtown Merchants Association met weekly, or as needed, in a suffocating small room purposely without the comfort of air-conditioning, with the intent of keeping meetings short and to the point. To be profitable, new and potential proprietors needed to launch their businesses during the crushing heat of late summer just before school began. The little room was originally the attic above the Main Rx Pharmacy and all-around general store that boasted the town's only snow-cone-making machine. The unventilated and smothering room reeked from decades of smoke residue deposited from cigarettes, cigars, and pipe tobacco. The wooden plank floor was stained by those who preferred chewing their tobacco but rarely hit their targets when spat toward. The walls had been painted white maybe once in the past twenty years but were now sallow and musty. The only adornment was an American flag in a broken stand that, appropriately, Lorry thought, leaned to the right. It had forty-eight stars.

Lorry Cullen was not intimidated by the miserable room or the three men. She sat still and poised upon a stout wooden chair with her toes barely touching the floor. Her confident but not-too-cocky stare toward the members of the Downtown Merchants Association made them fidget as she waited for them to make up their hesitant minds in the putrid squalor of the rank little room. Lorry Cullen had submitted a well-thought out and prepared business plan, had secured all the necessary city and county permits, and shown in the prospectus that she was very well financed. She didn't care if the college students left in a cloud of dust every June; her business would remain open throughout the summer. She also knew that her innovative vision for her new enterprise could very well revitalize the sorry little two-block retail district. She would not compete with the already-established businesses, most of which shut their doors promptly at six o'clock in the evening. Closed on Sundays.

A corpulent, wolfish-looking man with an unlighted bare-butt Pall Mall dangling from the left corner of his mouth stared at Lorry. He was wearing a cheap cotton shirt two sizes too small, with armpit stains the size of dinner plates. He smiled condescendingly at her and then lazily folded his hands on top of his greasy pompadour. He had tiny yellow teeth. The man to his left, who looked so much like the man in the middle that Lorry assumed they must be brothers, mimicked the gesture, only without the cigarette, as if on cue. It turned out, after introductions had been made as an afterthought, the two men were indeed brothers. The dominate man in the middle was Dan, and the man to his left was his younger brother, Stan Jr. They owned the hardware and farm store started by their father, presumably Stan Sr., right after World War II. The man seated to Dan's right was small and slim with a receding hairline and a wispy little start of a mustache. His name was Harley. He owned the gas station and auto repair shop that boasted a collection of license plates from every state in the union, except Alaska and Hawaii. But Harley figured that since they weren't connected, didn't really count. The shop had been passed down from his father. Harley also owned the theater and grocery store passed down from his father-in-law. He had a pleasant and friendly countenance that Lorry took a cursory liking to. He often quietly belched and seemed very embarrassed by this affliction, which the other two men ignored. His thinning blond hair was combed over from his right ear to his left. Lorry became momentarily mesmerized by his prominent Adam's apple, which bobbed in his skinny neck whenever he swallowed.

"So tell us again, darlin'?" Dan drawled in a lazy and conspiratorial tone. "What do you call this thing?" He glanced at the prospectus and spelled out loud, " B-I-S-T-R-O. How do you say that again?"

Lorry Cullen ignored the full frontal display of Dan's exposed girth and recited with precision the phonetic reply. "It's pronounced B-E-E-S-T-R-O, bistro. The spelling is different from the pronunciation."

Dan struck a match to light his Pall Mall but thought better of it after receiving an intimidating scowl from Lorry indicating that he'd better blow out the match and put that cigarette right back where it came from. Dan obeyed with a sheepish grin.

"Well, girly," he whined dismissively, "we think it's a long shot." He absently thumbed the prospectus like a deck of cards. "I mean, you're only gonna be open on weekends?" He closed the prospectus, dropped it on the table, and casually spun it around. Stan Jr. and Harley abandoned their copies in the same fashion. "And you're gonna have live music too? Who are you gonna to get to come all the way out here in the boonies to play?" Now reminded of the turbulent times in college campuses in 1968, he added, "Besides, it might attract, you know, the wrong kind of element."

Lorry had prepared for this confrontation, and with a full measure of calculation, she fixed a predetermined angry stare seemingly upon all three men at the same time. Her unflinching reply was calm and fearless. "As you can read in the prospectus, gentlemen, my business partner will provide the music. She sings. We will serve dinner from six o'clock until eight thirty, well after the other restaurant in town has closed for the night. She will perform from nine o'clock until midnight. We will seat up to thirty-five for dinner and allow up to seventy-five for performances and still be in compliance with your occupation codes. Gentlemen, as you know, we are geographically located exactly in the middle of nowhere. We have a built-in clientele of ten thousand college students all looking for something to do on the weekends, and I don't believe the counterculture will reach Three Forks anytime soon, if ever. We will provide the exact venue they're looking for. Or would you rather have demonstrations and burned-out buildings?"

As if they had been practicing, all three members of the Downtown Merchants Association removed their hands from the tops of their heads, folded their arms, and slouched in their metal chairs. The fat from Dan's thighs oozed over the sides.

"Well, darlin'," Dan drawled on, "we just think it's too much of a long shot. I mean, you're only what? Twenty-one? We think that you should just stay in school and . . ."

Feeling attacked by their condescending attitude, Lorry Cullen authoritatively took to her feet and placed her tiny hands on her tiny hips. The abrupt action startled the three men, who had rarely been faced with an obstinate act of any kind.

"Do not patronize me, sir. My name is Lorraine. It is not *darlin'*, *sugar*, *hon*, or *sis*. My name is Lorraine, and I would like to think, gentlemen, you would come to realize that the increasing number of empty buildings in your miserable little downtown district is not exactly a Norman Rockwell portrait of what a prosperous and thriving small town should look like. And for your information, I finished my degree in three years, and I shall be starting law school in two weeks." Lorry Cullen was also very fond of making dramatic hand gestures to enhance her more-passionate points.

The three members of the Downtown Business Association stared at Lorry in slack-jawed amazement. Dan's Pall Mall fell out of his mouth and rolled on the floor until it came to rest near his right foot. Later they would exclaim that her eyes had turned bloodred and hot steam had most certainly shot out from her ears. After a long and loud whispered conversation that included many hand gestures and facial distortions, Stan Jr. pounded his fists on the table and snorted, "Hell, I don't even remember who owns that building, and anyway, it's been empty for months. How did she even get permits?" They seemed to have forgotten that Lorry was even in the room.

Before their conversation could go further, Lorry Cullen interrupted them in a no-nonsense voice, "If you would examine the prospectus, gentlemen, it will reveal that my business partner and I own the building." With a cunning little grin, she added, "Well, that is, along with our dads."

Panting and greatly perspiring, like punch-drunk street fighters, the three members of the Downtown Merchants Association surrendered and slouched down as deep as their chairs would allow. Dan looked down and gingerly picked up the prospectus as if it were now a document of great importance. He managed a gruff retort, "Huh. So you don't really need our permission, do you?"

"No, we don't," Lorry Cullen replied with confidence but cordially added. "But we want the right thing for you and your town. And we feel it's crucial to have your approval."

Lorry Cullen then sat back down in her chair, like a queen upon her throne, and folded her hands on top of her tiny lap. With a sweet and inviting smile, knowing she had won the three men over, added, "We want to be good neighbors and even better friends. And I, or I should rather say we, me and my business partner, strongly feel that you would want the same. Yes?"

The three members of the Downtown Merchants Association quickly and quietly caucused once again. Dan, with his eyes cast slightly downward, compliantly asked, "What will you call your place, Lorraine?"

"We're calling it Ginny's Bistro. That's my business partner's name and my best friend."

Dan raised his chin. "Oh, and also, Lorraine, we were just talking. Would you consider joining the Downtown Merchants Association? Maybe we could meet at your new bistro?"

Lorry smiled. "I would like that very much, gentlemen. By the way, my friends call me Lorry. You can too."

Lorry Cullen shook hands with Dan, Stan Jr., and Harley and, with a burst of energy and excitement, thanked them for their valuable time, made a quick pirouette toward the door that led downstairs to the store and outside. She could feel their eyes upon her as she made her exit and heard Harley exclaim, "Wow. She's something else, yeah?"

Lorry took that as the compliment it was intended to be. She floated downstairs, left the store, and once released from the stagnation of the small office, greedily sucked in as much fresh air as she could. She blinked hard a few times to adjust to the strong sunlight reflecting off the sidewalk, gathered up the back of her hair, and secured it with a small barrette. And although it was already eighty-five degrees and climbing, she felt refreshed. She took off her coat and unbuttoned the top three buttons of her blouse. That done and feeling as comfortable as she could expect, she walked with quick little steps north on Main, toward the building that, in two weeks' time, would open as Ginny's Bistro, a small one-story brick structure located at the end of Main, where the sidewalk ended. Tufts of weedy grasses grew through the sidewalks cracks. The space had been vacant for the past two years, and Lorry Cullen kept her eyes on it, with the hope it would be available when she and Ginny were to that point in time when her business plan could be put into place.

Approaching the intersection of First and Main, she came upon a solitary figure, a young man, who, as she drew closer, appeared to be a rather fine-looking young man at that. He seemed lost or perplexed, perhaps both, and in apparent need of direction as Lorry noticed he was studying a small hand-drawn map of downtown. He now held the piece of paper at eye level to shield the sun's glare off the sidewalk. He was twirling the hair behind his right ear and was so deep in concentration that Lorry considered stopping to offer him help. But when she realized he was so oblivious to her approach, she quick-stepped past him, but not without first judging him to be a very, very fine-looking young man, tall and straight with an athletic build. They were the only two people on that side of the street, and Lorry expected him to at least take a surreptitious glance her way. She wondered how anybody could find themselves lost in this comatose two-street town, and besides, she had no time to waste, especially on someone who was obviously just another aimless freshman, no matter how good-looking he was.

The building Lorry was walking toward had been occupied by many failed establishments, most of them restaurants, throughout the '50s and '60s, all perishing in the hot summer months when the customer base predictably disappeared. Lorry Cullen had designed and formulated her business plan as an undergraduate and, at the end of spring semester 1968, submitted the project as her final and formal presentation before graduating. Her professor was so captivated by her work that he urged her to copyright the document before others discovered her ideas to claim as their own. She immediately complied and received some notoriety within the academic community for her accomplishment, mixed with a few cynical murmurs that, while the plan looked presentable, in theory, it still needed to be proved credible. The skeptics had ostensibly never enjoyed a pizza and for certain had never been thrilled to their core by the voice of Ginny Simmons.

# The Gift

Lorry Cullen and Ginny Simmons have been best friends since the second week of school when they were placed at the same table in Ms. Brown's fifth-grade classroom. They were eleven years old. The pairing took place after Lorry's original table mate, an insufferable little boy with dirty fingernails, had persistently disrupted her and teased that even first-graders were taller than she was but nonetheless insisted on being her boyfriend. He reeked from infrequent hygiene practices and dubious toothbrushing skills. He reminded Lorry of Eddie Munster, and having her fill of him after the first two weeks of school, she successfully persuaded Ms. Brown that the boy be either moved to the front row or banished to the back of the classroom as long as he was away from her. Ms. Brown complied with her prize pupil's request without pause and reassigned Ginny from the first row and the boy in her place where an eye could be kept on him. This new arrangement suited Ginny as she very much wanted to become friends with Lorry but was too shy to approach her, even during lunch.

Lorry Cullen's first words to Ginny Simmons were "Golly, you are so pretty."

Ginny blushed at the compliment. "Oh no, I'm not, but thank you."

It was during rehearsal of the fifth and sixth grade combined choir when Lorry, who had to stand in the first row to be seen, heard Ginny's stunning, beautiful voice and told her with her I-know-everything-grin, "Your voice is sensational, Ginny. I bet one day you'll become a great singer."

Ginny shook her head frightened of the notion. "Oh no, I don't think I could ever do that."

But Lorry, whose parents encouraged her to follow and act on her instincts because they were almost, almost always right, insisted, "But you could be a singer if you wanted to be. You have a gift."

Ginny Simmons indeed had been born with the gift of voice. She loved to sing but preferred hiding deep within the anonymity of large groups or in the sanctity of her bedroom, where she would stay awake as long as she could, listening to her transistor radio. Teachers at school and her church choir leader tried with little success to lure her into performing solo to show off her voice as something they had discovered. With Lorry's encouragement, however, she sometimes agreed, but only if they both felt the song was a good fit and she could remain within the security of the main choir body. Audiences strained their necks to locate the beautiful girl with the beautiful voice that stood out above all others. Her teachers informed Ginny's parents that she was pitch-perfect, a term neither of them understood.

"You need to put this young lady in as many talent shows as you can," her parents were told, badgered really. "Let us know what you decide. We'll be happy to help." The very idea, the very thought of anything like this, totally unnerved Ginny, who nearly became a petrified casualty in the battle over her talent. Sometimes she felt as if she should completely forget any notions of sharing her gift.

When they were fourteen, Ginny caught a feverish case of strep throat, and her parents quarantined her in the house for ten days. The only visitor allowed was Lorry Cullen, who had persuaded Ginny's parents that, because she had just recovered from her own strep infection, she was, therefore, immune to probably everything. She further argued with competency and excessive hand gestures that, due to their close friendship, she was the one to blame for Ginny's condition and must be allowed to see her in order to cheer her up. Ginny's father smiled as he always did when he could not resist his daughter's diminutive best friend's sweet form of obstinance and asked her to stay for dinner, which she did.

Illness notwithstanding, the two shared everything through-out their junior high and senior high school days, except for clothes. Lorry had to either buy her apparel from the children's sections of department stores or make her own clothes, always with Ginny's help. Lorry Cullen didn't suffer the angst and anxieties of her adoles-cent years as much as she pursued it and helped Ginny navigate her own challenges, especially when it came to boys who were drawn to her beautiful face, her long blond hair, and emerging figure. The two girls seemed to have a lot of first dates, one and done, or hitched and ditched, as they liked to say. Boys lacking maturity found Lorry too direct and competitive, as was her way. One fellow complained to a buddy that Lorry Cullen's favorite form of communication was the argument. During these times, Lorry assured Ginny that she was not as insecure as most thought, but was quiet and shy, making it diffi-cult for boys, who preferred talking about themselves, to draw even a few words out of her, let alone a conversation. Lorry ultimately deter-mined that she was not short but petite, not pugnacious but perky. Ginny was not aloof or haughty; she was reserved and bashful. Lorry concluded these results as simple prepubescent nonsense and very much looked forward to their college years, where she assumed there would be an abundance of mature men. Almost, almost always right.

Since their fifth-grade pairing and to the end of high school, Lorry and Ginny had become passionate devotees to music. Over the years, they had built an impressive and sizable collection of 45s and albums and listened to them without pause. They eagerly waited for the Sunday-night weekly broadcast of America's Top Forty and would alternate commandeering each other's living rooms. They knew the words to every song, the moves to every dance, and in the secure surroundings of a living room, Ginny performed both with infinite joy. It was during these evenings when Lorry Cullen recognized and became convinced that Ginny Simmons possessed not only a uniquely gifted voice, but also a rare and intrinsic talent with artistic skill one heard maybe three or four times in a lifetime. Both gained acceptance to Northern University when it became time for college, the huge urban school near home where one could disappear into the masses, not to be seen again until Christmas vacation. Rather, they opted for the obscure and distant Northern State University, Northern's ugly little cousin, about seven hundred miles inland from the coast, in the small agricultural town of Three Forks. It was an easy choice that their parents encouraged. They wished their daughters to grow and pursue their goals with the independence of making their own choices without their opinions, whether asked for or not.

*   *   *

Lorry reached the end of Main and entered the building that, in two weeks' time, would open as Ginny's Bistro. She stood in the entryway, let her eyes adjust from the bright sunshine, and without hesitation, began to supervise the renovations and construction. Gone was the rancid residue and odor of past restaurants, replaced with the tingling scent of ammonia. The dining area was finished, and the stage would be ready by the end of the day. She now applied her energy to the daunting task of hiring the right crew to cook, serve guests, bus tables, wash dishes, and clean up after closing. She felt uncharacteristically anxious over this process as few applicants fit the conditions as defined in the business plan, not to mention willing to work weekends. Lorry had hired five college students so far, but the business plan required six employees with at least two weeks' training, and she couldn't stand the notion of deviating from her plan. In the middle of wondering where number 6 would come from, the door opened, and a young man entered, silhouetted by the bright sunshine against the dark interior. Upon noticing that Lorry had to shield her eyes from the light, the young man quickly closed the door and waited for her eyes to readjust. Lorry asked with the abruptness of one whose train of thought had just been derailed, "Can I help you?"

"I hope so," came a quiet reply. "I have an interview at two o'clock." He handed her a sheet of paper. "This is my application, but I'm not sure whom to talk with."

Lorry snatched the application and answered him without looking up, "You talk to me. I'm Ms. Cullen." She glanced at her watch. "Hmm, and you're right on time too. Well, that's a good start." Lorry

Cullen then looked up at the young man's face. She drew a sharp breath, startled by his intrepid dark-blue eyes and a wonderfully honest face. The young man appeared two to three years younger than Lorry was and absently twirled the hair behind his right ear. He wondered if he'd already done something wrong.

He looked vaguely familiar to Lorry, and she asked with a quiver in her voice, "Have we met?"

"No, ma'am," he politely replied with a bashful smile. He pointed to the outside. "But you did just pass me on the sidewalk up the street a bit." He extended his right hand, which Lorry took without a second thought. "I'm Matt. Matt Jensen."

# Matthew

Matthew Aaron Jensen entered this world in May of 1950, wearing a sweet and innocent smile that seldom washed away. From infancy to being a teenager, he left a happy imprint on anyone who took notice of him, especially his four sisters, aged four to twelve years his senior. Upon arriving home from the hospital, his sisters greeted this new little stranger with spirited interest and passed him around like a bowl of popcorn.

"Oh, look at his eyes," the oldest sister burst with delight. "They're so blue." She whipped around to Mom, nearly dropping the baby on his head. "Do you think they'll stay that way?" she hopefully asked. "All of us have brown eyes."

Mom quickly snatched Matthew away and looked into the tiny yet intense midnight-blue eyes of her son. He returned her stare with an infectious and bashful smile, the likes she hadn't seen in her other children until they were at least three months old.

Mom whispered, "I sure hope so." She cradled him tight and gave Dad a quick smile and a wink, knowing what he was thinking: "At last, a boy." Growing up, Dad and Matthew played catch as often as they could, even in the rain. This is noteworthy in the Pacific Northwest, especially the part locals refer to as the Wet Side, which rarely receives no more than eighty cloudless days throughout the year. As wet and green as is the West Side of the Cascades, it counterpunches the brown and dry East Side.

The girls knew the household dynamic would change when Matthew needed a bedroom of his own, forcing the girls to double up, not so unheard of in a middle-class family full of baby boomers and living in a diverse blue-collar town just south Seattle. But they were so taken with their new baby brother that any resentment was short-lived and dismissed. And despite his unique position, the girls were quick to pick up that Mom and Dad treated him the same as they were treated, or as much as possible anyway.

In a home of five children whom Mom and Dad named with great affection the Wild Bunch, Matthew grew up affably content to watch and listen to the constant motion of slamming doors, crowded bathrooms, blaring music, and incessant laughter. He was naturally unpretentious and thoughtful, with an innate sympathetic reflex to help anyone he felt might be in need. He also possessed uncanny intuitive powers of observation. And so quiet his parents twice forgot to pack him into the station wagon before a family trip. It didn't take long before one of the girls snickered and asked, "Aren't you forgetting someone?" Dad would screech to a stop, U-turn for home in a panic, but be relieved to find his son patiently waiting on the front porch, twirling the hair behind his right ear. Mom scolded the girls for not alerting them. Laughter would break out as this was a routine spectacle, and they knew she was merely trying to blame them for her forgetfulness. Mom clutched her young towheaded son and, with her tears pouring out, apologized to him over and over. Matthew hugged her back and, in his gentle manner told her everything was okay and to please not be sad. He then looked at his sisters with his mesmerizing little smile, as if saying, "We got 'em again."

One Sunday afternoon as Dad was working outside in the yard, something he did often just for a little peace and quiet, the next door neighbor called over the fence, "How's that brood of yours doing, Art? There sure seems to a lot of coming and going."

Dad removed his Seattle Rainiers ball cap, scratched his head, and replied, "Well, pretty good, I guess. Never a dull moment, that's for sure." He leaned his rake against the fence and joined his neighbor, who kindly handed him a cold beer. "They all seem to have an overactive sense of humor, especially Matthew, although he's a pretty quiet kid. You'd think he'd want to be right in the middle of every-thing, but he seems content enough to just watch. He mostly keeps to himself and listens to music, obsessed with it, actually. Sometimes I wonder if he's just trying to stay out of the way, like me, don't ya know?" He tugged on his beer and, with due consideration, added, "He's a little unpredictable, always full of surprises. Bev had him at the doctor for a checkup last week, and the office has a false ceiling, you know the kind with panels that have the tiny holes in them? After looking at them for a while, he asked, 'Hey, Mom? Who wood-peckered those holes up there?'" Dad took a final swig of beer and chuckled. "Last night at dinner he asked us why birds don't get elec-trocuted while they're sitting on phone wires." I laughed and told him, "Just lucky, I guess." Dad suddenly got a faraway look in his eyes. "He's happiest when he's helping somebody, anybody. What a gift."

Matthew was so unperturbed and unruffled by the affairs of life that many times his sisters harassed him just to watch his reac-tion. Such goings-on were worth the potential but rarely parceled out discipline since little brother always enjoyed such great fun with his sisters. Matthew giggled with weak effort to try to worm out of their clutches, when sister number 2, Emily, pinned him to the floor and then tickled him into paralysis. Sisters 3 and 4, Lucy and Tess, grabbed his arms and wrestled him onto a chair where sister number 1, Katie, tied him up and then dragged him to the backyard patio until Mom called for dinner. Frightened, as her Mattie seemed to have vanished again, Mom searched the house from top floor to basement and in all the usual places. She naturally feared the worst. As her panic set in, Dad would arrive home from work and franti-cally join in the search. The girls, unable to control themselves any longer, broke into laughter. Exasperated, Mom and Dad raised their arms in surrender and asked what they'd done to him this time. With sublime satisfaction, Lucy confessed, "He's on the patio, Daddy." His sisters then retrieved their delighted little brother with the bashful smile, lifted him as if he were Caesar, and carried him to his place at the dinner table. Thoroughly vexed, Dad would ask, "Will someone please untie him so maybe we can have a peaceful dinner together for once."

Not to be undone or outmaneuvered, Matthew became quite accomplished with his own harmless, yet entertaining, pranks. His favorite, and one that never failed to amuse, was to sneak into the girls' bathroom late at night, ingeniously lift up the toilet cover and seat—strictly forbidden in a house with four teenage girls—and lay awake until he heard the splash and subsequent scream from the one who had just bottomed out. The high-pitched outcry of being stuck in the toilet, sometimes loud enough to wake the neighbors, created hysterics within the household but found Matthew bent in laughter, with which the rest of the family would join in when he squealed with delight, "Splashdown! Gotcha!" The victim would pry her damp rear end out from deep within the toilet, chase Matthew around the house until he was caught, and tickle him until he was sufficiently breathless and made to promise never to cause anyone to bottom out again. His sisters often retaliated, sneaking up behind him while he was cutting the lawn and opening up the garden hose on him. Prepared ahead of time, Matthew would hide a stash of water balloons, and the wet rumpus was on. Dad came home from work to find the lawn half cut, the mower on its side, and his kids lying down together side by side, eldest to youngest, sunning themselves dry in the backyard.

With his yard work only half finished, Mom and Dad reluctantly assigned additional chores to Matthew only to discover that their even-tempered son thoroughly enjoyed himself. He never considered extra tasks, no matter how unpleasant, as punishment. He inexplicably and cheerfully helped his sisters with their own extra chores to the point of embarrassment as they would receive the praise for their brother's hard work. But Matthew proved to be without conceit and would never think of betraying his sisters, or anyone else for that matter, an attribute that fascinated his sisters and made them adore and treasure him over and above what they thought was possible. During dinner on Matthew's tenth birthday, his sister Katie, home from Northern State University for this event she would not dream of missing, whispered to Mom, "He's golden, isn't he?" Mom teared up and nodded.

One unusual, tranquil evening in the Jensen household brought an unanticipated and astonishing incident that left a pleasant and unforgettable memory on the entire family. It occurred shortly after sixteen-year-old Emily's piano lesson with Mrs. Winkleman, an elderly woman who lived across the street in a rambling house with at least half an acre of lawn. Her ten-year-old brother, Matthew, climbed atop the piano bench and, with crisp expertise, flawlessly played every piece of music from Emily's lesson by memory and his own ear, including Beethoven's Moonlight Sonata in C-sharp Minor. Little was said of this phenomenon until Dad, while scanning the evening newspaper, heard the piano being played in the other room and proudly remarked that Emily was getting pretty darn good. It was brought to his attention that Emily was sitting next to him on the sofa, reading a biology textbook. She wasn't playing; it was Matthew. Dad looked at Emily in total bewilderment, as if he'd never seen her before, folded the paper on his lap, and quietly mused, "No way. Is it really?" One by one the entire family cautiously, almost ghostlike, gathered in the living room, listening to this prodigious, barefooted little brother, whose feet didn't even reach the petals. They could do nothing but gaze in stilled amazement.

This sensation was brought to Mrs. Winkleman's skeptical attention, and a deal was struck. If Matthew would cut the massive lawn for Mr. Winkleman, a detested task for his part, she would give Mathew free piano lessons in exchange. Matthew happily replied that the arrangement sounded fine to him, then asked what they would do during the winter.

Mrs. Winkleman, a woman difficult to impress and even harder to please, frowned at the boy and raised a single eyebrow. "Well, young man, we'll just have to figure something else out, won't we?" she answered.

After two months, Mrs. Winkleman told Mom and Dad that she had brought out every dusty and faded piece of sheet of music she owned. Matthew's talent was joyously baffling to her, and all she could tell him from this time forward was to simply practice. She gave Matthew a rarely given hug and gave Mom and Dad the number of an acquaintance who could take the boy to a higher level. They were quick to enroll their son with a more accomplished instructor. Matthew continued to cut Mr. and Mrs. Winkleman's lawn for free until he left for college.

Matthew developed a persistent, yet reasonable, preoccupation and fascination with making music and easily mastered every instrument he chose. Except for the oboe, which he figured nobody could master, so he didn't feel too bad. Regardless of genre, music seeped through the pores of his skin and flowed through the blood in his veins. For Christmas when he was twelve years old, his sisters pooled their money and bought him an electric guitar, a small amplifier, and five guitar lessons. After learning the basic chords, he taught himself the guitar and banjo with the same passion with which he had learned piano. He enrolled in every music class offered by his school and was often asked by teachers to accompany school productions or other special events, including weddings, parties, reunions, and even an occasional funeral. During summer vacation, he would ride the bus downtown and play in sandwich shops during lunch hour or sometimes on the street just for fun.

One day when Dad and a few of his fellow lawyer friends went out to lunch, he noticed a crowd gathered on the street outside his office. He soon recognized his son's unique voice and guitar style and then saw Matthew busking for pocket change. Dad elbowed his way through the crowd and dropped a single dollar into Matthew's guitar case, already heaped with bills and coins.

Matthew enthusiastically cried out, "Wow. Thanks, Dad!"

"You're welcome, son," Dad wryly replied. "Now go home and mow the lawn." The crowd vigorously laughed, clapped, and congratulated Dad on having such a talented son.

His music teachers also had friends, and friends of friends, who were in constant need of backup musicians for bands or groups. Matthew was always highly recommended. It was too bad, they would tell each other, that he was too young to play in the bars. He never hesitated to help, but found he was uncomfortable when receiving the praises from others. He found it much less difficult to offer praise to others rather than to receive praise for himself. One night after sitting in on lead guitar, when the regular was nowhere to be found, Matthew was asked by the group's leader to hold out his hand and, to his astonishment, found himself holding two one-hundred-dollar bills, quite a windfall for a sixteen-year-old.

"You're good, kid," he was told. "You should join the union." When he got home, he asked Dad what a union was.

Back when he was ten-years old, it was announced that Katie, his twenty-two-year-old sister, was engaged to be married. It was at this time that Matthew discovered a disturbing trait within himself; a sudden overwhelming feeling of desolation had seized him. It was something that he could only confide in to Dad. An undefinable sadness surged through him when he realized Katie would be leaving home for good. He felt dejected and conflicted even with all the wedding excitement going on around the house. Dad told him his feelings were natural but maybe he was taking things a little too hard; after all, getting married was a pretty normal thing and a happy occasion too. Even so, it was difficult for Matthew to put his feelings into words, especially at ten years old. He found himself jubilant one moment and dismal the next. And he felt guilty and helpless as these emotions swept through him, like being marooned on a vast, deserted wasteland. During these moments, he withdrew to his bedroom as often as he could. He found comfort in music and became consumed by it.

One Saturday afternoon, he heard five quick knocks on his bedroom door. It was Katie's secret knock; she didn't wait to be asked in. She sat on the bed next to her brother and put an arm tightly around him. He leaned into to her and quietly cried.

"I'm going to miss you, Mattie," she whispered. "I'm going to miss you so much."

"Me too," he answered. "It's really hard already. I don't know what to do."

She gently eased her embrace, straightened him up, and smiled a teary smile. "I need you to do something for me, buddy."

"Okay. What?"

"Well, since Dad is walking me down the aisle, I need you to walk Mom down the aisle right before us. Will you do that for me, Mattie?"

Matthew wiped his eyes and nose with his shirtsleeve and nodded. "Sure. I mean, if you need me to."

Katie wrapped him in a suffocating hug. "You don't know how much I need you to do this for me, Mattie. Thank you." She kissed his forehead, stood up, and grabbed his arm. "So let's practice, huh?" She stuck out her elbow. "Get up and grab on, you little goof!"

He immediately felt better with Katie on his arm as they practiced walking back and forth in the upstairs hallway. When he least suspected, Tess, Lucy, and Emily leaped from a bedroom, pounced on him, and helped Katie wrestle him to the floor, where he was tickled into breathless, blissful paralysis. This was their own little love language toward their brother.

In what seemed an impossibly short time, his sisters left one by one to discover their own paths, whether it was going to college, getting a job, traveling, or getting married. And for every time this happened, Matthew felt the indescribable and frightening grip of sadness crawl through his body and brain. He heard their voices in his head, but they were gone.

All alone in a quiet house, Matthew often contemplated these random periods of disturbing and sad thoughts, pondering where they came from. Once again, he made his concerns known to Dad, who silently studied this quiet son of his for some time before he spoke.

Finally, he said, "Mattie, you have the sweetest and kindest soul of anyone I've ever known. And an uncommon ability to feel what others are feeling, to know what others need before they know it themselves. Follow your heart and your conscience, and you'll discover inside yourself the wonderful young man we all know you've already become. I'm so proud of you, son. Great things lie before you. Just let them come to you, because I know, you'll always do the right thing."

Despite Dad's kind and encouraging words, Matthew felt waves of complex contradictions swim through his head. He didn't feel normal, at least what he reckoned normal to feel like. He felt disconnected and detached. But he did make up his mind; from that moment forward, he would try his best not to disappoint Dad and Mom, his sisters, or anyone else who came into his life, as much as he could anyway. But something, a feeling of vulnerability, lay deep inside, one that made him wonder if he would be able to match up to the challenges life presented. Would he succeed when times and events became difficult? Could he persevere through the conditions and the seasons of life?

Much later in his life, he would suffer through these apocryphal premonitions on more than one occasion. These awkward, troublesome entanglements and inhibitions lurked deep in his soul and rarely abandoned his thoughts. He became ever critical of himself and at times melancholy, preoccupied with misguided self-examination to the point of mental exhaustion.

Perhaps what he needed was simply a change in scenery. Perhaps he should go away.

# Yes, My Queen

Lorry held her gaze on Matt Jensen until his shuffling feet told her that she was making him a bit uneasy. She shook her head sharply to regain her composure, cleared her throat, and invited him to sit down so they could talk. They sat around an ancient solid oak table with six chairs around it. Matt noticed there were six other similar-looking tables with matching chairs all situated before a small raised stage in the final phase of construction. Electricians were busy setting up and testing the stage lights back and forth between the houselights.

"Don't let them bother you," Lorry said while concentrating on his application.

Matt replied, "It's okay. No bother at all." He noticed that the electricians, and everybody else for that matter, avoided eye contact with Lorry Cullen as they worked around her.

When the houselights flashed on, Matt noticed what appeared to be hand-stitched tapestries covering most of the tables. Earth-toned, beige, and light green, it felt comfortable, warm, and inviting. Artificial ferns poured out of macramé hangers, which dangled from the ceiling. Posters of old movie stars and celestial events covered the walls. The smell of freshly baked bread wafted from the kitchen.

Lorry cleared her throat again and began in her distinctive let's-get-right-to-the-point tone. "I need someone for restaurant work," she hurriedly said. "You'll have to bus tables, wash dishes, clean bathrooms—especially the women's—and stay to clean up after closing.

You'll have to make sure everything is ready for the next day before you can leave for the night."

Matt bobbed his head, indicating he understood, and Lorry repeated for emphasis, "The kitchen and bathrooms must be spotless and ready for the next day." Matt nodded again that her conditions were very clear.

Eyes filled with hope, she asked, "Do you have any experience with this kind of work?"

Matt pointed to an unread page of the application that listed over fifteen references. Lorry's head jolted back, impressed as she read glowing reports of Matt's work ethics and capabilities. "You don't mind working weekends, Matt?"

"No, Ms. Cullen. It's how I'm putting myself through school."

Lorry delicately held the application and realized she was acting like a condescending member of the Downtown Merchants Association. Her instinct told her to give the kid a chance. She looked again into his penetrating blue eyes as if they were daring her to ask him another question. She pursed her lips together and offered, "We start training a half hour from now. Can you be here?"

"Yes, Ms. Cullen, I sure can," he replied with a bashful smile that almost, almost made Lorry melt. "Thank you very much." Matt stood and once again offered his hand and helped her to her feet, a gesture that staggered her.

"All right then, Matt. I'll see you at three o'clock sharp." Lorry turned and quick-stepped toward the stage, thinking, *Now that's how you make a good impression.* The electricians hid from Lorry as she hopped up on the stage.

Matt sat back down to wait for the training session to start and continued to take the place in. He heard someone in a back room viciously pounding out "On the Sunny Side of the Street" on an out-of-tune piano. A woman's wonderful voice could be heard even through the construction noise. Matt sensed she was desperately trying to keep time to a pianist who was pounding on the keys like he was administering CPR. He twirled the hair behind his right ear and thought, *Jeez, that's just awful.*

At three o'clock sharp, five people emerged from the kitchen, cheerfully talking among themselves, and sat at a table next to Matt. The beautiful voice struggling against the erratic piano playing became louder and then softer when he saw Ms. Cullen emerge from a back room with the sour look of disgust on her face.

Lorry saw Matt sitting alone. "Would you mind joining the rest of us, Johnson?" She pointed. "Everyone, this is Mark Jackson. He's new."

Matt raised his hand to about ear level. "Um, actually it's Matt. Matt Jensen."

Clearly preoccupied, Lorry made a dismissive motion with her hand, and the rest of the crew amiably introduced one another to Matt. Lorry quick-stepped around the table and addressed the crew like a Marine Corps drill sergeant. All eyes followed her. The awful sound from the back room started up, causing a brief distraction. She pointed to Matt. "Since *Matt* is the new kid here, I'll remind all of you what we'll be starting here two weeks from today." She stared at Matt to make sure she had his full attention. "Because our main clientele will be our fellow college students, we'll be serving a simple fare at an affordable price. Pizza. Just pizza and nothing else but pizza, at least for our first year." She made a quick pirouette and continued with Matt's eyes glued to her. "Every pizza will be fourteen inches in diameter, no smaller, no larger. Because we're dealing with perishable food items, I've limited the selection to four varieties: cheese, sausage, pepperoni, and a combo. Take-out orders will be welcome but not without at least a one-hour notice in advance. I will tend the phone. Our beverages will be water and soft drinks. We will serve from six thirty to eight thirty. At that time, the kitchen will close. That will give you time to arrange the dining area for performances and start washing dishes. I want as little clatter as possible coming from the kitchen when Ginny begins performing at nine o'clock. Anybody coming just for the performance will be charged a two-dollar cover charge. During performances, we'll serve bread, cheese, and fruit all prepared beforehand. There will also be wine, one white and one red. I thought of getting a liquor license, but it's like trying to infiltrate the CIA, just too much of a hassle. Besides, anyone serving hard liquor has to be over twenty-one years of age. Now, you all have your assigned jobs. Cooks will need to be here two hours before opening to bake the crusts, bread, and to prepare toppings. Bussers and dishwashers must arrive one hour before opening to prepare tables and organize dishware. You will be under the cook's charge."

The unpleasant sound from the back room stopped, and an angry man's loud voice could be heard by all. Lorry hesitated and pursed her lips for a moment and made a slight turn before stopping. "Any questions then?"

Matt raised his hand among a quiet hush of voices around the table. They all knew what he didn't, that it was a rhetorical question and should not be replied to. "Yes, Jensen?" Lorry demanded.

"Wh-what's going on back there?"

Lorry looked tired and worried. "It's a rehearsal," she said quietly. "Ginny and our new accompanist are trying to put together our opening night's performance. Fortunately, they have two weeks to figure things out. Okay, anything else? Anyone?"

Matt raised his hand and Lorry put her hands on her tiny hips, her patience running thin. "What *is it*, Jensen?"

"Have you considered a soft opening?"

Lorry almost shouted back, "A soft opening? And what exactly is a soft opening?"

Matt stood and leaned against his chair. He noticed his fellow crew members squirm in their seats as he walked toward Lorry. "A soft opening is like a dress rehearsal. You know, a practice run to work on any, um, unforeseen issues. A few customers are invited, and we all work as if it was the real thing. Only it's all for free."

Lorry Cullen stood in shock, totally unaware. She'd never thought of such a thing, and it wasn't in her business plan. She recognized the value of such an event and was also very impressed that the idea came from a dishwasher and a freshman dishwasher at that. She found Matt in front of her and spoke almost as if she were speaking to herself. "Well, I-I think that's something very important to think about. Yes, yes, of course we should have a soft opening, definitely. Thank you, Jensen."

Matt looked down at her with his bashful smile. "Well, Ms. Cullen. It's just an idea. I'm sure you would have thought of it."

Lorry found herself once again mesmerized by his dark-blue eyes. She gathered her senses and asked just above a whisper, "Any other questions?" She looked at the rest of the crew but found nothing but wide-eyed stares. She extended her hand to Matt. "So we're all good, right?"

Matt clasped both his hands around Lorry's and held them tight. He smiled at her and ventured a reply he'd often use with his sisters, "Yes, my queen."

Lorry narrowed her eyes into a no-nonsense stare, relaxed, and laughed. "I think you're going to work out fine, Jensen."

"I hope so, Ms. Cullen."

"Please, Matt. Call me Lorry."

# Just a Sixteenth Note
# Late (or Early)

"How's our new guy doing? Matt?" Lorry asked the other kitchen member, Debbie, who was polishing silverware.

"He's great," Debbie replied with enthusiasm. "He's a really hard worker, has the routine down pat." Debbie winked at Lorry. "He's pretty nice to look at too."

Lorry moaned, "Oh, come on, Debbie. Is this going to be a problem?"

Debbie pouted a little. "Hardly. He doesn't talk. I mean, he hasn't said two words since he started. He's very polite."

"Quiet, respectful, and hardworking," Lorry judged with a grin. "What's not to like?"

"You forgot handsome, Lorry."

"Did I?"

Preparations were precisely on schedule for the soft opening, with the exception of the contentious music director. Ginny, thinking that the fault was hers, had tried and worked hard to accommodate the musician's direction, but the two couldn't tie the songs together. Lorry hired the man, Bruce, who was a graduate student in music theory and composition at NSU but had come to regret the decision, and the two exchanged harsh words more than once. It was plain that Ginny's confidence was greatly damaged, and she sat slumped down with her arms tightly wrapped around herself whenever Lorry and Bruce went toe-to-toe. The two sat together in the rehearsal room right after Bruce had stormed out, threatening to quit. Ginny was near tears.

"What are we going to do? This isn't working out, and we have to be ready in two days." Both knew that it didn't matter how many cheap pizzas Lorry sold; if the performances weren't good, there wouldn't be anybody to serve them to.

"We're stuck with Bruce for right now," Lorry fumed. "And he knows it too. I'll start looking for somebody to replace him." She looked around the room and sighed, "But I don't know where to begin." Auditions would be difficult at this point as fall semester was just under way.

Ginny painfully stood, her body sagged in defeat, her joy of singing vanquished.

"I'm going for a walk." She left the stuffy rehearsal room and entered the cool, air-conditioned dining area. Walking in a slow circle around the empty room, she couldn't help but admire the exceptional work Lorry had done in setting up the restaurant and training the crew. She felt the magnitude of the stress, knowing the entire venture rested upon her. But she also knew deep within herself that she could be successful with the right accompanist and instrumentation. Bruce, "the maestro," seemed more interested in establishing himself as the main performer. He was turning Ginny into a secondary role, a backup player. She lightly touched the hanging ferns, the tapestries and smiled at the large blackboard near the entrance that announced campus clubs along with up and coming events, especially the Frisbee club and the Four H saddle club for the folks from town. She and Lorry wanted the bistro a place where people could feel comfortable and safe.

She was surprised to hear dishes banging from inside the kitchen. The crew was off for the afternoon; neither Ginny nor Lorry wanted them to hear that things weren't going well in the rehearsal room. Ginny opened the kitchen's swivel door, peeked inside, and saw who she surmised was the new guy Lorry had told her about. He was so absorbed in fussing and fidgeting over the placement of each pizza pan that he took no notice of Ginny.

"Well, hello there," she said softly.

Completely startled, Matt reacted with a shriek and dropped the metal pizza pans he was in middle of stacking.

Ginny covered her mouth. "Oh, I am so sorry. I thought you heard me come in. You must be the new crew member Lorry told me about. Mark, I believe?"

Matt was on his knees, picking up the dropped pans, and replied with a chuckle, "It's Matt. Yes, I'm the new guy."

"I'm Ginny Simmons. It's nice to meet you."

Matt placed the pizza pans on the shelf and turned toward Ginny. "Thanks, it's nice . . ."

Matt was stunned speechless. Standing before him with a pleasant smile of perfect teeth, which sparkled like jewels, was the most strikingly beautiful young woman he'd ever seen. He judged her to be about five feet and six inches tall with glorious blond hair that loosely fell to the middle of her back. Her face was pale but flawless. He followed her high cheekbones and examined her delicate doelike brown eyes that glowed like a beach fire on a dark night. Her graceful neck connected to her slender body, which remained motionless before him.

"To meet you too. I'm Matthew. Matt."

"Well, Matthew. I'm sorry to have interrupted. I just wanted to say hello."

"It's okay," he replied. "No harm done. Are you the singer we've been hearing?"

"Yes," Ginny warily replied. "That's me."

"You have quite a talent, if you don't mind me saying."

They stood perfectly still, each curious about the other. Ginny was used to being stared at, but not as genuinely as this, and Matt wasn't used to anybody staring at him. He eventually made a slight motion and pointed to the remaining dishes in the dishwasher. "Well," he mumbled and cleared his throat, "best get to it I guess."

"Right," Ginny answered. "We'll see each other again, no doubt."

Matt nodded once, unable to make a reply.

The crew assembled the next day promptly at eleven thirty in the morning as per Lorry's instructions. In a very unlike fashion, however, Lorry was nowhere to be seen. Matt sat in silence amid the chatter that had started in Lorry's absence, when the entire group was startled by a furious explosion of expletives coming from the rehearsal room, where none were allowed to enter. They heard Lorry scream, "We have only thirty hours before the soft opening. Why can't you get it together?"

An enraged and overbearing man's voice screamed, "I'm not the problem. Your vocalist is the one who can't get anything right."

"Oh, that's bullshit!" Lorry screamed back.

The crew looked wide-eyed at each other, including Matt. The door to the rehearsal room whipped open, and a short man with shaggy, unkempt hair and a desperate attempt to grow a beard emerged. He shouted, "I'm done. I can't work with a no-talent loser like her." He stared straight ahead and rushed toward the exit, expecting to be called back with an apology that never came. Abandoned pages of sheet music lazily floated to the floor. Matt stood and carefully picked up the sheets, keenly studied each one, and walked toward the rehearsal room.

"Matt, don't," Debbie hushed. "We're not allowed in there."

As he approached the entry to the forbidden room, he could hear Ginny crying and Lorry fuming. "Let's just push the date back," he heard Ginny say. "We can tell them we had a failure. We don't have to be specific."

"We can't Ginny. Tomorrow is already set up, and we don't want those guys from the Downtown Merchants Association to be a bunch of I-told-you-so smart-asses." Lorry had invited Dan, Stan Jr., Harley, and their families to the soft opening.

Matt softly knocked. "Excuse me?"

Lorry snapped around and hissed, "Oh, what in the hell do you want, Jackson? Can't you see we're busy?"

"We couldn't help but overhear the trouble you're having."

Lorry was ready to explode but caught a glint in his intrepid eyes that told her he might have something useful to say. "Well," she demanded to know, "what is it?"

Matt shuffled his feet and twirled his hair. "Your piano player was always a sixteenth note off. Sometimes early, sometimes late."

Lorry was caught by surprised. "What are you talking about, Jensen? What does that mean?"

Rather than answer, Matt tactfully added, "And he always started Ms. Simmons out in C major. Anybody can tell she's a natural E-flat major."

Lorry's face turned an aflamed shade of bright red, her fury building. She repeated, "What does that mean, Jensen?"

"It means she's singing in the wrong key."

"Oh, really?" Lorry challenged and defiantly motioned to the piano. "I suppose *you* can do better?"

Matt breathed deep and sat on the piano bench. He slowly twirled the hair behind his right ear and kicked off his shoes. "Keep in mind that this is the backup instrument," he said. "The real instrument in is Ms. Simmons's voice."

Neither Lorry nor Ginny understood. He bashfully smiled at Ginny. "Ready?"

Ginny warily nodded, and in an instant, Matt began the introduction for "On the Sunny Side of the Street" in the proper key. Ginny found her voice and easily sang the vocal. She finished the song with a delighted and satisfied look of finally connecting to the music.

Matt shrugged. "See? E flat major."

Lorry placed her tiny hands on her tiny hips with grudging concession. "All right, Jensen, you made your point. Is there anything else?"

Matt shyly replied, his eyes straight ahead and slightly downcast. "This piano is out of tune." He was so innocent and sincere that Lorry didn't know how to reply.

"Fine, then. At least that's one thing we can fix before tomorrow."

Matt offered, "I'd be happy to tune it for you. I'm sure I can borrow the tools from the music department. I mean, they don't know me like they know you."

Lorry surrendered her arms and suppressed a smile. She looked at Ginny, who, by this time, had recovered from the uncompromising Bruce and beamed with confidence. "Is there anything else, Jensen?" she sighed.

Matt answered, "I'm sure your playlist is set for tomorrow night. I'll be glad to help out until you can find a replacement." He asked for the seven songs selected for the soft opening and studied them to make sure all the major root chords could accommodate E flat major. "Oh, sure," he brightly said. "It's all piano. I can cover these, I mean, if you'd like me to." He looked at Ginny's eager eyes and then back down to Lorry's hard stare.

"You're sure you can play this music?" Lorry dubiously asked.

"Yes, ma'am."

She looked at Ginny. "Do you think it's all right?"

Ginny softly answered, her body in motion, "Yes. No problem."

Lorry seemed reluctantly satisfied. "Okay, Jensen. You're our guy for tomorrow."

Matt looked at Ginny. "Maybe we can rehearse tonight? Around seven o'clock?"

Ginny threw him a sunbeam of a smile that lit up the room. "Absolutely."

# Soft Landing

Matt had the piano, an older but sturdy Baldwin baby grand, tuned up about twenty minutes before Ginny was due to arrive. She found him sitting on the floor in the rehearsal room with the sheet music for the soft landing spread around him. Concerned that she'd scare the living daylights out of him for a second time, she moved silently into the room and leaned against a wall. She curiously watched him study each page with unabridged concentration. He held a pencil firm between his lips, with which he would make notations every few measures.

"I'm familiar with a couple of these," he said without looking up. "But I'm going to have to learn some of these songs in a hurry." He raised his head and smiled at Ginny. "Unless Lorry will let me read off sheet music tomorrow night. Do you think she'd mind?"

Wondering how he knew she was there, Ginny replied, "No, not at all. I mean, considering this must all be very new for you."

Matt shrugged and waved over the sheets. "They're mostly show tunes. I'll be okay, passable anyway."

He studied Ginny and politely asked, "How are you doing? That's the real question, right? Do you feel ready for all this?"

Ginny's eyes darted back and forth. "I'm not sure at the moment. Sometimes I kind of suffer from massive stage fright."

"Well then," Matt began enthusiastically, "best get to it." He gathered the sheets of music off the floor and stood. "Is this the piano we're using tomorrow night?" Ginny nodded that it was. "Why don't we roll it out so you can get a feel for the stage?"

Ginny agreed and eagerly offered, "Do you need some help?"

"No, thanks. It's on castors, so it should be a cinch." He handed the music to Ginny, released the castors, and easily pushed the Baldwin through the rehearsal room and to the stage area and asked, "Where are you thinking of putting this?"

Ginny pointed to the far right corner of the stage. "Bruce, your predecessor, wanted over there."

Matt answered quickly, "If we put it there, I'm afraid it might drown out your voice too much. Remember, the instrument supports your voice, not the other way around." He studied the stage with great concentration from all points of the dining area then pushed the piano to the left side of the stage, but not quite in the middle.

"Let's try it here," he suggested. "You'll be able to pick up the notes better, and we'll have good eye contact. That will be important, especially tomorrow night. Also, I'll look around for a carpet for the floor."

Ginny thought, *Bruce was never this nice or helpful,* and felt her confidence grow. "Sounds great," she said.

"So," Matt asked, " how do you like to warm up? Any special way?"

Ginny was completely caught off guard. Bruce had never allowed her to warm up her voice. "I'm not sure," she replied. "How do other people do it?"

Matt shrugged his shoulders. "Well," he considered, "there are a few techniques. Some vocalists like to run scales, and others just match notes until they feel ready." He noticed that Ginny didn't know what to do, so rather than embarrass her, he made a suggestion. "Why don't we start by matching notes, okay? That will help me learn your range. Do you know Roy Orbison has a five-octave range? Pretty amazing, don't you think?" Ginny shook her head, indicating she wasn't aware of that. "Well, anyway," Matt continued, "let's start by matching notes."

Ginny fidgeted in place. "Before we start, can I ask you a question?"

Matt replied, "Yeah, sure."

"Why are you barefoot?"

Matt blushed, and Ginny thought he was annoyed like Bruce would have been. Instead he shyly smiled. "Um, I always have. I don't really know why. I guess it just feels more comfortable. Maybe I get a better feel for the pedals. I don't know." He laughed. "Shoes are confining."

He struck middle E-flat, and Ginny immediately matched the note. He dropped an octave to bass clef, and again Ginny matched the note in perfect pitch. He played back and forth, bass clef to treble, raising and lower octaves. Ginny responded to every note in her clean, distinct tone. Finally, Matt struck a high E-flat. Ginny struggled at first, but by forcefully engaging her diaphragm, she hit the note precisely on key and held it as long as she could.

"Nice, Ginny," Matt encouraged. "Five-octave range, just like ol' Roy."

Ginny was astonished. "I-I didn't know I could do that."

"Let's run some scales, all right?" Ginny excitedly nodded. Matt played them all: C major, C-sharp minor, D-flat, E-flat, F-sharp, G, and A minor, up and down the keys until he said with a grin, "I think you're pretty much warmed up, Ginny."

Ginny laughed. "It sure feels like it. I'm sweating."

Matt tilted his head and smiled, "Girls don't sweat, Ginny. You elegantly perspire."

They practiced the seven songs for tomorrow night's soft opening, and in a way Bruce had never offered, Matt said, "You have to tell me what's right for you, Ginny. We want to do this your way."

She walked to the piano and sat down beside him, causing Matt to uncomfortably slide a few inches away from her. She noticed the pencil notations Matt had made on the sheet music. They indicated the specific dynamics, the accents, crescendos, and decrescendos in the way he was to present the music.

She asked, "Would you mind having a dress rehearsal, Matt? Say, around four o'clock?"

He was quick to accept and then began to gather the sheet music. Ginny turned off the lights and began to leave. Neither noticed it was after midnight. After locking the door, she looked up and down the deserted street and sighed. "Lorry is supposed to be here to pick me up. I guess she, um, got held up somewhere. She had a date tonight."

"Let me walk you home then," Matt offered.

"Oh no, Matt, I'm sure it's far out of your way."

Matt looked up into the clear, quiet night, washed bright by the Milky Way. "Wow. What a perfect night. I think I'd enjoy it."

Ginny gratefully accepted Matt's offer. "Well, okay. That would be nice." She pointed to the hill rising above First. "It's that way."

They walked south on Main, turned right onto First, and climbed the hill. Neither was very adept in the art of conversation, so not much was said along the way. After twenty minutes of climbing the hill, Ginny stopped and said, "Here we are." She stared into his distinct midnight-blue eyes, which seemed to glow, even in the dark.

She was almost ready to invite him inside, when Matt said, "Good night, Ginny. You're going to be great tomorrow." He shook her hand, turned sharply, and walked back down First toward home.

"Thank you, Matt," Ginny whispered, but he was too far away to hear.

Minutes later, Lorry arrived, her clothing disheveled and her hair uncombed. "I stopped at the bistro, but you'd already left. I'm sorry." She couldn't help but notice Ginny's dreamlike trance. "How did it go tonight? Do you think he can do it?"

Her reverie broken, Ginny replied with wide eyes, "He's perfect," and smiled.

*　　*　　*

Lorry Cullen had second and third thoughts over inviting Dan, Stan Jr., Harley, and their families to the soft opening. Maybe inviting a group of her college friends, who would not be as critical, would have been a better idea. Earlier in the day, she had stopped by Dan's farm store just to confirm how many people she should expect. Dan lazily rubbed his chin and said, "About eighteen I'spect. Can you handle that many?"

"Yes, Dan," she replied acerbically enough to let Dan know that she didn't appreciate his attitude.

Dan nodded an apologetic nod and then sincerely asked, "How's it all coming together for you, Lorry?"

Lorry sighed. "Well, except for a temperamental pianist who walked out on us yesterday, everything is going fine. We found a replacement that Ginny seems to like, but I haven't heard him yet. He was my dishwasher, so that means I'm down one kitchen hand, at least for tonight."

Dan looked at her thoughtfully for a few seconds, put his pinky fingers in his mouth, and loudly whistled. "Hey, Bobby!" he shouted. "Come in here."

Before long, a rawboned youth with stringy long hair and terrible acne emerged from the back warehouse. Dan jerked his head toward Lorry. "This is Bobby, my oldest, just graduated from high school. I think he's looking for somethin' else to do besides buckin' bales for me all day long."

Lorry instantly recognized that hiring Bobby would go a long way into gaining Dan's good graces. Dan knew it too.

She looked the skinny youngster up and down. "I need a dishwasher, at least for tonight. I'll pay you three fifty an hour, and you'll work from five o'clock until midnight."

Bobby nodded that he understood. Lorry glanced to Dan, who bobbed his head in appreciation. "He'll be there at five o'clock sharp," he said while staring Bobby down. "Now go get cleaned up, son. And get a haircut."

Dan turned to Lorry and said, "Best make that seventeen."

Lorry bowed her head and smiled a coquettish smile. She cocked her head to the left and looked up at Dan. "See you at six o'clock." She turned to leave and, over her shoulder, added, "Sharp."

*   *   *

The sweet aroma of baking pizza crusts pleasantly drifted through the bistro as Lorry addressed the staff. "Listen up, people. There are a few last-minute changes." She gestured toward Matt. "Johnson here is going to fill in for Bruce, who, as you saw yesterday, decided to part ways with us." She looked at Matt. "Remember, Johnson, it's just for tonight, capisce?" Matt nodded that he understood and made no attempt to remind Lorry that his name was Jensen as she continued talking while circling the staff. "I'm going to canvas this town and school for a permanent replacement during the next two weeks. And I have a kid coming in tonight to take Jensen's place in the kitchen." Debbie frowned at this news. "Our guests will be here at six o'clock, and we'll serve them as if this were the real thing. Ginny will start at seven o'clock, which I know is early, but I think we'll be dealing with a bunch that likes to be in bed by ten o'clock." The staff laughed. "And remember, this is much more than a soft opening. Tonight we'll prove to these people that we belong here." She looked at Matt. "Any questions?" Matt shook his head to indicate that he had neither any questions nor tidbits of helpful information. Lorry checked her watch. "It's now three o'clock. I'll see all of you at five o'clock, and please be ready to go."

After the staff departed, Lorry looked at the stage, placed her tiny hands on her tiny waist, and demanded, "What is the piano doing there?" She spun about and gave Matt a menacing stare.

"We put it there last night so Ginny could get familiar to the stage," Matt dutifully answered.

"Hmm, good idea, Johnson," she grudgingly acknowledged. "I assume you're ready?"

"We're going to have a dress rehearsal at four o'clock, just to work out any possible kinks," Matt said.

Lorry threw her arms up. "We don't need any kinks tonight, Jensen. Got it?"

"Right, Lorry." Matt bashfully smiled. "No kinks. I promise."

Lorry dubiously shook her head and turned away.

At three thirty, just hours before the soft opening, Lorry heard someone playing scales on the piano by the stage very rapidly and with meticulous efficiency. She immediately stopped her task at hand and cautiously quick-stepped to the stage area. A five-foot-long, four-foot-high planter full of artificial ferns had been moved to separate and hide the piano from the dining area. She timidly peeked around the planter to find Matt warming up.

"I usually just crack my knuckles," Matt said, leaving her to wonder how he knew she was watching him. He faced her and shyly admitted, "But since tonight is special, I figured I should warm up a little before Ginny gets here."

Lorry blankly nodded and silently retreated. "Would you tell Ginny that I have to go buy my books for this semester?" She quickly added, "But I'll be back no later than four thirty."

Ginny arrived at four o'clock and rapidly paced around the stage, urgently nervous. Matt noticed and offered, "Don't worry, Ginny. You'll be fine."

Ginny was on the verge of tears, her head down, while rapidly pacing around the stage. She was rigorously wringing her hands. "I can't do this, Matt. I can't sing in front of a crowd by myself. I mean, I've never done anything like this before. There's just no way, no way at all."

Matt walked over and stood before her, eye to eye, his midnight-blue eyes brightly shining. "Trust me," he softly told her. "Watch me, I'll help you." He took one step closer, only inches from her face. "You need to always remember: You're perfect."

Lorry, carrying a bag full of law books that possibly weighed more than she did, arrived soon after. She dropped the books with a loud thud, looked at Matt, and said, "All right, let's hear it."

She walked to the far end of the bistro's dining area to check the sound. The instant Ginny and Matt began, she was overwhelmed by amazement, not only with Matt's precision on the piano, but how comfortable Ginny seemed with the accompanist as if her every worry had instantly vaporized and been blown away. Lorry had been listening to Ginny for nearly eleven years, but never with such clarity and precision. At the end of the set, she absentmindedly sat down, her mouth agape in wonder. Collecting her thoughts, she finally spoke, "It sounds like you two are ready."

With her confidence rediscovered, Ginny clapped her hands with delight. "I told you, Lorry. I told you he's perfect!"

Lorry looked to Matt, who was uneasily fidgeting on the piano bench. "Well," she muttered, "it seems so." She walked away in astonishment, not the easiest feat to accomplish.

Matt asked Ginny to join him at the piano and handed her four pages of sheet music. "I checked this out from the music library," he said. "Do you know this song?"

Ginny nodded. "I've heard it, but I've never sung it before."

"Let's use it as your encore," Matt suggested.

"Encore?" Ginny precariously replied and repeated, "What encore?"

"There will be an encore, Ginny, believe me." Matt reached behind the piano bench and grabbed a music stand. Handing it to Ginny, he said, "I think, just for tonight, you can use sheet music, if you it makes you feel more comfortable. Just watch me, and you'll be fine."

Precisely at six o'clock, Lorry Cullen opened the entryway doors to find Dan, Stan Jr., Harley, along with their wives and children, already waiting outside. Dan was wearing a button-down shirt and tie as long as a '56 Cadillac. His sport coat appeared two sizes too small. Regardless, he managed to fasten one button. The smell of cheap beer seeped out of him. Stan Jr. was similarly dressed, only his clothes fit a tad better. Harley was wearing a brand-new pair of Levi's that looked so stiff Lorry wondered how he was going to sit. He had on a new western-style shirt buttoned to his chin. His wife hastily pulled off a tag from behind.

"Oh my," Lorry exclaimed. "You all look so nice. Please, come in, come in." She escorted the shuffling group to the tables in front of the stage. The adults sat together, and the children spread out on tables to either side.

Dan bent down low and whispered to Lorry, "Did Bobby show up on time?"

Lorry smiled encouragingly. "He sure did, Dan." She added, "He's a really good worker too."

Dan arched his eyebrows in surprise. "Well, that's unexpected good news."

Lorry nodded to the servers, who sprung to their duties, bringing glasses of water and menus. "We'll give you folks a few minutes to look over the menu," Lorry said. Dan and Stan Jr. looked a little forlorn when they discovered that beer was not offered and even more so when they noticed No Smoking signs posted on every wall, even in the men's room.

After exactly four and a half minutes, three servers swiftly appeared, one for each table. "What can we make for you tonight?" they asked in unison.

Dan spoke for the entire group. "We'll have three of everything," he announced, but let each person select their own soft drink. Baskets of breadsticks, lightly spread with olive oil and a touch of garlic, were quickly provided and quickly consumed. Lorry ducked into the kitchen and asked the cooks where the olive oil and garlic came from. She was told that it was Matt's idea and suspiciously took a bite of one. "Wow," she grudgingly admitted, "that's good."

"We spread a little on the crusts too," one of the cooks reluctantly admitted. Lorry responded with a "We'll see about that" look but said nothing.

Exactly seven and a half minutes later, fifteen steaming-hot pizzas were delivered, and the guests eagerly sampled each type. The servers now let their guests enjoy their dinner, except for briskly refilling soft drinks and water. Lorry appeared every five minutes and rather apprehensively asked how everyone was doing. Dan gave her a gracious nod of approval.

After exactly thirty-five minutes, three bussers, including a very nicely cleaned-up Bobby, emerged from the kitchen to clear the tables. Five minutes later, four bottles of wine, two white and two red, were placed at the adult table. Plates of cheeses, fruit and warm bread, lightly spread with olive oil and garlic, soon followed.

Without warning, the houselights dimmed, causing general murmuring that came to an abrupt stop when the stage lights came up revealing Ginny standing at center stage, glowing like Glinda, the Good Witch of the North. She wore a casual yellow cotton dress, which hemmed just below her knees, and was wearing a light, faded jean jacket. Her blond hair fell loosely past her shoulders, with a small blue ribbon tied to the side. As the guests gasped at her beauty, she began to sing "On the Sunny Side of the Street" slowly and a capella. Standing out of the sight of her guests, Lorry raised her hands and mouthed, "What are you doing?" Ginny smiled and winked as if to say "Wait and you'll find out." After holding the final note on the first line for about five measures, she stopped and looked at Matt, who nodded. She began the song again in the upbeat style of its true intent. Matt came in on the downbeat of the first measure and played as only a true professional would play. Lorry Cullen was impressed. But beyond that, the guests were delighted and gave their vigorous approval. At the end of the seventh song set, Ginny motioned her appreciation to Matt and indicated he should stand to receive the recognition Ginny thought he deserved. He reluctantly stood and offered a little wave in appreciation. The admiring crowd pleaded for an encore.

Lorry took the stage and thanked one and all for making the soft opening a success. Still, the group, especially Harley and his wife, insisted on an encore. Lorry turned to Ginny, who, to her surprise, nodded. "Okay, folks," Lorry announced. "Here's my best friend, Ginny Simmons."

The crowd applauded and then hushed as the stage lights fell dark with a single spotlight focused directly on Ginny. She sang Hoagy Carmichael's "The Nearness of You" unhurried and tender, as if she and Matt were the only two persons in the room. Matt expertly played in a slow tempo, indicating to Ginny her cues with simple nods and smiles. Dan and his wife stood up and affectionately danced until the piano stopped and Ginny's voice came to a peaceful and tranquil end.

Ginny beamed, glowing in her success, and graciously acknowledged Matt, who preferred to remain nameless and invisible.

Dan, Stan Jr., and Harley congratulated Lorry on a job well done. Dan even gave her a little hug, which Lorry very much appreciated.

Harley's wife leaned down and whispered in Lorry's ear, "We'll be here every Saturday night. And we'll bring our friends too."

Lorry gathered the staff to congratulate them for their excellent work. The rare praise was accepted with claps and cheers, especially from Bobby. The crew returned to their cleanup work, and Matt began to gather his music. Lorry and Ginny became engaged in spirited and excited conversation for a few minutes, and then Lorry walked over to Matt, who was just ready to leave and help in the kitchen.

"Matthew?" Lorry asked. "Could we have a word, please?" She gently hooked her arm around his and slowly walked him to the stage, where Ginny anxiously waited.

"Matt," Lorry began, "we'd like to you to be our accompanist and help with the music decisions until we can find someone permanent. Would you take that into consideration?"

Matt looked into Ginny's eager eyes and at Lorry's coy smile. He remembered Dad's advice, that he had an uncommon ability to feel what others were feeling, to know what others felt before they knew themselves. "Sure," he brightly replied. "I'd be honored."

Lorry didn't take his quick reply without a little suspicion. "You don't want to take a few days to think it over?"

"Nope."

# Free Ride

Lorry and Ginny chatted nonstop while sitting across each other in the house they shared on First Hill. They were happy and confident by how smoothly the soft opening had gone.

"Everything went according to the plan," Lorry said with satisfaction, "except for the intro to the first song. Whose idea was that?"

Ginny laughed. "Matt thought it would help stretch out my voice if I held the first measure a little longer. And he was right, wasn't he, hmm?"

Lorry grudgingly agreed and began to wonder about this enigmatic stranger, Matt Jensen. He was difficult to engage unless prompted, and his replies, though amiable, were painfully pithy. His talent was apparent, as was his willingness to ease Ginny out of her massive stage fright before an audience, even if it was just Dan, Stan Jr., and Harley.

"He seems to know his place," Lorry offered rather offensively. "He knows you're the attraction. I do like that about him. I mean, I thought you were going to have to pry him off his seat just to take a little recognition, but I just can't help wondering if that naive boyish charm of his is just an act."

Ginny said, "I think he's just shy, especially with women. When he walked me home last night, he stayed about five feet away from me. He's not like Bruce, who wanted to be the center of attention." Ginny sensed there was much more about her new accompanist than met the eye. "Also, I think he has a lot more talent than he's showing us. He doesn't wear shoes when he plays. Didn't you notice he was barefoot? Anyway, there's just something about him. He brings out the best in me, you too, if you'd give him half a chance."

Lorry reluctantly smiled. "Well, maybe. He does seem very sincere. Debbie was crushed when she found out he was leaving the kitchen."

"He is quite handsome, isn't he?" Ginny sighed with a touch of drama.

Lorry didn't argue the fact. She stood up and yawned. "I have a nine o'clock class in the morning that I have to get ready for." She looked at Ginny, who was moving toward her own bedroom. "It was a good night, Ginny. The first of many, I just know it."

*   *   *

Very early in the morning, two days after the soft opening, Matt Jensen was downtown, about a ten-minute walk from campus, leaning against the brick exterior of the Main Rx. He wondered why it wasn't called Main Street and wondered why First wasn't called First Avenue. He ended up concluding that since Three Forks had just the two main arterials it probably didn't matter that much. He dug his hands deep into his pockets, closed his eyes, raised his chin a little, and allowed the rising sun to fill his face. A few minutes passed when his reverie was broken by a car screeching to a sudden stop, followed by a horn blast. He slowly opened one eye and saw Lorry Cullen parked diagonally between the parking line stripes. She gunned the engine, shut it down, and climbed out.

"The store doesn't open for another hour," she announced to Matt even though he already knew that. "What are you doing here?"

Matt offered a brief explanation, "I'm waiting for the bus. It's supposed to arrive any minute."

Lorry rolled her eyes. "Oh, the bus," she dismissed. "It's never on time. You could be here all morning."

In the distance they heard the low rumbling of a diesel engine dropping down its gears and making the turn from First onto Main.

"Expecting someone?" Lorry asked with a hint of distrust. "Or are you leaving town?"

"Neither," Matt answered, "just expecting some packages."

Lorry was keen to know exactly what packages Matt was expecting, but rather than simply ask, she let her curiosity take over. They watched in silence as two bleary-eyed passengers gingerly descended the steps of the bus, turned, and unsteadily walked down Main toward the campus. The driver emerged and opened the storage compartments.

"You must be waiting for these," he asked grumpily and eyed Lorry up and down. Lorry quickly pointed to Matt, who nodded and helped the driver unload what looked to Lorry to be guitar cases.

"Are those what I think they are?" she blurted out.

"Yes," Matt replied. "Two guitars, one acoustic, one electric, and a banjo." He looked deep inside the compartment, reached in, and pulled out a small amplifier. "I thought we might try these to expand the play list." He shyly added, "If you and Ginny think it will work out."

"Humph," Lorry snorted. "I suppose it's worth a try. Good thinking, I guess." She stopped and thought for a second. "Where did these come from, anyway?"

"Oh," Matt said matter-of-factly, "they're mine. My folks sent them over."

"Well," Lorry mused, "you must have very nice parents."

Matt smiled at her. "They're the best."

Lorry viewed the instruments, the amp, and a small cloth bag that Matthew buried in his jacket pocket. "And how were you thinking of getting these to the bistro? That's way too much to carry."

Matt smiled, strapped one guitar case on like a backpack, put the banjo under one arm and then picked up the other guitar with his right hand, and picked up the amp with his left. "Nothing to it."

Lorry checked her watch. "Listen, I have about ten minutes before my class begins. Toss all this into the back seat, and I'll give you a ride."

Matt smiled at her. "Thanks, Lorry. I'd really appreciate that." He stored his instruments and equipment into the back seat and, upon noticing the front bench seat was set in its most forward position, crammed his six-foot, two-inch frame inside. His knees were almost to his ears.

"Most people insist I move the seat back for them," Lorry airily sighed.

Glad they didn't have far to go, Matt turned his head with some effort and smiled at her. "Well, they're not driving, are they?"

Lorry was hoping for some lively and witty back-and-forth banter, but all she got to her twenty questions were concise, indirect answers, like he was hiding something from her.

"Where did you grow up, Matt?" she began. Matt told her the town he grew up on the coast in a town called Hillwood.

"Oh, no kidding?" Lorry said with surprise. "Right next door to me then. I'm from Lakemont Terrace. What made you decide on NSU? It's kind of far from home, wouldn't you agree?" Lorry knew his answer would require more than his usual two- or three-word reply and anxiously waited for Matt's response.

He didn't know how to begin. He wasn't ready to tell Lorry that there were a lot of reasons he was at Northern State. Two of his sisters attended NSU. In fact, Emily was in her final year of medical school and was the head resident at the Three Forks hospital. So far, both had been too busy to meet up with each other. He wouldn't tell Lorry that he turned down a full ride to Northern University just to work his way through Northern State because he felt he and his parents should help Emily as much as they could. At least she had an admirable goal. Matt wasn't sure what he wanted, but he knew what he needed. He needed to be on his own. He needed to learn how to make friends and how to be a friend. He felt an urgency to invent himself, to discover if he really was the man whom Mom and Dad and his sisters insisted he had already become. He needed to prove it for himself. He was desperate to understand, regardless of his natural tendencies to ease the burdens of others, why he sometimes felt out of place and time. How could he so easily care for others but live in fear of finding another who equally cared for him? He struggled to understand what caused his occasional bouts of melancholy.

"Seemed like a good fit" was his simple five-word answer.

Lorry asked, "Where do you live?"

"I pledged a fraternity," Matt said, without telling her which one.

"Really?" Lorry exclaimed acerbically and, trying to get a rise out of him, added, "I never would have figured you for a frat boy."

Matt was unfazed. "Seemed like . . ."

Lorry finished his reply, "A good fit, right. So tell me, how old were you when you started piano?"

"Eight."

"I presume you've had years of lessons and training?"

"A few years. Yes."

"And the guitar? The banjo? I've always thought the banjo was an odd instrument."

"A few lessons but pretty much self-taught."

"What's in the bag, Matthew?"

Matt struggled in the cramped space to retrieve the cloth bag from his jacket pocket. He produced a recorder and two harmonicas.

At this point, Lorry began to seriously bait him. "Are you any good?" But she quickly added, "Never mind that, I'll find out soon enough. What I mean is, can you read music, or do you just play by the seat of your pants? Ginny can read music. She's very good, as you know."

Matt lightly ducked his head and brightly smiled. "Yes, I can read both notes and tablature." If he was offended, it didn't show.

Not knowing want he meant by tablature, she decided to just try to find some common ground. "Who's your favorite group?"

"The Beatles."

"Mine too," Lorry said. "What's your favorite song?"

"'I'd Rather Go Blind,'" Matt replied.

"That's not a Beatles song, is it? I've never heard of it," Lorry tightly said.

"No. It's by Etta James."

Lorry rolled her eyes. "Okay then. What's your favorite Beatles song? Matt." She added a little emphasis to his name.

"'Day Tripper.'"

"'Day Tripper'? That's not a song you can play on the piano. What are you thinking?"

Matt smiled and agreed, "No, it isn't." He pointed to the guitars in the back seat. "But we can on those."

Lorry came to an abrupt stop outside the bistro, like an F-14 hitting the deck of the Kitty Hawk. She handed the front-door key to Matt. "Give this to Ginny after rehearsal tonight, would you?" Matt nodded, and Lorry added, "Maybe I'll drop by for a listen."

Matt unfolded himself from the front seat of Lorry's giant Buick, stretched a bit, removed his gear from the back seat, and stacked it on the sidewalk. "I appreciate the ride, Lorry. Thank you."

Lorry narrowed her eyes at Matt, the way some people would take as a silent warning. "Ginny is very good, Matt. She has something really special to offer."

Matt leaned inside the car and, with a little grin, replied, "As do you, Ms. Cullen. Thanks again." He gently closed the car door and gave her a little wave of thanks.

For the first time in her life, Lorry Cullen felt her cheeks grow hot and her face flush.

# Mattie!

Matt unlocked the front door to the bistro and stood inside just to take it all in. He liked the hardwood tables and chairs and the fixed aroma of freshly baked pizza crusts and bread. The decor made the dining area cozy and pleasant. If he were the kind of guy to say *charming*, or maybe *quaint*, he probably would. He admired Lorry and Ginny for their thoughtful presentation, especially the small stage, which was elevated to just the correct height to be seen from all points of the room. He was glad that Lorry accepted how he had hidden the piano from the audience's view but wondered how he could situate himself with the guitar and still remain unseen. He knew the proper placement of the amp would not drown out Ginny's voice but would rather enhance it. He set his equipment on the stage, locked the front door, and climbed the hill to the campus. He knew he'd have to tune his acoustic guitar and certainly the banjo, but he looked forward to the task after his classes ended for the day. He was back at the bistro by four thirty that afternoon, knowing it would take at least an hour to restring and tune his newly arrived instruments into rehearsal condition.

Ginny arrived for practice at six o'clock, along with Lorry, who still remained unconvinced but was curious to find out just how good Matt Jensen could play the guitar. Matt heard them talking to each other as they came in. Ginny walked directly to the stage while Lorry peeked in and out of the kitchen just to make sure that Bobby had everything in order. He did.

Lorry walked to the middle of the dining area and loudly asked, "How's it going there, maestro?" Matt ignored the disdain in her voice.

"Just finished tuning this banjo." Matt stood, placed it on its stand, and very poised, announced, "Ready to go. Shall we get to it?"

"Yes, by all means, please get to it," Lorry retorted. She handed Matt a sheet of paper and explained, "These are the songs we've picked for opening night. Now, you have to remember that I'll be hiring someone permanent, but we figured you should be prepared nonetheless."

"Yes," Matt replied, his eyes glowing with amusement. "I believe you've mentioned that, a couple of times."

Lorry allowed Matt a moment or two to look over the playlist, and she noticed he promptly began twirling the hair behind his right ear. By now she knew this was his habit whenever he was either deep in concentration, lost in his thoughts, or both.

"Something wrong?" Lorry asked in an intimidating tone.

Matt forced himself to stop his twirling and instantly dropped his arm to his side. "Um, why do you ask?"

There was no way Lorry was going to reveal her secret knowledge of Matt's body language. "Just wondering," she nimbly replied. "So what do you think? Can you handle these tunes?"

Matt's hand rose toward his right ear again, but he stopped midair and looked at Lorry, who had a very satisfying and crafty smile on her face. Ginny wondered what was going on between the two.

He handed the playlist back to Lorry and evenly said, "To be honest, it looks like it's straight off *American Bandstand.*"

Irritated, Lorry placed her tiny hands on her tiny hips and challenged, "And what's wrong with that? Don't tell me now that you're some kind of prima donna." She took a step toward Matt and pointed a tiny finger at him. "You just remember, mister, Ginny is the attraction, not you. Got it?"

Matt shifted his feet back and forth and then buried his hands deep into his pockets. He politely said, "I can assure you, Lorry, I'm the least-temperamental person you're ever likely to meet. It's just . . ." He hesitated, unsure if he should continue.

"What? It's just what?" Lorry demanded.

Matt drew a deep breath and exhaled. At the same time, he removed his hands from his pockets and crossed his arms in a thoughtful pose. He nervously tapped his toes and wet his lips. "Ginny has much more talent than to waste on *Top 40* songs." He pointed to the list with which Lorry held in a tight grip. "Especially 'Yummy, yummy, yummy . . . I've got love in my tummy.'" He shrugged his shoulders. "You asked for input, right?"

Ginny's eyes were wide with astonishment. She could never remember anybody talking like this to Lorry, not even her own parents.

Lorry began to circle around Matt, not hiding her rancor. Finally, she asked with a bit of insight, "What exactly do you mean by that, Matt?"

Matt fixed a steady but respectful gaze on Lorry but slowly turned from her to face Ginny. He had a head full of words he wanted to say but struggled to find a useful expression.

"Don't accept the notion that you have to cover the very same music that can be just as easily heard on the radio," he gently said. "You're too good for that." His eyes remained fastened to Ginny's eyes. "You want people to come here for the pleasure of listening to you and look at you." Matt paused to gather his thoughts and made a small hand gesture toward Ginny. "Your talent, your voice. You have what everybody else wants, your extraordinary gift. But I think that just singing familiar songs, although you probably have to sing a few pop tunes, I suppose, won't reveal the true depths of your gift." He shrugged his shoulders. "You shouldn't limit yourself to *Top 40* or show tunes or soul or R & B or protest songs or even folk. You have unlimited potential with your voice, only—" Matt abruptly stopped speaking; he was totally embarrassed and ashamed. His insecurities surfaced. He had never spoken so boldly to anyone and feared his words could be possibly taken as mean-spirited and contentious.

Lorry impatiently stomped her tiny little foot. "Only what?" she demanded.

In a blazing moment of clarity, Matt suddenly found himself able to speak fluidly and genuinely. "I'm not trying to be difficult, believe me. You had enough of that with Bruce." He continued to gaze directly into Ginny's eyes. "You have the amazing ability and opportunity to be different from anyone else. It's quite a blessing, really. You have the talent to be creative by sheer aptitude." He stopped to think, his eyes wandering. "What's that word? Not electric. Oh, eclectic, that's it." He nodded eagerly to Ginny and to Lorry, who had come up beside her. "Your songs should reveal your joy and passion. Make every note, every song your favorite, your own. You have the voice, the talent to free the trapped notes and lyrics from sheet music and pour out your soul and your spirit into any song you choose. I mean, you love to sing! Share that love with your audience. Don't put yourself in a position of regret because you've put boundaries on your talent. That would be such a shame." He felt his face grow hot with distress; he had never spoken so boldly and was embarrassed. "I'm sorry," he whispered. "I've said too much."

Lorry's disposition remained militant, but she noticed an expression on Matt's face that showed her that he was eager, almost desperate, to help.

Matt turned toward the piano to begin practicing the playlist, but Lorry hooked her arm around his and spun him about with surprising strength. She recognized the truths Matt had spoken and the help he was offering Ginny. She looked up at Matt, her face eager with hope. "You can do this for her, can't you?"

Matt's eyes darted back and forth from Lorry to Ginny and then firmly on Lorry. His reply was nearly inaudible. "Yes," he said. "Yes, I can."

Lorry Cullen sat down and blew out a heavy breath. She was bewildered, almost stupefied by what Matt had just said to Ginny, who was equally astonished at this young man, who stood blushing before her.

Lorry contemplated all that was said. She knew that Matt's observations were spot-on. She fanned her face with the playlist a few times, crumpled it, and tossed it on the floor. But before she could cross-examine Matt further, the front door flew open with a loud bang. A woman, a little older than Lorry and Ginny, hurried inside and, with a delightful shriek of joy, shouted, "Mattie!"

Matt's face lit up like a full moon on a clear night. He gleefully shouted, "Emmy!"

Emily rushed to Matt, tightly embraced him, and repeatedly pressed kisses over his cheeks and forehead. Lorry and Ginny, quite startled by this sudden interruption, reluctantly looked at each other with puzzled expressions.

Ginny leaned into Lorry and whispered, "Girlfriend, you think?" Both felt a guilty pang of jealousy that ostensibly came from nowhere.

"She could be, I guess," Lorry whispered back. "She's older than he is, though."

Ginny leaned toward her. "So are we."

"I went to your frat," Emily said with a lively smile. "It took ten minutes before anyone realized you even lived there. Honestly, Mattie, why don't you at least try and make some friends?"

Matt smiled at her and shrugged.

Emily breathlessly continued, "Anyway, I called home, and Mom told me you'd asked for your guitars. Then I was just at the gas station and overheard some guy talking about how great this place is, and I kind of put two and two together. I mean, if music is involved, we all know you'll find yourself right in the middle of it all."

"Well," Matt replied, "I'm technically a dishwasher."

Although thoroughly intrigued, Lorry was tired of being ignored. She noticeably cleared her throat to gain their attention.

"Oh dear," Emily exclaimed, "I've interrupted. I'm so sorry, but I just couldn't wait to see you, Mattie. I've been on call all week and just got my first break. I'm sorry I didn't come earlier." Emily playfully poked Matt in the ribs. "But you could've found me, you know?"

Matt replied with an absent minded smile and bobbed his head in agreement. He turned from Emily to face Lorry and Ginny. "I'd like you to meet my sister," he proudly announced, " Dr. Emily Rose Jensen, MD." Lorry and Ginny blew out inconspicuous sighs of relief.

"Emmy, I'd like you to meet my new friends." He emphasized *new*. "This is Lorry Cullen and Ginny Simmons, the singer. And this is their place."

Emily, Lorry, and Ginny cordially greeted one another with handshakes, and Emily again apologized for the interruption.

"So what do you two think of my baby brother?" Emily said with unabashed pride. "Quite the prodigy, isn't he?"

Matt murmured, "Actually, we're just starting. I'm just a temp."

Emily slapped her Matt's arm. "You big goof. You haven't played for them yet?"

Matt nodded toward his guitars. "They only got here today."

She reached up and pinched his cheeks the way Grandma used to do. "Mattie, Mattie, Mattie," she happily sighed. "Show them what you've got, for crying out loud."

Emily turned and addressed Ginny, "The fellow at the gas station said you have the most beautiful voice." She tightly clutched her brother's arm and put her head on his shoulder. "He'll make you better."

It wasn't said with conceit or blustering bravado; rather, it was a statement meant to give Ginny confidence and encouragement. Fortunately, Ginny and especially Lorry received it as such.

Emily continued, "Although you should know"—she smiled broadly—"Mattie tends to see the world a little differently than the rest of us."

"Yeah," Lorry replied in total wonderment. "We've just started to figure that out for ourselves, right before you got here."

Satisfied that Matt could very well be the permanent musician they needed, both Lorry and Ginny converged upon Matt, who struggled to keep his balance.

"So it's Mattie, is it?" Lorry blithely asked. "May we call you that too?"

Emily rose and kissed her brother once more. "You most certainly can," she cooed.

"He shall forever be your Mattie."

# Side by Side

"I'm curious, Ginny," Matt asked. He was leaning back in a chair with his hands on top of his head. "What gave you and Lorry the idea to start all this?" The grand opening of Ginny's Bistro was five days away, and the two were taking a break during practice. "I mean, this seems like the perfect place, especially with all the college kids. And from what I've heard, local folks are excited about it too."

Ginny explained that Lorry had created the idea and presented the plan as her final project in her honors business marketing class, every single detail. She continued to explain that Lorry had earned her undergraduate degree in three years by attending summer school and taking correspondence classes. By doing so, she could take four years to complete law school, but she had no interest of practicing. She was going to be Ginny's manager when and if her professional career began.

She gave Matt a bright smile. "That's the grand plan, Mattie. I'll finish my degree at the end of spring semester and will support myself with this place and help Lorry out if she needs it." She waved her graceful arm about in a sweeping motion around the bistro. "Call it a training ground, if you will. That's why finding the right accompanist was so important." She reached over and gently rested her hand on Matt's forearm. "You fell right into our arms, my friend."

Matt went uncomfortable and rigid. He cleared his throat and managed to barely ask, "What are you studying, Ginny?" He didn't offer what his major was as he was still undecided.

She replied, "Linguistics and languages."

Matt was pleasantly surprised by this news. "Really? So you speak different languages?"

"Yup, I speak French and Italian. And you?"

Matt scratched his head. "I pretty much stick to the mother tongue." His mind swarmed with ideas of what this meant for Ginny's musical selections and asked, "Have you ever heard of Edith Piaf?"

"Pourquoi oui, bien sur, mon ami," Ginny happily replied.

Matt twirled the hair behind his right ear. "I'll take that as a yes, then?"

Ginny gave him a seductive wink. "Ah, oui, mon cheri."

Matt methodically and rapidly tapped the piano leg with his foot and twirled his hair. His eyes grew wide.

"What are you thinking about, Mattie?" Ginny asked.

Matt forced himself to stop his fidgeting. "I'm thinking how great you'll sound singing Edith Piaf accompanied by an accordion." He took a chance and added, "If you ask me, Ginny, I think you're already a professional. How many years of voice training have you had?"

Ginny lowered her eyes. "I've never had any professional training. Do you think I should?"

Matt laughed. "Did you know that Judy Garland had only one singing lesson? It lasted about fifteen minutes. Ella Fitzgerald and Bing Crosby never had one, and neither did Sinatra." He grinned. "I don't know about Gracie Slick. But like I told you, Ginny, you're a pro, a natural. Voice lessons would only hurt you." He twirled his hair. "At least, that's what I think."

She reached for his hands and cupped hers around them. "Thank you, Mattie. Thank you so much. I really needed to hear that from you."

Matt hesitated for a moment. "You play the guitar. Lorry told me. A lot of these songs will benefit with you on guitar and me on piano."

"Well, I'm clearly not as good as you are, Mattie. I don't know about this idea."

"And you play the piano too. Lorry told me. We can do it with the right music. What do you say?."

Ginny mulled this over. "Well, all right. But only if I can play with any degree of competency."

Mattie smiled. "Now there's a thought that never entered my mind."

Matt watched the veils of insecurity fall away from Ginny. He liked her; she reminded him so much of his sisters. Underneath the uncertainty and self-doubt, Ginny's talent was emerging. She was so eager to sing and perform yet totally modest about her genius. And totally unpretentious about her beauty. She accepted Matt's ideas and guidance with enthusiastic delight and in turn came up with ideas of her own.

Lorry entered the rehearsal room and decided to just be still and watch Ginny and Matt work together.

"Okay," Ginny uneasily began, "I just want to go over this one more time." She glanced at Lorry and then to Matt, who was sitting on the floor, his back against the piano. "We'll have one set of eight songs, a thirty-minute break, and then eight more songs, right?"

"I guess so," Matt agreed. "And you know I was thinking that we can perform maybe seven or eight new songs each week. We can keep the leftover songs the same, or we can present them in different arrangements from the week before. That way, the audience always gets something new, and you can expand your range and your repertoire."

Ginny took a deep breath. With Matt's calm, common sense, and considerate approach, she was beginning to relax about the upcoming performances and began to feel secure and more determined to succeed.

Matt turned to Lorry and explained, "We've been rehearsing thirteen numbers to go along with the seven from the soft opening." He pulled several pages of single-lined notebook paper from a Pee-Chee and handed them to Lorry. "I have some songs you and Ginny can look over."

Lorry critically scanned the song lists Matt had put together. "Mattie, are you kidding me? How many songs do you have here?"

"I quit counting after 150," he replied, and he quickly added, "But there are five or six categories or . . . what's the word . . ."

"Genres, Mattie." Lorry frowned while still looking over Matt's song lists. "They're called genres."

"Right, right, right. Genres," Matt quipped. "And you'll notice that Michael is *not* rowing the boat ashore, nor are we on the eve of destruction. And I don't even know what Kumbaya means, so that's out too." He pointed to the opening night's playlist. "But look at Ginny's first number. It's quite exceptional, considering where we are."

"'Downtown'?" Lorry exclaimed. "Please say you're kidding me."

Ginny giggled. "Oh, we're not kidding at all. It's ironic, it's funny. Downtown Three Forks, get it?" She smiled at Matt. "Actually, it's Mattie's idea."

Lorry did see the irony, and she smiled, thinking of the meager little downtown of Three Forks. She laughed. "Yes, it is funny. It is."

*　　*　　*

The next evening, Lorry and Ginny arrived for rehearsal and found Matt tuning his Gibson L-3 Arch Top acoustic guitar. It was a gift from Grandma, who had had the instrument fully restored and restrung with wire strings before presenting it to Matthew on their last Christmas together before she passed away. It had been in the family since the '30s, Grandma had told him. Matt treasured the guitar; it was his most prized possession. Attached was a very elaborate leather strap, obviously handcrafted. For some reason, the strap caught Ginny's attention, and she carefully examined it. The seams and scoring were intricate and flawless. She noticed letters etched in, and she read them to herself, "We love you, Mattie, KS, TE, ER, LA."

Ginny delicately ran her fingers up and down the polished leather. "Mattie?" she called, and pointed to the lettering. "Are these initials or something?"

Matt picked up the guitar and admired the special strap. "Yes," he said, and explained, "Kathleen Suzanne, Tess Elizabeth, Emily Rose, and Lucy Annette. My sisters made this and gave it to me for my birthday a few years ago. Pretty cool, huh?"

"You have four sisters?" Ginny exclaimed. Matt nodded and Ginny continued, "Are you the youngest?"

Matt replied, "I am." He laughed. "When I was little, Dad would look at me and wonder out loud, 'Good God, Matthew. Why can't their cycles all be at the same time? Why?' It didn't dawn on me what he meant until I took health class in the ninth grade."

"Speaking about Emily Rose," Lorry casually said, "I actually ran into her today."

Matt swiveled his head and shot her a suspicious glance. "Nobody runs into Emily unless they're in the emergency room."

"Oh, all right," Lorry admitted without any indication of remorse, "I looked her up, and we went for coffee." She gave Matt a sly smile. "She said some very interesting things about you, Mattie." Lorry spoke nonchalantly to Matt and faced him while speaking to Ginny. "It seems, Ginny, in addition to his piano and guitar skills, this young man apparently has quite a fine tenor voice."

"No kidding," Ginny replied with her own sly grin. "You know, Lorry. Most of our songs would sound much better with background vocals, don't you think?"

Lorry said, "Absolutely, and I think our new friend Mattie can deliver. Emily told me we should just tickle him, and he'll do whatever we ask."

Matt was now seated on the piano bench, bent over with his head buried deep in his folded arms. "Please don't tickle me," he pleaded, his voice muffled.

"Then you'll do it? Will you sing with me?" Ginny excitedly asked.

He sat up and faced them. Like it or not, he knew he was done for. "Is this a deal breaker, then?" He sighed.

Ginny said, "Yes, sir, it's either that or Lorry tickles you into submission."

Matt studied their catlike grins and raised his hands in defeat. "Well, I suppose we should set up some mics."

Their voices blended smoothly on the first song they practiced, as if they had been singing together since the beginning of time. Both had the ability to instantly memorize both music and lyrics. Matt instinctively knew his cues, the strength and tenderness of each background vocal, and the timing of when and when not to enter into each song. Ginny loved to rehearse with him. He was just so easy to get along with. He was never critical of her efforts while learning new material, which came easy to her. Still, Matt would gently point out any subtle changes using the charts as his guide.

He insisted she take occasional breaks. "Give those pipes a rest," he advised. "Over time it will strengthen your vocal cords, your diaphragm, and your breathing. Just ten minutes or so, that's all you need, and then we'll start again."

During her breaks, Ginny would carefully study this young man who had appeared from nowhere. He was tall, about six feet, two inches tall, with a slim but athletic build. His blond hair was highlighted by the most intense dark-blue eyes she had ever seen, and she had seen quite a few. Ginny had no end of male suitors and admirers, most of whom simply played with her emotions. She watched him in fascination during her breaks. His only interest was making her better as a singer, as a musician, and as a performer. Mattie would study the sheet music with an intensity she had never seen, concentrating on one piece of music after another. He had a talent for anticipating and hearing the notes in his head before he played them. He gently rocked back and forth to the rhythms of the music. Sometimes he would direct a song with his hands, his head bobbing in rhythm, his eyes closed, imagining each song in time.

With each passing day, Ginny endeared herself to him with soft and tender expressions. She developed a great fondness for him and wondered if he felt the same toward her. Mattie constantly made it clear that he was just an employee, but he had become much more than that to her. She wondered if her penchant for him would eventually turn into something serious. He was certainly unlike anybody she had ever met before and as humble as they come. He'd asked her to join him at the piano to show her notations he'd made on the music. He circled every specific dynamic or key change. "You see right here, Ginny? You always want to try and think a measure or two ahead. It will really help with your breathing."

Everything he brought to her attention worked and made sense to her, and Matt was very clever in arranging each piece of music that would bring out the best of her talent without merely mimicking original renditions. He cheerfully and almost excitedly explained to her when a song should be presented gently and with tenderness or when to unleash her voice with power and emotion.

"Okay," he would suggest, pointing to a specific measure, "you see this diminished triad right here? You want to hold this last note as long as you can, even after I stop playing, okay? Give it a try." It was the same advice for chord progressions, a minor fall or a major lift.

Ginny stood on the stage and sang without hesitation, her joy of singing renewed and fully healed from the persecution and verbal abuse Bruce had laden upon her. There was no drama, no condescending attitude, just gracious help without any recompense but a paycheck.

*   *   *

One evening, Ginny decided to show up for practice early, hoping to watch Matt tune his guitar and banjo. Instead, she found him sitting at the piano, thoroughly engrossed on several pieces of sheet music and twirling the hair behind his right ear.

"Catch you at a bad time, Mattie?" Ginny asked.

"No no no," Matt replied, and looked at Ginny with a friendly smile. "Let's start out by matching notes, okay?"

Ginny was a little puzzled. "Okay, sure."

Matt drew a breath and held it briefly before exhaling. "Match each note and hold it as long as you can. Sound good?"

Ginny nodded, and then Matt struck A. Ginny held the note as long as she could, but Matt would not give her the chance to stop and recover. He immediately tapped middle C, then one note up to D, and ended with B-flat. He climbed an octave, and Ginny matched from F to E and back and forth, holding each note as long as she could. Matt nodded his approval and asked her to sit down next to him.

He pointed to the music sheets on the page holder. "It's called 'In Trutina,'" Matt quietly explained. "It's a bit of a change from our usual stuff." He handed the sheets to Ginny. "It's a simple melody, but with your voice, it will be fantastic. I think it's the most beautiful song I've ever heard."

"Mattie," Ginny exclaimed, her worry revived, "I can't do this!"

Matt reassured her. "But you just did."

"No!" Ginny cried out. "The lyrics. I can't sing these words. Uh-uh, mister. No way."

Matt said, "But you speak Italian, right?"

"This isn't Italian, Mattie. This is Latin," Ginny moaned.

"Oh." Matt paused and then thoughtfully remarked, "I thought they were pretty much the same thing."

Ginny brightened and laughed at his naïveté and innocence. "No, Mattie. They're not the same thing."

"Well," Matt offered, "I think you should give it a try. Don't worry about the language. I mean, you're linguistically inclined, right?"

Ginny read the sheet music again and recognized the beauty of the song. She nodded in agreement. "Yes, let's try it. But I can't promise I'll ever sing it onstage." They would practice the song at least once during every rehearsal until the day arrived when Ginny felt confident to sing it before an audience.

She moved toward Matt as close as she could without scaring him. "My goodness, Mattie," she said, spellbound, "is there anything you can't do?"

Matt took a deep breath. "Math," he replied. "I can't do math."

He yawned and stretched, then he rubbed his hands together. "I'll see you tomorrow, okay? Only four days left."

\* \* \*

Late that same night, Lorry and Ginny were found discussing the importance of their opening in just four days. Although confident, they were a little anxious too, as both had a lot riding on each other's success.

"So you tracked down Mattie's sister today." Ginny laughed, as it was so like Lorry to do something like that.

"I did," Lorry answered. "I just wanted to find out a little more about him. Lord knows he's not going to volunteer anything on his own." She adjusted from a sitting position, lay down, and propped herself up on an elbow. "It's obvious Emily just loves him to death, as do his other three sisters. Did you know about them?"

Ginny replied, "Yes, I just found out about them tonight." She anxiously asked, "What else did Emily say?"

"Well," Lorry began, "apart from music, he doesn't really have any other interests." She snapped her fingers and pointed to Ginny, "Except—and this is a stunner—I looked it up to find out if it was true. Mattie was an All-League quarterback last year. Emily said it was the first and only time he'd played any sport. And here's the clincher: he turned down a full-ride scholarship to Northern to come here instead."

Ginny moved to the edge of her chair in shock. "Oh, no way. Really?"

"It's true," Lorry answered. She fell silent into her thoughts; her eyes wandered around the room. "He is, as we already know, extremely shy but not introverted. Emily said he has a natural, intuitive desire or power or something in him that seems to make everyone around him better just by being who is. He always sees the good in people and loves to offer his help if needed. Emily said he has true humility and is totally without guile, but I think she's probably a little biased." Lorry paused, wondering if she should continue. She pursed her lips and quietly said, "But there are imperfections. Emily said that he infrequently falls into some kind of mysterious downcast mood. A funk. Anyway, that's how she put it, but I'm not sure Emily could really explain it, so she let it go." Lorry paused again, then she said, "Honestly, I can't see him acting like that, can you?"

"No, I can't," Ginny answered, "but we're just getting to know each other." She clasped her arms around her knees and smiled. "So tell me. Are there any girls in his life besides his sisters and you and me?"

Lorry laughed. "Emily said he's witty, funny, and charming but totally clueless and mystified when it comes to girls despite the fact he's been surrounded by women his entire life. He just can't, or won't, seem to realize when a girl likes him . . . and apparently, there have been quite a few."

Ginny sat still and thought, *But I like him. And he does make me better. He's the first person who's never tried to change me into someone I'm not.*

Two days later, Ginny emerged from her bedroom, dressed to the nines, to show off her fine figure. She wore a new pair of blue jeans with a black belt, a white blouse with a light red sweater, and toeless red high heels. Her face was made up to perfection, and she wore a pleasant aroma of perfume.

"Well, look at you," Lorry exclaimed. "I thought dress rehearsal was tomorrow night, huh?"

Ginny smiled and shrugged her shoulders. "I don't know. I just felt like dressing up a little. Are you coming down tonight?"

Lorry gestured to the stack of law books and notepads surrounding her. "No, I need to study tonight. I have to stay a little bit ahead, you know?"

Ginny nodded sympathetically and asked if she could borrow her car. "I should be back by ten o'clock or so. Try to stay awake, okay?"

Ginny opened the already-unlocked door to the bistro, knowing Matt would have been tuning up for at least half an hour. She locked the door behind her and walked to the middle of the stage.

"I'm about done tuning," Matt said without looking up, and he added, "Also, I think I should use this metronome while we're practicing some of these songs. I feel like I'm rushing a few of them. What do you think?" He stood and turned to see Ginny smiling at him, her body glowing off an aura of light.

Matt nearly dropped his guitar. "Wow!" He took a clumsy step backward, gently shook his head, blinked hard, and repeated, "Wow. You look amazing. But I thought dress rehearsal was tomorrow." He blinked hard to gain his composure and slightly lifted his head. "Is that Rive Gauche you're wearing?"

Ginny gave him a quizzical look. "Well, you certainly know your fragrances."

Matt replied with a sophisticated sigh, "It's my area. Actually, I give Rive Gauche to my sister Tess every year for her birthday."

*So,* Ginny thought glumly, *does he think of me like a sister too?* She responded to Matt's puzzled expression and rebounded enthusiastically, "Let's go over the list one more time, shall we?"

The first set would begin with the already-agreed-upon "Downtown" by Petula Clark, followed by "I'm a Fool to Want You" by Billie Holiday, both songs accompanied by piano. Following those were "I Will" by the Beatles, with Matt on the banjo. He would then return to the piano for the Temptations, "I Can't Get Next to You." It would be their first duet and followed up without a pause to Nina Simone's "My Baby Just Cares for Me." Matt would play the piano, and Ginny, the guitar, for "Someday Soon" by Judy Collins, followed by the traditional "Simple Gifts" played on the piano. The set would end with "Oh! Darlin'" by the Beatles. Ginny loved rehearsing with him; he made practice fun and enjoyable. They would soon come to know each other so well they could anticipate every nuance of every song with just a simple nod and smile.

"You really want to belt out the last song with all you have," Matt encouraged. "Make it so they can't wait for the second set."

"It's quite the varied presentation, isn't it?" Ginny said with an easy approval. "I'm excited and already a little nervous."

Matt replied, "Well, I think that's the way it probably should be, yeah?"

Ginny looked around the stage. "By the way, Mattie. Where are you going to set up for the guitar and banjo?"

He pointed to a hidden chair on the back corner of the stage. Two microphones had been set up, one high to catch Matt's harmonies and one low to amplify the banjo and guitar.

Ginny smiled. "That's a little obscure, don't you think?"

Matt shook his head. "I prefer not to be seen, especially since you're the one everybody is coming to see. I'm just a backup, remember?"

Ginny tilted her head and grinned. "Well, we'll just have to see about that." Before Matt could protest, she sweetly asked, "Let's take a look at the second set. It seems we have an a capella duet. You can't hide from that now, can you?"

Matt shifted his eyes back and forth and quietly replied, "No. I guess not."

"Good," Ginny said with great satisfaction, "I'm going to love singing side by side with you."

Lorry had done her due diligence in promoting and advertising the grand opening of Ginny's Bistro. She advertised in the Three Forks and NSU newspapers. She had Bobby staple posters on telephone poles, and she bought time on KCOW, the local AM station. The campus FM station wasn't allowed to accept advertising dollars but did allow a lengthy interview. Lorry knew the DJ.

A queue of over one hundred people eagerly awaited the doors to open at six thirty, far more than the bistro could accommodate. Lorry allowed the tables to be filled with the dinner guests and encouraged everyone left in line to please come back for Ginny's performance at nine o'clock.

Precisely at that hour, the houselights dimmed, and the stage light sparkled on Ginny. The audience gasped at her beauty. She was visibly nervous but remembered something Matt had whispered to her just before she took the stage, "Remember, you're perfect." She looked at him now, and he smiled that bashful smile that always made her tingle. He nodded and played the introduction to "Downtown." The audience recognized the irony and responded with such enthusiasm that the stage shook. Standing in the back, Lorry smiled and realized, as did the audience, the compelling chemistry between the singer and her accompanist.

Ginny's extraordinary voice penetrated every inch of the bistro and was heard out on the street, where a crowd had gathered. Her energy and her confidence built with each song, her body freely connecting to the rhythms and patterns of each melody. The timid, and doubt-filled singer transformed into a fiery and dynamic performer, confident in her skills to make the transition from saintly to sultry. Every time she looked over to Mattie, he gave her a smile and a nod, assuring her that everything she was doing was terrific The first set came to an end with the dramatic and soulful rendition of "Oh! Darlin'." With a standing ovation before her, Ginny announced a thirty-minute break and asked the audience to please stay for the second set. She threw the crowd a brilliant smile, left the stage, and immediately reached for the glass of water that somehow Matt knew she would need.

Lorry blindsided and hugged them. "Oh my! That was sensational, absolutely sensational. You should hear what everybody's saying out there. Honestly, I just don't know how you two do it. I'd be scared senseless."

"Whew, I need to sit down," Ginny confessed. She looked at Matt. "We're going to just kill the second set, aren't we, partner?" It was the first time she referred to him as her partner.

Matt wiped sweat from his forehead. "Yes, ma'am. I believe so. Maybe you should rest a bit, okay? Also, I'm still a little reluctant to join you onstage, you know, next to you."

Ginny reached up and ruffled his hair. "Don't make me tickle you, Matthew."

The barricade that hid Matt during the first set had been removed, and he was now in full view of the audience. He had his first good look at the crowd and found Emily, who waved to him from the front row, holding some guy's hand and beaming with pride. Matt gestured to his sister, wondering who the fellow was, and Emily replied with a big smile and playfully displayed her middle finger. Matt laughed out loud and was instantly met with a scowl from Lorry.

"Now, Matthew," she said, "this is a restaurant. You have to wear shoes when you're onstage."

Eyes downcast, Matt withdrew a flimsy pair of flip-flops from his back pocket. "Will these do?"

Lorry rolled her eyes. "They might unless the health inspector comes around."

The houselights dimmed for the second set, and the audience applauded in anticipation. Ginny stepped to the stage, which was now fixed with two stand-up microphones, side by side. She graciously accepted the generous applause, nodded to Matt, who began to play Patsy Cline's "Crazy." There was no hesitation between numbers, and Matt followed with the classic "As Time Goes By," after which Ginny began clapping her hands in quick rhythm. She encouraged the audience to join along with her, and they did so with joyous enthusiasm. Matt vigorously pounded the keys, and Ginny sang, "I Wonder Where My Baby Is Tonight" by the Kinks. After the commotion died down, Ginny sang the soothing "Warmth of the Sun" by the Beach Boys. Matt's soft background vocal lent magic to Ginny's delivery. He then picked up his banjo, and Ginny ardently beckoned him to join her.

She cheerfully greeted the audience for the first time of the set. "I'd like you to meet the band," she exclaimed with a little dip of her knees. "Mattie? Would you come up, please?"

Matt weakly smiled. A banjo pick was firmly placed between his lips as he offered a shy wave in appreciation to the crowd's warm applause. He could hear Emily shrieking her approval. He loosened his shoulders, kicked off his sandals, and began picking "Wimoweh" in the style of Pete Seeger. That finished, he returned to the piano and began his favorite Edith Piaf melody, "La Vie en Rose." To the crowd's delight, Ginny sang the song in perfect French. She motioned Matt back to the stage to perform their a capella number, a traditional Irish love song that Matt introduced with the recorder, "Do You Love an Apple." Again, their voices blended with precision, their timing spot-on. Matt ended the number with another recorder solo.

The final number was Matt's favorite song, at least for the moment, "I'd Rather Go Blind," by Etta James, whom Matt thought was a genius. Ginny performed the number with such drive and passion that many in the audience broke into tears, including Emily and Lorry. Matt's electric guitar solo was met with a standing ovation.

Ginny's gift of voice had now been presented to the world, or at least to Three Forks. The crowds, inside and outside, thundered their approval, and as Ginny left the stage, the audience screamed out demanding an encore. She was quick to oblige.

"This town has an ordinance about establishments staying open after midnight." Ginny laughed. "But we'd like to play one more for you."

Matt knew she was exhausted as he began the encore "In the Wee Small Hours of the Morning." Rather than singing to the audience, Ginny sang directly to Matt. Their eyes locked on each other, their voices melted together, and their souls seemed bound to each other.

As the song and the evening came to their celebrated end, Ginny, her face flush with the elation of success, motioned for Matt to join her on the stage and share in her happiness, her joy, and her accomplishment. She was unaware of the effect she had had on the audience, with the power she held in her talent. She danced a little jig of celebration and then took Matt's hesitant hand, tightly clasped on to it, and raised it high in the air. Without any warning, she wrapped him in a tender embrace and, with the crowd's approval, kissed him softly on his cheek. Matt was unaware of the effect he had on Ginny.

Standing near the front entrance, Lorry gasped aloud and covered her mouth with both hands. For the first time she saw how perfect Ginny and Mattie were together, standing side by side in strange but wonderful chemistry, as if they had been predestined, eternally made for each other.

# Brothers

A single day doesn't pass by without history being made some-place in the world. But to imagine a historical event occur-ring in Three Forks? This was certainly out of the ordinary, which exactly what a historical event is, after all. Lightening had struck and her name was Ginny Simmons.

In the first three months of operation, Ginny's Bistro brought revival, rejuvenation, and enterprise to downtown Three Forks. Prospering new businesses offered internships to college students; a Saturday outdoor market sprouted, which added smiles to the faces of Dan, Stan Jr. and Harley. They finally came to recognize the advan-tages of students who had a little money to spend. Dan liked the random seating style Lorry had devised for dinners, which allowed him to proudly announce to whomever would listen how he had really helped Lorry and Ginny get their place off the ground. College students, faculty, and city and country residents eagerly staked places in line as early as noon on the days the bistro was open, all hopeful for a table or a front-row seat to listen to Ginny. Lorry considered expanding the menu, but the business plan did not allow for that until the third year, if they were successful. Lorry Cullen liked to stick to her plan.

The eclectic music selections allowed Ginny to fully demon-strate and project her voice, proving to herself and the audiences that she had no flaws. She could deliver any song that she, Lorry, and Matt—mostly Matt—chose to present. Matt had a knack for arrangement and was determined not to place any boundaries on Ginny's talents. By their sixth month, Ginny and Matt played and sang together with comfort and confidence. The audience became happily captivated when Ginny became flirtatious and coquettish with Matt when the song begged for it, especially "Would You Like to Take a Walk" performed in a duet like that of Louis Armstrong and Ella Fitzgerald. It became customary when Matt took the stage with Ginny for the second set that she would greet him with a tender embrace and a delicate kiss on the cheek, something Matt was still uncomfortable with. What Lorry considered as peerless after their first time onstage together had, in her mind, become perfection. Although fiercely casual, Ginny and Mattie clearly fused, in sync in their presentation. And although Matt continually demonstrated that he was indeed the kind, considerate, self-sacrificing young man whom Emily had described, neither Lorry nor Ginny knew anything about him outside the bistro walls. They knew he lived in a fraternity, but he never mentioned which one. Where did he spend his time away from work? What classes did he take, and what was his major? How could he instantly memorize songs and never need to fall back to sheet music? Who were his friends, and most importantly, whom did he date, if anyone?

"Lord knows he has his admirers," Lorry mused as she watched girl after girl vie for his attention, without success.

The spring of 1969 brought the relief of warmer temperatures after a brutal, long, cold winter. Lorry and the staff served free lemonade to those outside lined up on the sidewalk, waiting for the bistro to open. The doors promptly opened at six o'clock, and the tables were quickly and randomly filled with customers. Lorry would explain to the disappointed folks denied entry that they were at capacity for dinner but the doors would reopen at eight thirty. Those who chose to remain in line would be immediately seated and served up until eight o'clock, should anyone leave early. She also took takeout pizza orders that were hand-delivered to the waiting crowd. She had hired a friend, Raul, a massive young man who played offensive left tackle for the NSU football team until a blown ACL forced him to quit. His scholarship had been duly revoked, and Lorry gave him the job of "maintaining the peace outside" so he could fund the rest of his schooling. Raul kept everyone on their best behavior.

At eight thirty in the evening, as Ginny and Matt were warming up and tuning in the rehearsal room, Lorry quick-stepped in with a rather-displeased look on her face. "Mattie," she grumbled, "there's a bunch of goofballs sitting at one of the back tables who keep asking for you. They're causing a bit of a nuisance."

"Goofballs, you say?" Matt casually replied. "Oh my." The remark earned him a slap on the arm. "Why don't you just sic Raul on them?"

"He's busy outside."

Matt cautiously looked around the room and whispered to Lorry, "Let's have a look. We can't allow any goofballs in here, can we?" That earned him another smack.

Matt and Lorry peeked over the big planter box shielding the piano and parted the ferns to have a good look. Lorry stood on a chair. Matt smiled broadly. "Oh, those are my friends. They said they might come down tonight." He winked at Lorry. "They think I work in the kitchen."

Lorry put her arm around Matt's waist and purred, "If these rascals keep showing up, you might find yourself right back in front of the dishwasher."

"Do you want me to talk to them?" Matt asked.

Lorry waved him off. "Oh no. They're fine," she hushed. "I just didn't know you had any friends."

Matt replied with mock agitation, "Of course I have friends, Ms. Cullen." He laughed. "I don't think we'll ever be mistaken as the greatest thinkers of our time, except for Randy, he's pretty smart. I suppose that's why we get along so well."

"Well," Lorry continued, somewhat disgusted, "they told Tasha, their server, that they've run out of money. We have paying customers outside waiting to get in. What do you want me to do with them?"

Matt smiled toward his friends. "I'll cover their bill."

"Yeah, you will, mister, right out of your paycheck," Lorry retorted with a laugh. "So they don't know what you do here?"

"Nope."

"Well," Lorry concluded, "it will be worth just to see the looks on their scruffy little faces once they find out." She looked Matt's friends over again. "Who's the one in the middle?" she asked. "He's actually kind of cute."

Matt took one last peek and grinned at Lorry. "That's Lionel."

Matt hurried back to the rehearsal room and took a quick glance at the playlist for the evening. "Ginny?" he called out. "Would you mind changing out 'Faded Love' for 'The Night Rider's Lament' tonight?"

Ginny replied, "Sure. Why, what's up?"

Matt answered with a mischievous grin, "My friends are here tonight. You know, Lorry's goofballs. You'll make one them melt right into his chair with that song, especially if you dedicate it to Marty. He fancies himself a cowboy."

"Why, Matthew Jensen," Ginny exclaimed with delight, "I had no idea you were capable of such chicanery. What's his last name?"

"Nevin," Matt said anxiously. "Marty Nevin."

"Well, then," Ginny shined. "What do you say we make this night a little more special, hmm?"

"All right," Matt replied slowly and a little confused. "What are you thinking?"

Ginny walked to him and took both his hands in hers and, with a flirtatious smile, said, "What do say we bring the house down tonight. We can start the first set with 'Feelin' Alright.' I'll make the dedication to your friend for the sixth number and then switch out the last two with 'In Trutina.' We can finish with 'Shout.'"

Matt's blue eyes twinkled like the evening star. "Why, Ms. Simmons. You seem to have a bit a chicanery in you too . . . It's nice."

Matt cozied up to Lorry as the bistro's tables and chairs were being arranged and set up for Ginny to begin at nine o'clock. "I'm glad we did a sound check this afternoon."

"And why is that, Matthew?" Lorry only used his full name when she thought he was up to something that would contradict her plans. She didn't like last-minute changes, especially to the play list, which was always discussed and agreed upon every Tuesday.

He bent low and whispered, "I think Ginny's feeling a little, uh, spunky tonight."

Lorry's head jerked back. "Did you say spunky?"

"Spunky. Yes," Matt replied, deadpan. "I'm just going to go with it and follow her lead. Get ready for some improvisation." He gestured to the back table to where his fraternity brothers were huddled. "I told her they were here tonight." His head bobbed, and he grinned. "She made a few changes to the playlist."

Lorry stomped her tiny foot. "Oh, Mattie. You know I don't like that. If anything goes haywire tonight . . ."

Matt threw up his hands. "Hey, I'm innocent this time. It's all Ginny."

Matt began to walk toward the stage but suddenly spun about to find Lorry staring at him with her hands on her hips. "Oh, and you might want to think about bringing Raul inside tonight. You don't know what these guys are capable of doing." He gave her a wink and walked away, smiling.

Lorry left her many responsibilities in the bistro and quick-stepped to the rehearsal room, where Ginny was finishing her breathing exercises. "Ginny? Are you all right? Did Mattie do something to you?"

"Yeah, I'm great," she beamed. "I can't wait to get started tonight."

Lorry couldn't help but notice that Ginny was even more radiant this evening, strikingly beautiful, and glowing with confidence. She eyed her suspiciously. "Did you take something?"

Ginny laughed. "Of course not." She studied Lorry and took her hands. "You're the only true friend I've had, Lorry, and I treasure that friendship. But I know what it's like for Mattie, how difficult a time he has to make and keep true friends, like we are to each other. And now his friends are here tonight thinking he works in the kitchen. They don't know much more about him than we do. Don't you think that's odd?"

She let go of Lorry's hands, took a step back, and beamed with pride. "I'm going to show him off tonight, whether he likes it or not. I'm going to show those frat brothers of his that he's beyond special, that he's a person worth knowing, and that you and I are his friends too, his true friends, and that we care about him . . . and that I have feelings for him."

Tears formed in Lorry's eyes, a rarity at any time. She blinked several times and gave Ginny a weak smile. "Then go out there and raise the roof tonight, for both of us."

Matt appeared at the doorway. "We're set to go whenever you're ready, Ginny." Lorry rushed to him and hugged him before quick-stepping to some place where she was sure to be needed. Matt had a puzzled expression and looked at Ginny, who slightly shrugged and smiled at him.

"Okay," Matt said warily, "ready when you are, I guess."

Ginny hooked her arm around his. "First, show me where these friends of yours are sitting."

Matt hesitated. "Um, well, okay." He led her to the big planter box and peered through the ferns. Matt pointed to a table in the very back of the bistro. "There they are," he quietly said.

"What are their names, Mattie?" Ginny anxiously asked.

Matt pointed from left to right. "See the guy with the tall, frizzy red hair shooting into the sky? That's Owen."

Ginny giggled. "He looks like one of those cartoon characters who's scared all the time."

"Yeah." Matt chuckled. "It's quite the 'do, isn't it? Anyway, sitting next to him is Ty. The one in the middle to Lionel. He and I are going to share a place next year, and I think Lorry's already taken a little shining to him. So the guy with the cigarette behind his ear is Marty. He's the one you're dedicating the song to."

"Hmm," Ginny observed, "he doesn't seem too pleased with our no-smoking policy."

Matt smiled and shrugged. "No, probably not. And next to him is Randy."

Ginny turned to Matt. "They look like pretty good guys, Mattie. You know they're in for a big surprise tonight, right?"

Matt cleared his throat uncomfortably and checked his watch. "Only two minutes. We best take our places." He bent close to her and whispered into Ginny's ear as he did before every performance, "And remember. You're perfect."

Lorry had positioned herself near the brother's table, not close enough to be accused of spying but close enough to hear the conversation. She watched as Lionel stood up and apprehensively approached her. "Excuse me, miss?" he cautiously asked. "But do you work here?"

Lorry tried to look as innocent as she could. She batted her eyelashes several times. "Why, yes, I do, handsome. Can I be of any help?"

Lionel fidgeted, just trying to speak. He pointed to the brothers. "Well, we have a friend who works here too. Matt Jensen, do you know him? We just wanted to say hello, um, before we go."

"You're leaving so soon?" Lorry asked, thoroughly enjoying the moment. "Won't you stay for the performance?" She made a barely noticeable nod, and Tasha jumped to serve the brothers table with plates of cheese, fruit, and bread.

"I'm sorry, miss, but we don't have enough money for all this," Lionel explained with urgency.

Tasha replied with a grin, "On the house, gentlemen. Enjoy!"

Lorry gently pushed Lionel toward his table. "I think you'll see your friend around ten thirty. Enjoy the show." She considered serving them wine but figured since they were all underage that that would be a bit of a risk. Besides, she could smell cheap whiskey, which they had obviously smuggled in, coming from their table. The dark-haired fellow on the far right already looked totally wasted. They didn't appear to be the typical egocentric fraternity boys, Lorry noticed. She liked that about them.

The air-conditioning in the bistro was so ineffective on this warm evening that Lorry had it shut down and asked for all the doors and windows to be opened. Upon this discovery, a festival-like atmosphere began outside for those who were denied entrance. Pizzas were served outside until eight thirty, and Lorry explained that a city ordinance prevented them from serving wine outside, but most folks were packing their own beverages. It was NSU, after all. City police made frequent passes, but Raul kept the crowd well behaved. He even smiled once.

The usual murmuring of anticipation began when the house-lights dimmed, only to break into wild applause when the stage lights illuminated Ginny, standing alone at center stage. Lorry moved even closer to the brothers' table and grinned when their collective eyes widened in wonder. She found it hard to keep from laughing as she listened to their first observations.

"Holy shit, would you look at her?"

"I'm looking, I'm looking."

"She looks like a movie star."

"No, she looks like a swimsuit model."

"More like a centerfold. She has assets."

"I don't think she's wearing a bra."

"She's a goddess."

Ginny dazzled in absolute brilliance and waved to the audience. She gave Matt a grin and a slight nod, and he instantly began the introduction measures to "Feelin' Alright" by Dave Mason. Her body automatically went into motion with the melody. Her long blond hair spun haphazardly. Her body language and the delivery of the song flowed from her with joy and freedom, which were spiritedly embraced by the audience. On this night, music would truly liberate any of her lingering inhibitions and fill the great expectation she had always held for herself. On this night, she would show off Matt's talent to play the tickling rolls and frills of the blues, the gentleness of a ballad, the drive of rock 'n' roll, and uplifting tenderness of a spiritual. She turned to him during his piano solos and beamed her delight, sharing a unique passion for their music and for each other. She clapped her hands when the music was lively and encouraged the audience to do the same. It was the best they had ever been together.

After the first number, Ginny pointed to Matt and yelled out to the crowd, "He's going to give us a little blue-eyed soul tonight, you guys!"

The audience howled their approval and wildly raised their arms and hands high into the air. The table of brothers, who had yet to realize their friend Matt was the blue-eyed-soul man, remained quiet and subdued. Matt followed with "I Almost Lost My Mind" by Ivory Joe Hunter. There was no pause between numbers; it was one song after another in rapid succession. "A Shot of Rhythm and Blues" by Arthur Alexander, "Everyday (I Have the Blues)" by B. B. King, and "My Baby Just Cares for Me" by Nina Simone, after which Ginny finally took a break and took a sip of water.

"Whew," she exclaimed, "I'm ready for something a little slower."

She allowed the audience to settle back into their seats and smiled at Matt. "Ready, partner?"

Matt nodded and began a gospel arrangement that caught the crowd off guard. Ginny sang "His Eye Is on the Sparrow" in wide-open gospel fashion, stunning the audience into silence. The only standing ovation came from Owen, the skinny kid with the frizzy, unkempt hair at the brothers' table.

Ginny brought a barstool to the stage, sat down, and fanned herself, while Matt moved to the darkened corner of the stage with his acoustic guitar.

She thanked the audience, both inside and outside, once again. "We're going to do something new this evening, and that's to dedicate a song to someone very special who is joining us tonight for the first time. This is 'The Night Rider's Lament,' and it goes out to Mr. Marty Nevin."

From the brothers' back table came an incredulous shout, "Who?"

Ginny smiled. "I guess we know where Mr. Nevin is sitting tonight." The audience laughed and strained to find Marty's whereabouts.

Still standing nearby, Lorry covered her mouth and laughed as five muffled voices spoke at once, "Why didn't you tell us you know her, Marty? What the hell?"

"I don't know her." Marty adamantly scowled; he felt like he'd just swallowed sand.

"Well, unless there's another Marty Nevin here tonight, which we seriously doubt, she seems to know you."

They stopped talking when they heard a guitar strumming by a person obscured in darkness on the back edge of the stage. Ginny sang the song with a slow, mournful voice, and Marty melted into his chair in embarrassment and delight at the same time. As the song concluded, Ginny gestured to the back table. "We sure hope you enjoyed that, Marty Nevin."

"Oh, he did, all right. He's three shades of red," a voice other than Marty's shouted out with glee. The audience cheered and raised their glasses. "To Marty," someone shouted. "To Marty," everyone shouted in return, "whoever he is."

The stage lights dimmed to a single beam on Ginny. She stood still and gathered her strength for "In Trutina." She looked at Matt for a confidence booster. He smiled back, put his hands under his rib cage, and raised it, reminding her to breathe deep and project. He played the almost-inaudible introduction for Ginny and nodded her cue to begin. For the first time, Ginny's beautiful soprano was unleashed, and the bistro crowd became atypically silent. The crowd listened, captivated, as Ginny fastidiously wove through the lyrics with perfect enunciation, holding notes for incredible periods as her voice filled the bistro to the brim. She perfectly performed every accent, every crescendo and decrescendo. Matt stopped his piano accompaniment for the final eight measures, closed his eyes and listened to Ginny, thoroughly infatuated by her voice. He was actually shivering, thrilled by her presentation. The audience remained silent and stunned as her final note drifted to an end. The single spotlight faded to black, and the crowd instantly leapt to their feet with seismic applause, and for the first time in her life, Ginny Simmons had brought an entire audience to tears.

She stood still as the stage lights warmed back up, and she bowed and proudly gestured to Matt, who suddenly began the final song of the set. The audience immediately recognized the music to the Isley Brothers' "Shout." In a minute's time, the audience was ecstatic with the wondrous shift from opera to rock and roll. Ginny bounced and jumped up and down as she led the audience in participating back and forth through both parts of the song.

"Oh, my," she panted after the song ended. "I think I need a little break and maybe a change of clothes too!" She gave a conquering smile to Matt and then to the audience. "We'll be back in thirty minutes. Why don't you go outside and cool down. It's awfully warm in here. Once again, thank you all for coming. We're so very glad you're here with us tonight."

Marty Nevin rushed outside, grateful for the cooler air. He lit up a Marlboro and remained utterly confused about the dedication. He looked with baffled innocence at the brothers, and before they could speak, he pleaded, "I have no idea. Really."

All of them were astonished by Ginny's versatility, as well as her beauty, and how her accompanist could make her sound like Judy Garland for one song and Janis Joplin for the next.

The young woman whom Lionel had spoken with earlier came outside and greeted them, "How did you gentlemen like the first set?"

All five of them uncomfortably shuffled their feet and stammered that they thought it was fine.

"And which of you is Marty Nevin?" Lorry loved playing them.

Marty drew deep on his Marlboro and exhaled. "I am."

Lorry winked at him. "Well, Marty Nevin. You must be a very special guy." Marty shrugged, unconvinced. As cool as he thought he was, he remained in total shock over the special recognition he had received from Ginny.

She stepped up to Lionel, who panicked when she took him by the hand. "Why don't we all go back inside for the second set, handsome. I know you're going to love it." She led the very shocked Lionel back inside the bistro as Marty and the others shuffled in close behind.

During their break, Ginny changed from blue jeans and a cotton blouse into a yellow spaghetti-strapped sundress. She fluffed up the hair off her neck and tied it back with a blue ribbon. She said, "This feels better. What do you think, Mattie?"

Matt had been concentrating so hard on tuning his banjo that he was unaware that Ginny was even in the room. She looked fresh and wonderful. "Wow," he said softly, "you look great, very pretty as always." He was not nervous about playing in front of his buddies but was a little uneasy. He fumbled with his words and finally managed to say, "Um. Best get to it, I guess."

She hooked her arm around his and walked him backstage. "You'll be great, Mattie. As always."

Ginny took to the stage, smiled to the crowd, who had warmly greeted her, turned toward Matt, and announced, "I'd like you to meet the band, ladies and gentlemen. Mattie? Would come up, please?"

With some deliberation, Matt climbed the four steps to the stage with his usual bashful smile, a guitar pick between his lips, and gave his little half wave to the admiring audience. Ginny embraced him and softly kissed his cheek.

"He's going to start us out on the piano," she informed the crowd, and released Matt, giving him a little slap on his bottom as he left the stage, barefooted, to the piano.

Lorry, still standing near the brothers, watched their reaction from slack-jawed disbelief to eyes widened in amazement, their hands clasped over their mouths.

In a voice just loud enough to be heard throughout, Ty exclaimed, "Oh, I don't believe this. I just don't fucking believe this . . . Oops, I suppose I should've kept that to myself."

Mattie looked their way without showing any acknowledgment and shot Ginny a shy grin as if to say, "Yup, those are my buddies, all right."

The second set started out fast, featuring Matt's piano skills and vocal harmony to the Rolling Stones' "Let It Bleed." He played the piano like Ian Stewart would have played, combining the blues with a boogie-woogie blend of soul and rock and roll. The brothers stood and loudly whooped and yelled out Mattie's name with surprise, excitement, and wonder.

Ginny retrieved a tambourine from under her stool and watched as Matt strapped a capo on the second fret of his acoustic guitar and rejoined her at his place beside her side at center stage. Her eyes grew wide in anticipation while Matt quietly counted down the a capella introduction to "I've Seen All Good People" by Yes. Matt played the intricate chords and notes, and Ginny tapped the tambourine with a percussion mallet in slow rhythm and time. Their voices blended in exciting harmony during the presentation, and upon finishing,

Ginny leaned toward Matt. Their foreheads met, and they smiled at each other, knowing they had done their best. She reached up and gently caressed Matt's cheek.

The two barstools and one microphone were removed from the stage, and Ginny and Matt shared a single mic as Matt gently began to strum "Would You Like to Take a Walk." Ginny placed her hands behind her back and coquettishly swayed back and forth with a flirty little smile, their faces only inches apart, her hands on his shoulders. The audience cheered after Ginny gave Matt a little peck on the cheek when the song ended.

Matt gently placed the guitar in its stand, picked up his banjo, and did a last-minute tuning. He picked the instrumental version to Roger Miller's "Oo-De-Lally" one time through and then joined Ginny in singing the pleasant little melody. The audience was delighted and charmed, responding with robust applause and "One more time," loving the quick transition of genres. Matt put the banjo down on top of the piano, now in full view with the planter box full of ferns removed. He took his place at the piano as Ginny stood alone to sing the melody to the Robert Burns poem "Ae Fond Kiss." Matt played flawlessly and in a fashion that enhanced the presentation of Ginny, who sang in her best Scottish brogue. The beautiful yet mourning lyric brought tears to the eyes of many in the crowd, inside the bistro, and to those who had gathered outside. As the song closed, Ginny unhooked her mic, held it in her hand, and to Matt's surprise, walked to the piano and sat down next to him. She leaned into him, put her free arm around his shoulders, and they sang "You Send Me" by Sam Cooke, and once again their practices had resulted in Matt's timely tenor blending remarkably to Ginny's perfect lead vocal.

They stepped back onto center stage, and while Matt was strapping his banjo and finger picks back on, Ginny announced, "We're going to feature Mattie on this song, and please feel free to clap and sing along." Ginny began clapping her hands and tapping her feet in quick 4/4 time; the audience matched her enthusiasm. Matt picked the banjo like Earl Scruggs did to the well-known "Fox and the Goose." After the banjo introduction, Ginny and Matt leaned into the single mic and sang the words. The audience tried to keep up, but soon, scattered voices spread throughout the bistro. Matt didn't mind a bit. As the last number for the evening came upon them, Matt picked up his guitar; the stage lights dimmed once again to a single beam on Ginny, who affectionately sang "PS, I Love You" to Matt's gentle guitar. He didn't play the last four measures, which allowed Ginny to close the song with the only instrument that counted, her voice. She beckoned Matt back to the stage and bowled over the audience, especially the still very awestricken brothers in the back, when she embraced him around his neck and passionately kissed him on the lips. Matt's knees buckled, and his arms hung limp at his sides. He kissed her back. She slowly released him, and with happy tears in her eyes, she grabbed his hand, and they bowed, side by side, to the buzzing audience. Loud whistles came from the back of the bistro, and the audience demanded an encore. Matt whispered something to Ginny, and he was met with a vigorous nod. He picked up his electric guitar, made a slight adjustment to the amp, and then handed a tambourine to Ginny. Their faces went dead serious, which left the crowd to wonder what might be in store. Abruptly, Matt shouted out, "One, two, three, four," and began his favorite Beatles song, "Day Tripper." Ginny playfully accented the tambourine rolls and shakes inches from the face of Matt, who ducked his head away and smiled at her as she sang the harmony to his lead vocal into the single mic, again their faces only inches apart. From that night forward, nobody sat during a Ginny Simmons performance; the audience was always on their feet.

Still glowing after the show, Ginny lingered near the stage and mingled with the gathering crowd. She was experiencing absolute euphoria and excitedly thanked everyone, shook all their hands, and graciously accepted every accolade. The still incredulous brothers remained at their back table, unable to move, and after the main crowd dwindled down to just a few, Lorry approached them and said that if they stayed any longer she was going to charge them rent. But in a sudden motion, Ginny rushed to them, sat down, and introduced herself. All five brothers extended their hands simultaneously.

"Now then," Ginny began with a wide smile, "which of you is Marty?"

Before Marty could identify himself, Owen zealously asked, "Have you accepted the Lord Jesus Christ as your personal savior?"

Ginny's head jerked back and her hand went to her throat in surprise. "Excuse me?"

Ty, who was seated next to Owen, gently slapped him on the back of his head, sending Owen's frizzy tall cocoon of red hair into motion. "Oh, for crying out loud, Owen," he gently admonished. "Not now, okay?"

Owen realized that perhaps this was not the most ideal situation for such conversation, and he offered up a quick apology. "You play a mean tambourine is what I meant to say."

Ginny reached out and touched his forearm. "Maybe another time, Owen, okay? I just wanted to meet all of you. Mattie considers him to be pretty lucky to have friends like you. Now I see why."

Lionel said, "Well, he's, um, never been too specific about what he does here. And we didn't know anything about you. You're amazing, Ginny."

Ty muttered under his breath, "I didn't even know his last name until tonight."

Ginny looked startled but realized by Ty's impish grin that he was joking.

"Is he still here, you think?" Marty asked.

"Oh no," Ginny replied. "He leaves right after the concert." She stood up to leave, and the five brothers gallantly and respectfully stood as well.

Ginny eyed them closely. "We're lucky to have him." She grinned and nodded. "And as you can tell, we're all very fond of him. But he is full of surprises, isn't he?"

The young man at the far right, Randy, knowingly and softly replied, "Nothing he does surprises me."

Ginny studied him; his eyes were glassy and bloodshot. Had he not been leaning on his chair, he most surely would have fallen flat on his face. He had the look of one whose muscle tone was in decline; his skin was covered with red blotches and bruises. And his hands, regardless of his attempt to cover them up, uncontrollably shook. He had the look of defeat.

# An Unnamed Melody

The five brothers, Owen, Ty, Marty, Lionel, and Randy, stealthily hovered above Matt's bunk. He was sound asleep in the fraternity's sleeping porch, where a code of absolute silence was strictly enforced. They still smelled like whiskey. Randy and Owen grabbed Matt's ankles, Ty and Marty took a solid grip of his shoulders, while Lionel clasped his hand over Matt's mouth.

"Oh, Mat-tie," Lionel whispered like Ricky Ricardo did, "I thin' you have some 'splaining to do?"

All Matt could do was roll his eyes from side to side and hope for an upperclassman, none of whom cared for any of the brothers, to silence the group with strict instructions to shut up and get out. Fortunately, this happened rather quickly as one of the members threatened to put them all on report. The five brothers loudly laughed but made a quick exit.

All five stumbled downstairs for breakfast, which was only a few hours after they had come home for the night, and sat in a quiet circle around Matt, who had the Sunday paper spread out before him and a cup of coffee in his hand.

Owen cleared his throat. "Morning, Mattie. Feelin' all right?"

Matt continued his reading. "Yup. How about you?"

"Well," Owen said, "I'm not feelin' too good myself."

"Do you little howling at the moon last night?" Matt asked without looking up.

Ty said, "We were there last night, Mattie. At Ginny's."

"I know," Matt answered and finally looked up with a grin. "I paid for your cheese plates."

"We met her, Mattie," Lionel said. "I mean, Ginny, we met her. Why haven't you told us about her or you and her, in this case?"

Matt shrugged. "Not much to tell. I work for her and Lorry, who, incidentally, is the one who took you by your hand last night. She thinks you're handsome."

"She owns the place?" Lionel exclaimed. "That little gal?"

Matt stretched and cautioned in good nature, "Don't let her size fool you." He smiled. "She has gumption."

Owen said excitedly, "Ginny came to our table and talked to us, Mattie. She likes you."

Matt stretched and yawned. "Like I said, I just work there."

Ty held up a finger to make a point. "So, Mattie," he began, "just to clarify, and please be candid. Are you and Ginny like a couple? I mean, are you going out with her? What's the story?"

Matt cracked a weak smile. "I'm the accompanist, that's all."

"So," Ty continued, "that whole Betty Boop routine she did around you, 'Would You Like to Take a Walk?' What was that all about, huh? And remember, we're brothers. You must speak the truth."

Matt returned to reading the paper. "It's just part of her act, I think. She does that whenever we play that song."

The five brothers held incredulous looks at one another, their collective eyes saying "How clueless is this guy? Jeez."

Marty walked behind Matt and put his hands on his shoulders. "And that kiss at the end? Was that just part of the show too?"

"Well," Matt replied, "I admit that kind of took me by surprise."

Marty said, "From where we were sitting, you didn't seem to mind it too much. And you want us to believe there's nothing going on between the two of you?"

Matt shrugged. "Nope, nothing at all. She's kind of like a sister."

Owen laughed. "Yeah, a sister who parked a big wet one on you."

Ty asked, "So you won't mind if one of us asks her out then?"

Matt sat upright, a surprised expression on his face. "No, of course not."

Randy, who had yet to speak because he was still drunk and high from the night before, began to rock back and forth in his chair. He and Matt made eye contact, and Randy smiled at him with a slight nod. Randy was the only one who understood this quiet friend of theirs.

Marty, his hand still on Matt's shoulders, said, "You're good, man. Really good. Thanks for the dedication last night, Mattie."

Matt tilted his head back and replied, "Well, I only play the good notes. But you're welcome."

Owen yawned, which caused a chain reaction among the brothers. He shook his head. "Uff. I'm going back to bed."

One by one the rest followed suit except for Randy, who moved to a chair directly across Matt.

"You are something else, my friend," Randy said with admiration, and then cracked open a beer for breakfast.

Randy Holloway had known Matt since their high school days. They both played quarterback although at different schools within the same district. However, their pathways to athletic success took different paths. Matt had never participated in any kind of sport until his senior year, when he shocked Mom and Dad with his intentions of trying out for the football team. His parents were naturally concerned, worried that Matt would be competing against others who had been taught the basic skills for years, as had Randy. Randy had lived a privileged life. Besides that was the woeful head coach, who had never produced a winning team and was on his last year before his retirement.

Randy's father, Vernon Holloway, was a duplicitous, vulgar, belligerent man who incessantly controlled and burdened his son with presumptive expectations that no teenager could possibly achieve. Vernon tended to bask in his self-importance and of those whom he could steal from. Time after time, year after year, Randy's many attempts to earn his father's love were met with disdain, and he learned from an early age that his father's attentions were based on performance, not on relationship. Vernon's pandering efforts to control, intrude on, and tamper with his son's life led to nothing but repugnant dysfunction, leaving Randy without the ability or competency to understand his connection with Vernon and, more to the point, a purpose for his life.. He began drinking, sneaking bourbon or whatever was handy, from his father's liquor cabinet when he was fourteen. By age fifteen, he was a functional alcoholic, stranded in a life and a future without optimism or hope. Miraculously, he continued to perform admirably on the football field and was All-League at his position until his senior year and his final game. Randy had led his team to three consecutive undefeated seasons and was well on his way to a fourth, an accomplishment that would earn him a scholarship to the perennial football power and cross-state rival, Northern University. From his behind-the-scene manipulations and promotions, Vernon considered the scholarship for his son a done deal. But during Randy's senior season, an unexpected athlete from a perennial last-place team had appeared from nowhere. He dazzled the opponents with his ferocity on defense and equally with his finesse at the quarterback position. He had been awarded the All-League award and snatched away the scholarship that Vernon had so carefully schemed for his son. After the championship game, the quarterback from the opposing team found his way to Randy, who stood dejected and alone on the sideline. He offered his hand and said, "You're an amazing player, I envy you." Randy, still grieved by defeat, looked up at his opponent and stared into the kindest dark-blue eyes he had ever seen and became fixated on a humility that was completely foreign to him.

"I'm Matthew," the boy said. "You played great. Best of luck to you."

Randy wasn't sure if it was coincidence or just karma that he and Matt pledged the same fraternity at Northern State. Randy actually had no choice as he was a legacy, his father having been a member thirty years prior. Thinking and hoping he was away from his father's unyielding meddling, Randy embraced NSU and the fraternity too. He had recognized Matt Jensen on the first day of pledging but was hesitant to approach him. They should have been rivals, they should have disliked each other, and he was surprised when Matt refused to belittle him, which was what Randy most certainly would have done had the circumstances been reversed.

Randy soon discovered the congeniality, quiet humor, and unpretentious nature of this bashful young man, and they quickly became friends. Not because of Matt's accomplishments, but because of his humble, quiet, and gracious personality. Matt Jensen had the kind of character that nobody else in Randy's life had.

And now, with his hands on top of his head, he sat across his friend Matthew Jensen and smiled at him. Matt looked back at Randy with his usual bashful grin and made a subtle shrug.

"You feel like going outside?" Matt asked. "It's a nice morning for a walk. It might clear out the cobwebs a little bit."

Randy gulped down his beer and slammed the bottle on the table. "Good idea, let's go."

They were the only two people out on Sunday morning as everyone on campus, and in town, usually wouldn't emerge until around noon.

"Why don't you come and see Ginny next Friday?" Matt asked brightly. "Maybe I can get her to dedicate a song for you."

'Yeah," Randy blandly replied. "'Tiny Bubbles' would be good. But I can't. My dad will be here, ruining my life."

Unfortunately for Randy, his father, in his never-ending pursuit to feed his insatiable ego, endured the arduous nine-hundred-mile round trip drive to NSU twice a month and every weekend during football season if there were home games. He had become a hero to the fraternity membership. He made lavish donations to the building fund and had hosted catered barbecues and parties. He brought cases of liquor and arranged for prostitutes, anything to gain the members' adoration. Every person, except the six brothers, Matt included, kowtowed to Vernon, and little fuss was made when he brutally belittled his son in front of the entire fraternity, calling him, among other things, the biggest loser the family had ever produced. Matt knew that Randy drank as an escape, and the two often discussed the situation. Matt felt a desperate need to help Randy in any way he could.

"He doesn't cut you much slack, does he?" Matt said.

Randy stopped walking and sat on a concrete bench outside the student union building. Despite the fact it had yet to open for the day, Matt was able to talk the early kitchen crew members at the union's café out of a couple of cups of coffee. Randy took out a cigarette, but before lighting up, he smiled at Matt and asked if smoking was permissible. Matt chuckled and told him since they were outside that it was probably all right.

"My dad has no desire to cut me any amount of slack," Randy said. "You know, he's threatening to cut me off if I don't pull straight As this semester."

Matt looked into his coffee cup and then up to the sun. The sky was full of dust and smoke from local wheat farmers burning the stubble left after harvest. Later that day, it would probably rain mud. "I just don't get it, Randy. I mean, you're smart, you're personable, and you're motivated. You made the dean's list. What more does he expect?"

Randy slowly moved his fingers through his hair. "He wants me to be more successful than he is. He wants me to be someone he can brag about to his country club cronies and then take the credit. But I can't seem do anything good enough for him. He's never going to be satisfied or happy with me or anyone. Except you."

"Me?" Matt exclaimed with a start. "But he doesn't even know me!"

"After last night, I'm not sure anyone really knows you." Randy bitterly laughed and then became disheartened. "But he knows who you are. He worships you. Remember last year's game?"

Matt was dumbfounded. "But that didn't mean anything. It was only a game, for crying out loud."

Randy said, "Maybe to you and me, but not to Dad." He had a vacant look in his eyes. "It was everything to him, and I failed."

Matt remained stunned. "But you didn't fail, Randy. You were brilliant."

Randy painfully grinned and put his hand on Matt's shoulder, appreciative of Matt's innocent virtue and sincerity. "I lost, and that's all that mattered to him."

Matt had a difficult time processing this and could make no sense of the dysfunctional relationship between Randy and his dad. As much as he wanted to, he couldn't console Randy and tell him that he knew what he was going through; it was completely unfamiliar and foreign to him.

"I suppose we all have people who influence our lives," Matt said, his tone conciliatory and soothing. "Sometimes it's good, other times, totally overpowering." He shifted uncomfortably. "I do know that nobody can or should force us in the choices we make. You're right, Randy, I don't understand what the deal is with your dad, except that it's difficult for you and difficult for me to watch, for all of us to watch. But I know you, and I know that, if anyone has the strength, the inner strength, to fight through this struggle and to free yourself from it, it's you."

Randy crushed out his cigarette and finished his coffee. "I hope you're right, Mattie," he whispered. "I hope you're right."

*　　*　　*

Lorry and Ginny were surprised to hear music drifting through the bistro when they arrived for Sunday's afternoon performance. Sunday concerts were much more relaxed than the high energy of Friday and Saturday nights. It was illegal in Three Forks to serve alcoholic beverages on Sunday, so Lorry served coffee and desserts. It was part of the business plan. Ginny performed for one hour, took a fifteen-minute break, and then sang for one more hour. Patrons requested songs from previous concerts and, to their delight, were graciously accommodated.

Although it was common for Matt to arrive early to tune, it was unusual to find him playing the piano. Lorry and Ginny furtively poked their heads around the big planter box and curiously watched Matt as he played transitional chords up and down the scale and then paused to write in the key signature, notes, and chords on blank charts.

"Hi, you guys," he said without looking up. "The coffee and desserts smell great."

Lorry and Ginny looked at each other, both wondering how Matt always knew when he was being watched.

"You're composing, Mattie," Ginny said. "You never told us you wrote music, although I'm hardly surprised."

Matt stopped. "It's nothing."

"It's beautiful, Mattie," Ginny replied, very impressed. "I can't wait to hear the harmonics. Are you a lyricist too?"

Before he could reply, Lorry eagerly asked, "What do you call this song, Mattie? When can you have it ready?" She observed a flash of worry and unhappiness on his face that vanished just as quickly as it had come. Ginny noticed it too.

Matt ignored their concern and gathered up the sheet music. "It's a work in progress," he said. "I don't know what to call it."

Lorry turned and walked to the supervise the kitchen. "Well, okay, Mattie. But you let me know as soon as your unnamed melody is finished. It's beautiful."

Matt could not tell them that the composition was already finished. He couldn't tell anybody that he wrote to soothe himself and to try to make some sense of Randy's path of self-destruction. He had no intention of ever playing the song in public.

Ginny sat beside him. "I met your friends last night," she said, and threw a bright smile. She put her arms around his shoulders. "I like them."

"Not nearly as much as they like you," Matt teased. Ginny blushed.

She withdrew her arm and folded her arms on her lap. "Randy has a drinking problem, doesn't he?" It was a statement rather than a question.

"Yes," Matt carefully replied, "he has troubles at home."

"You're trying to help him, aren't you?"

Matt hesitated, "I'm trying to, but I don't know what to do."

Ginny drew up and gave him a peck on the cheek. "We'll try and help too."

"Thanks," Matt whispered. "I'll take any help I can get. I think I'm a little over my head."

He suddenly cheered up, eagerly clapped his hands, and asked, "Now, what are you dazzling these folks this afternoon, hmm?"

*   *   *

"I think I made a fool of myself here last night with my dad," Randy told Matt. They were sitting on the front porch at the fraternity, enjoying the shade provided by the ancient elm trees that had been planted along the street decades ago.

"From what I've heard, it was the other way around," Matt replied.

Randy and his father became involved in a nose-to-nose shouting match in the great room inside the fraternity the night before. Randy had screamed at his dad to stop interfering and controlling his life with a veiled threat of "Or else." Both had consumed more liquor than common sense allowed for.

Vernon shoved his son to the floor and stood over him like a conquering hero. "Or what?" he shouted like he was using a bullhorn. "You couldn't zip up your pants without me showing you how, junior. You're a goddamn drunk, just like your mother." He spat on his son, still prone on the floor. "You're useless."

Vernon turned to leave but suddenly spun around. "Hey, where's this Jensen kid? That's who I want to meet. He's the only winner around this place."

Randy struggled to his feet and charged his father but was restrained by Ty and Marty.

Vernon bitterly laughed. "See what I mean? You can't even fight for yourself."

Someone among the shocked crowed mentioned that Jensen worked downtown at a place called Ginny's Bistro.

Vernon started for the front door. "Shouldn't be hard to find in this one-horse town," he snorted. "See you girls later." He stumbled to his car, revved the engine, and tore off down the hill toward downtown Three Forks.

Lionel ran to the phone and frantically dialed 0 for the operator. He needed to warn Matt or somebody that Vernon was heading their way.

"Ginny's Bistro, this is Lorry," her voice cheerfully answered. "Can I help you?"

"Oh, Lorry," Lionel hurriedly said, "I'm Mattie's friend, Lionel. I don't know if I remember me or not."

"Well, Lionel, of course I remember you," Lorry said even more cheerfully. "You're the handsome one."

"Um, okay," Lionel uncomfortably replied. "Listen, a very drunk and very angry man is headed down to your place right now. He's driving a big Lincoln. Anyway, he's looking for Mattie. You can't let him inside."

Lorry turned from cheerful to fiery in a heartbeat. "Is it Randy's father?" she asked rapidly.

Lionel wondered how she knew, but he managed to stammer, "Ye-yes, it is."

"Don't worry, Lionel," Lorry said assuredly. "We can handle him. Oh, and, Lionel?"

"Ye-yes?"

"Thanks for calling."

Lorry quick stepped outside to alert Raul, and at that same moment, Vernon Holloway slammed down the brakes of his Lincoln, left it parked in the middle of Main, and stumbled toward the entrance. Raul instantly met him on the curb, grabbed him by the back of his shirt, and with little effort, shoved him back into his car with a warning never to come back. Vernon, frightened and dumbfounded, gunned the engine and sped away to an unknown destination. Afterward, Lorry dialed the fraternity and impatiently waited for someone to find Lionel.

"Hello?" Lionel asked, gasping for breath.

"Lionel, it's Lorry down at the bistro. Thanks again for the warning. The situation is well in hand. Ginny and Mattie never knew he was here."

She could feel Lionel's relief over the phone. "Oh, and, Lionel?"

"Yeah?"

"We should get together sometime, okay?"

"Um, yeah, okay. Sure."

"Good night, Lionel." She hung up before he could say anything more.

"Why don't you come down to Ginny's this afternoon?" Matt asked Randy. "It's our last concert before school is out."

"I think I will," Randy replied, suddenly renewed. "I could use a little Ginny and Mattie magic tonight. You know, a swift musical smack to the forehead."

The bistro was filled to capacity when Randy arrived. Lorry had asked Raul to be on the lookout for him with the assurance that she could find a place for Randy regardless if it breached the city occupation code or not. Ginny and Matt's soft melodies and harmonies soon put Randy fast asleep, slumped down into his seat. When Ginny whispered to Matt if he thought Randy was all right. Matt smiled and whispered back that he'd had a rough night.

"He's just resting his eyes," Matt assured her. "Trust me, he can hear every little note we play."

It was the last performance before spring semester ended. Lorry closed the bistro during finals week but reopened the evening of commencement. It was a victorious evening for Ginny, as she had just earned her degree, and Lorry expected a celebratory crowd. She appealed to the Downtown Merchants Association if she could open an hour earlier than usual. The Downtown Merchants Association didn't hesitate since all members had planned to be in the audience that night, and Dan asked for a reserved table for six. It was the first and only time Lorry would honor such a request and told Dan she would see it done.

The bistro closed for two weeks, as the business plan dictated, in order for the dust to settle after the students, excited for summer vacation, made their predictable and defining departure. Ginny's would reopen for summer hours, Thursday through Sunday afternoon. Concerts in the city park, free of charge, would be held once a week. The Saturday open street market on Main would remain in operation during the summer. Ginny and Matt would set up outside the bistro for an hour and then resume the performance inside during the evening. Although crowds were plainly thinner, downtown Three Forks remained a beehive of activity.

For Randy Holloway, it became the worst summer of his life. Since he had no scholarship, Vernon made it a compulsory task that, if Randy wanted to stay in school, he had to work for him. His father's verbal abuse was cruel, at home and in front of the office staff for everyone to hear. Although Randy had become conditioned for this and desensitized, he counted the days until September, when he could return to NSU.

Fall semester of his sophomore year proved a disaster. Vernon had put Randy on his own version of probation for failing to earn straight As the previous semester, and Randy soon fell back into his bad habits. Matt told him of a free sobriety program at the hospital and volunteered to go with him, which they did but only once. Randy was afraid his father would find out through the many covert sources he paid to keep tabs on his son. He quit going to classes and by midterm was placed on the detention list. He progressed from alcohol to using pot and even heroin when he could find it. He was glad for his friends' offers to help, especially Matt's, but he was unresponsive. His father called him and, with spite in his voice, told him that he had called admissions to demand a refund on his tuition. He also withdrew his housing allowance and canceled his checking account.

"You're on your own now, you stupid shit," Vernon told him. They were the last words he would ever speak to his son.

Randy found part-time work on campus and slept on the couch in the house that Matt and Lionel shared. But he became a nuisance on campus and in town and frequently called Matt to pick him up from the campus police station. Matt worried about him but felt helpless. Randy's eyes were constantly glazed and vacant. His body continually shook, and he became painfully thin. When Matt noticed the bruises on his arms weren't healing, he took him to see Emily, who did everything she could to heal his body. But neither Matt nor Emily nor Lionel could do anything to fix a brain and heal a body that refused to be healed.

On a moonless and frosty October night, Lionel was startled awake by loud and continuous banging on the front door. He checked his watch and saw that it was twelve thirty in the morning. He stumbled to put on his pants, opened the front door to find two campus policemen holding up an unconscious Randy Holloway between them.

One of the cops spoke and nodded to the street, "We found this guy passed out on the sidewalk. Do you know him?"

Lionel nodded. "He's kind of staying here until he can find his own place."

The policemen let go of Randy, and he fell into Lionel's arms. "Keep an eye on him, huh?"

Matt arrived home, and the cops recognized him as the fellow who always came for Randy whenever he was brought in for drunk and disorderly.

One of the cops pointed to Matt. "You need to make sure this doesn't happen again. He could've frozen to death. And besides, next time we find him like this, we'll have to run him over to the county jail."

Matt promised that he and Lionel would keep their eyes on him.

"You better," the cop said as they turned to leave, "or he'll be sobering up in a cell and facing charges."

Matt nodded that he understood. He told Lionel he'd stay up with Randy until he came around. "I don't know what to do, Lionel? Do you?" Lionel shook his sleepy head that he didn't know either. Around 3:00 a.m., Randy woke up and noticed a blanket had been wrapped around him. He saw Matt asleep in a chair across the room. He picked up a paperback book and gently threw it at Matt, instantly waking him.

"Oh, hey," Matt asked with a yawn, "how ya feeling?"

"Like a road grader ran over me," Randy moaned.

Matt went to the kitchen and brought him a glass of apple juice. "Here, drink this, you might feel better." He also brought a box of soda crackers that Randy quickly ate.

Matt asked, "So what happened tonight?"

"I got drunk, I got high. Maybe I picked a fight or two and got knocked out. When I came around, I started walking here, that's when the cops found me kind of staggering down the sidewalk. I think I passed out." He shifted up to one arm. "I bet you told the cops that you'd keep an eye on me and that this will never happen again, didn't you?"

Matt shrugged with a smile and nodded. "Where do we go from here, Randy? My sister told me that you'd be welcome back into the sobriety program anytime, but nobody can force you to go."

"Wait, what? Your sister? Who's she?" Randy asked.

"Well, yeah, you remember," Matt replied. "That doctor we met with a while back, she's my sister."

Randy bitterly chuckled. "You do have a habit of showing up at the right time, man, I'll give you that. Probably saved me from a citation and a night in the county jail. I'm grateful for that, Mattie, I really am."

"It still doesn't solve anything, Randy," Matt answered. "Will you just think about talking to Emily? That's my sister's name."

"I don't know, maybe," Randy distantly replied. "I just feel beyond help, like I've hit rock bottom." He stared blankly at the floor for several minutes. "You're the best friend I've ever had, Mattie, and I know you mean well." He went back to his staring and then rolled back on the couch. Matt heard him say to no one, "But there's no way out but to . . . how did my life get so screwed up?"

Matt tried to stay awake but dozed off for a while. He woke up with a start and a deep-down feeling that something was wrong. He noticed the kitchen light was on and was certain he had turned it off earlier. He rushed to the kitchen and found the most horrific sight he had ever seen. Randy lay wildly twitching on the floor. A piece of surgical tubing was loosely tied to his arm above his elbow, and a broken hypodermic needle was next to his body, the tip still stuck in his inner arm. Pale red bubbles oozed from out from the needle's tip. He had cut his wrists with a paring knife and was now lying faceup in a river of dark, almost-black blood gushing out of his body. Matt screamed for Lionel (he didn't know how many times), grabbed some dish towels, and tried to bind Randy's wounds. He didn't touch the needle. He screamed again for Lionel, who finally came but was so horrified he couldn't move. He stared down at Randy and Matt and then threw up. Matt tried to hold up Randy's arms and pleaded for Lionel to call for an ambulance. Totally disoriented and frantic, Lionel managed to called the hospital. The ambulance arrived ten minutes later and the attendants immediately began first aid. They said Randy was still alive but they would have to move fast. Matt insisted he ride with them to the hospital, which the attendants refused to allow until Matt told them that Dr. Jensen was his sister. It was a short ride that seemed eternal. Matt cradled Randy's head on his lap and watched his eyes flicker open.

He weakly smiled and managed to whisper, "It's not your fault, Mattie, it's not your fault. Tell Dad I'm sorry."

After an hour of waiting, Emily solemnly walked to her blood-soaked brother and cradled him the way she used to do after he had fallen off his bike. She rocked him back and forth and allowed his tears to fall. "I'm so sorry, Mattie. He's gone." She let him cry. The unnamed melody drifted through his head.

Emily said, "Now, you must listen to me. You're in shock, and I insist on admitting you until this afternoon or until I'm confident you're all right. I'll call Lorry and Ginny for you, it'll be okay."

Matt was dazed with disbelief. He barely made sense of what Emily had told him but nodded anyway. He couldn't control his shaking, and Emily called for an orderly to bring a wheelchair and to take him upstairs to a room; she'd handle the paperwork. She administered a sedative to make him sleep, and she stayed with her brother, whom she loved so much and felt so badly for, until he woke up nearly eight hours later.

"What do you remember from last night, Mattie?" she gently asked, knowing she had to make him talk it through.

Matt tried to process his thoughts. When he spoke, his words were flat and staccato, his face unmoving. "I remember finding Randy on the floor and wrapping towels around his wrists. I remember the blood. I remember you telling me he was gone. That's all." He began to cry. "He was my best friend, Emmy, and I let him die."

Emily rushed to his side and held him, rocking him back and forth. "Shush, shush, shush. It's not your fault, Mattie. It's not your fault."

That evening, a single sheet of paper was stapled outside the bistro's door. It read as follows:

Ginny's Bistro will be closed until further notice in memory of our friend, Randy Holloway. We are greatly saddened by his death. May he rest in peace.

Sincerely,
Lorraine Cullen, Virginia Simmons,
and Matthew Jensen.

# Lorry and Lionel

Maybe it was the horrifying sight of Randy Holloway's mutilated body on his kitchen floor. Maybe it was the guilt he felt from his failure to protect and help his friend. Or maybe it was the unexpected and dreary six-hundred-mile drive from Three Forks to the coast for Randy's funeral. Matt found himself entangled in silent anguish without any ambition to engage in conversation with the brothers, Lionel, Ty, Marty, and Owen, as they began the solemn trip in Ty's 1962 Valiant. Matt stared at the countryside, his eyes as distant as the smoke-filled horizon. His aberrant sadness, his loss and frustration, the burden he had thought long ago outgrown and suppressed to the past, had surfaced with haunting cruelty. He could not help thinking over and over that, had he not fallen asleep, perhaps he could have kept Randy from damaging his body to the point of death. He could not stop thinking, regardless of the continuous efforts by Emily and the brothers, all of whom tried to convince him that Randy's decision to end his life wasn't his fault, and although he had emphatically tried his best to help, he should not blame himself. But Matt did blame himself. To the brothers' dismay, he remained doubtful and inconsolable. None of them understood how Matt could make his life so miserable; it did not seem to be in his nature. Even with the kindest of intentions, he had failed his friend and wondered why it was so easy for him to care for Randy but have no interest to invest and care for himself. After two hours into the drive, he arrived at the decision to will his despair away, to bury it deep into his soul, and never again allow sorrow and despondency consume him with such savage cruelty.

The impact of such sudden and permanent loss, especially to one of their own, was a new experience for the brothers, except for Marty, who had lost his father while still in high school. It was a quiet and somber drive to Matt's house, where they would be staying for the weekend. Mom and Dad were kind and gracious to the brothers and, despite the circumstances, were excited to meet Matt's friends, of whom he had spoken with great affection.

Vernon Holloway found no sympathy among the mourners. He sat alone in the front row of the temple during the funeral, a man whom very few, if any, respected. His wife and two daughters, unwilling to sit with him, were placed two rows behind. The rabbi made quick work of the memorial and rushed through the prayer service. No extra words were offered. The five brothers participated in the mitzvot, and none of them made eye contact with Vernon, let alone speak to him. Matt suggested they should at least offer their condolences, but Marty, ostensibly speaking on behalf of the group, bitterly said, "We're not talking to that son of a bitch." Matt made the solitary walk to say a few words to Mr. Holloway.

"Mr. Holloway," Matt said, "I'm Matthew Jensen. Randy was our good friend. I, I mean we, just wanted you to know how sorry we are for your loss." Vernon looked up into the kindest dark-blue eyes he had ever seen or at least had ever noticed. Matt returned his stare and had never before seen such a pitiful display of pain, remorse, and bereavement on a man's face. He wondered if it was sincere.

Vernon replied, his voice hoarse, "Thank you for being my son's friend, Matthew." He gestured toward the scowling brothers. "And the others too. Randy was lucky to have known you all. I wish I would have discovered that for myself."

"Yes, sir," Matt replied. He quickly turned to leave, but Vernon grabbed his arm.

"Keep in touch, Mattie," he whispered, "please?"

Surprised that Vernon used his nickname, Matt gave him a hesitant nod and then picked a small clump of soil, broke it up, and let it sift through his fingers onto Randy's casket. He left Vernon standing alone and hoped someone would forgive him as he stared into Randy's grave, crying.

Matt and Lionel found Lorry and Ginny in the parking lot, and Matt invited them to his parents' house for dinner.

Lorry looked at Lionel, who instantly blushed. "We'd love to, Mattie. Wouldn't we, Ginny?"

Ginny enthusiastically agreed. "Should we just follow you, Mattie?" she asked, eager to meet Matt's parents.

"Or," Lorry piped in, "maybe we should have Lionel ride along with us to guide the way?"

Lionel, tongue-tied as ever, stammered that he wasn't familiar with the city, so Lorry and Ginny had better follow behind Ty's Valiant. But he did ride with them.

Lorry kept about twelve inches off Ty's rear fender from the temple to the Jensen home and parked behind him on the street. After unfolding himself from the back seat, Matt looked across the street and saw an elderly man struggling to crank up his lawn mower.

"You guys go on in," he told them. "I'll be right back."

Mom and Dad greeted them at the front door and introduced themselves to Lorry and Ginny. Mom pulled Lorry aside. "Thank you for hiring Matthew," she said. "You've really helped him and with much more than just his college expenses." She rolled her eyes. "Now if he would only choose a major."

Mom excused herself to the kitchen with Owen on her heels. "It sure smells good in here, Mrs. Jensen," he cheerfully said. "Is there anything I can help you with?"

Mom raised an eyebrow but found Owen's request to be completely authentic. "No, thanks, Owen. I know my way around the kitchen fairly well."

Still, Owen persisted in his usual good-natured manner until Mom finally told him, "This is a one-butt kitchen, young man, and regardless of how skinny yours is, it won't fit. Now scoot."

Dejected, Owen turned to leave, but Mom gave him a hug and stuffed a piece of garlic bread in his mouth. She thanked him again for his offer and then gently pushed him out of the kitchen.

In the living room, Dad was pleasantly asking each of them where they had grown up and what they were studying. He wasn't invasive but gently brought some relaxation to them after the misery of the day, prodding them into thinking and talking of other things. Dad was good at that.

"You know," he warmly said, "Bev and I were a little concerned when Matthew decided to enroll at NSU. He's so quiet, you know? We thought he'd have trouble fitting in and making friends. I understand now why he speaks so highly of you all. I think he depends on you much more than he realizes."

Ginny said, "He's very special, Mr. Jensen, but I understand your concern." She looked at Lorry. "We hardly remembered he was working at the bistro, he was so quiet. But all of a sudden, he opened up, precisely when he discovered we were having a trouble with our music."

Ty spoke up, "He's one of a kind, Mr. Jensen. He's not like anyone we've ever met before. It's hard to . . ."

"To define?" Dad finished with a grin.

"Exactly," Marty replied. "He always seems to have the right answer, the right solution to everything. Except math, of course." They all laughed.

Owen, with a big smile on his face, entered in from the kitchen, looked around the room where everybody was casually chatting. "Hey, where's Mattie?" he asked.

Nobody knew where Matt had disappeared after they got home until Lorry, glancing out the bay windows, pointed outside. "There he is, across the street."

Dad looked and laughed. "Hey Bev," he shouted, "come and look at this."

She came out of the kitchen, drying her hands on her apron, and followed Dad's pointing finger to see Matt cutting Mr. Winkleman's yard.

Mom and Dad laughed together and explained that Matthew had been cutting the Winkleman's grass since he was eight years old.

"He traded Mrs. Winkleman's yard work for piano lessons," Dad explained. "She only taught him for about two months but he kept on doing their yard work for free until he left for college. She gave him cookies."

Six voices rang out in agreement, "That sounds like Mattie, all right."

Lorry made a premeditative maneuver to sit next to Lionel at the dining room table. Ginny sat across from her and Marty and Ty, each of them frantic to engage her in conversation.

"Well, now," Dad said with satisfaction, "it's been a long time since this table has been fully occupied. Dig in, everybody."

Owen piped up, "Mr. Jensen? Do you mind if I say grace first?"

Dad smiled and nodded. "Of course, Owen. I don't mind at all."

Owen prayed for God's blessing for their hosts, the Holloway family, and for the dinner they were about to receive. He ended with "In Jesus's name we pray. Amen."

Dad said, "Owen, you are a delightful young man, regardless of your hair." Owen tried to thank him, but his mouth was already full of mashed potatoes.

Mom and Dad had anticipated the weary day their guests had been through. They made pleasant conversation and kept everyone amused with stories of their five children, the Wild Bunch, as they grew up. All went well until Lionel suddenly let out a loud yelp of surprise. Lorry had begun to playfully rub her toes against his shin.

"Oh my, Lionel," Mom asked, concerned. "Are you all right, dear? You're sweating, and your face is so pale!"

"Ye-yes, fine," he managed to say.

Lorry gave Ginny a quick wink that made her giggle. Matt figured it out and laughed out loud. Soon, everyone caught on and began laughing at Lionel, whose face turned from white to crimson.

After dessert was served and the dishes were cleaned up, with Owen's eager help, Matt brought out new pages of sheet music that had been delivered to the house. The song was named, "Seven Bridges Road" by Steve Young. Ginny carefully studied the charts while Matt went upstairs to retrieve his first guitar. She agreed the song would be a good fit but that Mattie would have to sing harmony.

"I can carry the tune," she said. "Do you want to try it right now?"

"Sure, but I need to tune this guitar. It's been a while since I've used it, and the strings have probably stretched out a little."

Ginny looked at Mom, blinked hard, and smiled. "He tunes a lot."

Mom rolled her eyes. "Oh, we know, dear. We know."

The tuning finished, Matt spread the sheet music on the coffee table, and they performed the song at a moderate tempo. Even trying it out for the first time, they sang the song with perfect melody and harmony. Mom and Dad gasped in wonder. Emily had told her parents how special the two were together, but they had not expected such a gifted and professional sound. It was the first time they had heard Ginny's extraordinary voice and the magical, almost-mystical connection she and Matthew shared.

Marty and Ty listened from the back patio since Mom did not allow smoking in the house.

After they finished, Mom gushed, "Emily told us that you sing perfectly together."

"And you look perfect together too," Dad added.

"Well, thank you," Ginny replied. "I think so, too." She turned to Matt. "This one's a keeper, Mattie. And also, I think you should sing with me more often."

Everyone agreed except Matt, who reminded them that he was an accompanist, nothing more. He would provide backup vocals if the music demanded or was directed otherwise by Lorry.

"You may consider yourself to be so directed, Matthew Aaron Jensen," Lorry said, her voice soft and inviting. During the song, she had cozied up to a very uncomfortable Lionel.

She asked him, rather cunningly, "Lionel? I'm hoping you would do me a big favor."

Lionel stammered back, "Wh-what kind of a favor?"

Lorry answered, "Ginny is driving her own car back to Three Forks tomorrow, and I'd really appreciate it if you would ride along with me, you know, to keep me company. I'll pick you up here, or you can spend the night with me and my parents."

Lionel stared at her with his mouth agape and thought about Lorry's request. She smiled encouragingly at him. Finally, he managed to say he'd do it but that he would rather be picked up here at Mattie's house.

She touched his arm and said, "Great, I'll pick you up at nine o'clock tomorrow morning. We can have lunch along the way."

Marty quickly volunteered to ride with Ginny to keep her company too, an offer that she accepted. Ty scowled at him.

"I call shotgun in Ty's car," Owen cried out.

Matt leaned toward Ginny, his voice low, "She's had this treachery planned from the beginning, hasn't she?"

Ginny smiled. "And does that surprise you, hmm?"

It was, as Lionel would often recall, the most harrowing but interesting ride of his life. Lorry drove near the speed of sound, with reckless control, a single finger on the steering wheel. By the time Ty and Ginny had reached the designated place for lunch, Lorry and Lionel had already come and gone. Lorry assumed her attempts at conversation with Lionel might be difficult at first; he was naturally tongue-tied, but it seemed that Lionel didn't possess the skills to even put a coherent sentence together. He was pretty good with one-word replies though, so Lorry changed her tactics by engaging him in the common-ground knowledge they shared.

"So, Lionel, tell me," she began. "Is Mattie a good roommate?"

"Yes," he replied. "He's the best."

"Oh? And why is that, Lionel? What makes him the best?"

Lionel thought it over for a few miles. "Well, he's quiet. He's easy to talk to. He's very neat. He makes up his bed every day." He searches for a word that might impress Lorry. "Um, he's phlegmatic."

"Hmm," Lorry retorted, "it sounds to me like you live with a maid, is that it, Lionel? I mean, does he cook for you too? Does he make up your bed as well?"

"No," he replied, irritated.

"Okay, okay, Lionel. You don't have to get sore at me," Lorry scolded.

Lionel became contrite. "I'm sorry. I thought you were making fun of me, that's all."

"Well, I'm not making fun of you," Lorry snapped. "I'm trying to create a dialogue. Is that all right with you, Lionel?"

Lionel stared into the empty highway and wondered where all this was heading. He thought, *Does she like me or something?* "Sure, a dialogue is fine," he said with a sheepish grin.

He remembered Mattie telling him that even Lorry's friendly voice sounded like she was scolding someone. "He's genuinely modest," Lionel said. "I've never heard him say anything negative about anybody or anything. He's, well, he's like nobody I've ever met before. I think Randy's death has affected him more than we know. He thinks he's to blame, that it was all his fault."

"Well, that's absurd," Lorry retorted, thinking of Randy's vulgar father.

Lionel sighed. "It is to us, maybe. I-I don't know how to explain this, but he went kind of dark for a couple of days. He wouldn't talk, he wouldn't eat. He really didn't brighten up until dinner last night, after he helped that old guy across the street cut his lawn."

"Hmpf," Lorry replied. But she had seen it too. She had seen the light go out of Mattie's eyes. She was just not surprised, but shocked and concerned at how quickly Mattie's disposition could darken. They were all shocked by Randy's death, but she worried about how hard it had affected Mattie.

After a few silent miles had gone by, Lorry absently began humming the music to Matt's unnamed melody.

"That's Mattie's new song!" Lionel exclaimed. "How do you know it? He plays it every day on his guitar, over and over. It's nice, isn't it?"

"He plays it on the piano too," Lorry told him. "But he won't tell us if it's finished or not."

Lionel let a few more silent miles pass by. "I think, well, I'm just guessing, but I think it's just for him. He says it's therapeutic."

"Hmm," Lorry said with a conniving tone, "I'd like to get a copy of it. Do you think you could talk him into letting me have the chart? It's a beautiful song."

Lionel snapped back, "I think that's for Mattie to decide, don't you?"

Lorry smiled to herself. "Yes, Lionel. You're absolutely right." She knew right then that she had him right where she wanted him.

About fifty miles passed with neither speaking until Lionel, in uncharacteristic fluidity, offered, "You know, he practices every morning, at least on his guitar. We don't have a piano, so he goes to your bistro and practices there, every single morning before his first class."

This news caught Lorry off guard. "I didn't know that." She wrapped her fingers around the steering wheel like talons on a hawk.

Lionel continued, "He's pretty hard on himself, Mattie, that is. He's always telling me about the mistakes he thinks he's made, you know, while Ginny's singing. But I think he's pretty good."

"He's very good, Lionel. Gifted really. They both are," Lorry said. "And we've never heard him make a mistake. He makes Ginny better."

Lionel countered, "I think he makes everybody better."

"Yes. Yes he does," Lorry replied thoughtfully. "He most certainly does."

Lionel fidgeted in his seat. "Well, he's preternatural."

Lorry laughed. "My, that's quite the word."

Lionel ducked his head and smiled a little smile. "Well," he admitted, "I try and learn a new word every day."

"And what word would you use to describe me, Lionel?" Lorry teased.

Lionel smiled. "I can think of a few. Obstinate, puissant, portentous, intractable . . . foxy."

She put her hand on his thigh and purred, "I like that last one the best."

Lionel continued, "I also think that you're not as tough as you let on."

Lorry broke into a genuine smile. "Oh, you think so, do you?"

"Yes," Lionel replied. "Tough but tender. You're a trailblazer, Lorry. Mattie says you have gumption."

Lorry was impressed. "It's much more difficult for women to succeed in business than it is for men. In any field, really. But you're correct up to a point, I know I have a reputation as being kind of bitchy, but it's just a facade. A necessary facade, but a facade none-theless." She yawned. "Would you mind driving awhile, please?" She pulled over and stopped before he could reply.

Lorry settled into the passenger's seat like a contented cat. "Tell me, Lionel. Does Mattie have any girlfriends? I mean, does he go out with anybody?"

Lionel scratched his chin and knew this was dangerous territory. *Socratic questioning,* he thought. *She's sharp.* "No, not that I know of, anyway. He has a lot of friends who are girls, but just as friends. I've been trying to set him up with a girl I know from home, but he keeps coming up with excuses to avoid her. Although I can tell you that our place is always crowded with girls just trying to get his atten-tion. Guys too, just to hang out. They eat all our food. Emily comes over as often as she can. She cooks for us. She's nice." He wonders how much he should talk about his friend. "You know, he plays for a lot of sororities, he just can't turn them down. Sometimes I go too. Everybody likes him, but there's nobody special, except Ginny and you, of course."

"Nice touch, Lionel." Lorry laughed.

She turned her attention back to him now that common ground had been established. "Mattie told me that you grew up on a farm, is that right?"

Lionel had been taunted by fraternities during freshman rush because he was a farmboy, and he clammed up. Yes was the curt reply. But sensing Lorry wasn't going to make fun of him, he decided to continue, "Near Pine City. It's about three hours northeast of NSU."

Lorry said pleasantly, "And I assume you're majoring in some-thing that will help further your family's fortunes?"

"Yes, well, no," Lionel stuttered. "I'm not planning on going back after I get my degree." He straightened up a little and tightly held the steering wheel. "I want to travel, maybe go to graduate school." This was a brave statement from Lionel, who had never dis-cussed his intentions with anybody except his father, who gave him his blessing, and Mattie, who gave him encouragement, especially during a time when he was having a difficult time in school.

At that moment, Lorry decided to reel Lionel in. She unlocked her safety belt and slid next to him. After Lionel recentered the car onto the highway, she asked, "Do you like me, Lionel?"

Lionel shrugged. "Yeah, I guess so."

"You guess so, Lionel? That's a rather equivocal reply. You do know what equivocal means, right? I mean, either you like me or you don't, which is it?"

"Yes, Lorry. I like you. You're a bit straightforward though."

"So?" Lorry sharply said. "And what's the matter with that?"

Lionel seeped into his seat. "There's nothing the matter with that, Lorry."

"Well, it sounded like a criticism to me. Otherwise, you never would have brought it up."

Lionel scratched his head. "I'm not criticizing you, Lorry. I'm sorry."

Lorry returned to her own side of the car, refastened her safety belt, folded her tiny arms, and looked out the passenger-side window. Lionel was totally perplexed. He'd never met anybody like Lorry before and remembered that Matt had warned him not to let her diminutive size fool him.

As they pulled into Three Forks, he put his hand on her shoulder and broke the silence. "I like you very much, Lorry," he said. "Honest, I do."

Lorry took his hand and smiled. "I guess you'll have to show me where you and Mattie live. I just can't let you out here, can I now? Besides, I'd like to see the most popular house at NSU. Do you wash your sheets, Lionel?"

Lionel thought it a rather odd question. "Every now and then," he said. His face turned grave when he thought about the house he was about to enter and everything that had happened over the past three weeks. "I think Emily sent in a crew to clean up while we were gone," he distantly said. When Lorry and Lionel went inside, they found the entire house spotless; a vase of fresh-cut flowers was placed on the kitchen table. There was food in the refrigerator.

\*　　\*　　\*

Early the next morning, Lorry carefully peeked outside Lionel's bedroom, looking both ways before she headed to the bathroom.

She heard a voice call out from the kitchen, "Would you like a cup of coffee this morning, Ms. Cullen?" Matt innocently asked.

*Mattie!* she thought. *How does he always know?* She reluctantly peeked around the corner and saw Matt sitting at the kitchen table with a cup of coffee and the morning paper spread out before him.

"I just put on a fresh pot, and it's all ready," Matt said without looking up. "It seems you had a pleasant trip back?"

Lorry, wearing one of Lionel's NSU T-shirts, looked both guilty and triumphant at the same time. She sat down across Matt, "Yes, Mattie. I'd love a cup of coffee, with milk too, if the date hasn't expired." Matt made her breakfast too.

He smiled at Lorry, folded his palms together, and rested his chin on them. "So you and Lionel? A match made in heaven, if you ask me."

Lorry took a nibble of wheat toast. "Well, nobody asked you, Matthew, did they? Pass the jam, please."

Matt grinned as he passed her the raspberry jam. "This is Lionel's favorite, in case you're wondering. Sorry we're out of eggs, but this banana seems fresh."

"Toast and fruit is plenty, thank you very much," Lorry snapped. "But shouldn't we wake up Lionel?"

Matt shook his head, his dark-blue eyes twinkling. "Oh, let him sleep, Lorry. I'm sure he's exhausted."

Lorry threw the banana peel and hit him square on the face.

Thus became the tumultuous, on-again, off again twenty-year relationship between Lorry Cullen and Lionel Henslaw, marked with argument and competitiveness that caused separation, only for them to be reunited time and again. After Lionel earned his degree in agricultural economics from Northern State, he was offered a fellowship at Cornell, which he didn't hesitate to accept. He earned his master's degree and took a job as a midlevel analyst for the Department of Agriculture in Washington, DC, although it would cost him his marriage to a local woman from Ithaca, New York, who, after living in the city for six weeks, decided to move back home, where she eventually remarried a local fellow. Lionel became a servant to his work and quickly rose above his peers. Within five years, he was appointed as an undersecretary. In 1992, Lionel Henslaw was placed on the short list for the new president's choice for secretary of agriculture, a position he still holds to this day. He has traveled to thirty-five countries and has met fifteen heads of state. But work is the only place where he didn't feel miserable.

# The Wild Bunch

On the day Matthew Jensen turned twenty-one years of age, Lorry Cullen presented him with a small glass of red wine.

"How does it feel to be of legal age at the place you've worked at for the past three years?" she teased. No sooner had the celebratory drink been offered, it was withdrawn. "After the show, birthday boy."

"You never know, Lorry," Matt deadpanned. "It might make me better."

Lorry playfully poked him in the ribs and took a sip from his glass. "I hope you don't need this to make you better, Mattie." She hooked her arm around his and walked him to the rehearsal room.

Ginny was warming up but stopped and rushed to Matt, wrapped her arms around him, and kissed him on the cheek. "Happy twenty-first, Mattie," she said excitedly.

"Thanks, Ginny," he bashfully said. "All Lorry got me was a glass of wine she won't let me drink."

Lorry stuck out her tongue, quick-stepped to Matt, climbed as high as her tiptoes allowed, and kissed him on the other cheek. "There," she said, "is that better?"

"Very nice, Lorry. Thank you." He grinned. "No wonder Lionel is crazy about you. Or is he today? It's so hard to keep track."

Lorry let the comment pass but made a point to mention that Lionel was bringing a very special friend of his from back home in an attempt to get the two together. She innocently asked, "Do you know anything about that, Mattie?"

He felt his cheeks flush. "Yeah, he told me."

"Well, I've met her, Mattie," Lorry sang out. "And she's adorable."

Initially, Lorry seemed unconcerned when she mentioned Lionel's friend, when Ginny abruptly walked out of the room, her eyes brimming with tears. Lorry quick-stepped after her, leaving Matt alone to twirl the hair behind his right ear and wonder about Ginny's sudden mood swing. But no sooner had Ginny left, she returned.

"Ginny," Matt asked, concerned. "Is everything okay?"

She smiled brightly. "Yes, birthday boy. How about we raise the roof off this place tonight, hmm?"

Matt hesitantly replied, unsure of what was going on. "Okay, sure thing." He leaned down to her and whispered, "And remember. You're perfect."

*So are you, Mattie,* Ginny thought. *So are you.*

Ginny took the stage and gratefully waved to the excited audience. She made a quick look around until she spotted Lionel and his friend. She blew him a kiss that Lionel caught in midair and pressed against his cheek. The music selections had become a bit more contemporary over the past three years, but keeping with Matt's intuition and gentle persuasion, Ginny stayed determined and resolved to keep pushing her boundaries. Matt had remained as eclectic as ever, which included a clever banjo arrangement of Marvin Gaye's "What's Going On." Tonight she took her voice to a new level, thrilling her audience and especially Matt as she filled every inch of the bistro with flawlessly executed notes. Matt smiled broadly and bobbed his head to the rhythms and moods as Ginny sang each song better than the previous one. She gazed adorably at Matt, who sometimes was so intent on his performance he wouldn't notice. Other times when he'd see her long-fixed glances of adoration, he would smile, bob his head to the rhythm of the song, and point with his chin toward her. This was his way of letting her know that everything was all right and she was, as always, perfect. Ginny acknowledged her accompanist after every song with a graceful bow and then turned to accept the audience's appreciation of her talent. The final number of the first set found Matt seated in the dark corner of the stage with an accordion strapped around his shoulders and chest. Ginny sang an emotional rendition of Edith Piaf's "L'hymne à L'amour" with a precise and perfect Parisian accent. To Matt's surprise, however, she uncharacteristically lingered onstage after closing the song out. He twirled his hair.

"Before intermission," Ginny announced, "would you please join me in wishing a happy twenty-first birthday to our favorite guy in the world? Mr. Matthew Aaron Jensen!"

She motioned Matt to the stage with an urgency he'd never before seen. He reluctantly joined Ginny with an embarrassed smile. The audience chanted his name, the kitchen doors swung open, and Matt received a surprise beyond shock. His four sisters, Katie, Tess, Emily, and Lucy, were pushing a cart that carried an enormous cake aglow with candles. It was shaped like a piano. Totally embarrassed by the attention but elated to see his sisters together for the first time in many years, Matt ducked his head and pinched tears away from his eyes. Ginny, Lorry, Katie, Tess, Emily, and Lucy hugged and kissed him. He blew the candles out with a single breath and was presented a glass of red wine from Lorry. To the crowd's delight, he drank it down in a single gulp. He waved his thanks to the audience and, with Ginny draped all over him and his sisters in tow, headed for the rehearsal room and a well-deserved break as the second set, quite unbeknownst to Matt, would test his skills as never before.

None of them could remember the last time the Wild Bunch had all been collected under one roof, and Matt knew it took a lot of effort for Katie, Tess, and Lucy to leave their families and make the long trip to Three Forks. He hugged his sisters and held Katie in a tight, extralong embrace. Ginny watched with quiet interest at this family, now all seated cross-legged on the floor. They seemed to be speaking all at once, yet each could be heard distinctly. In the intimacy of his sisters, Matt took on a new persona; he was entertaining, witty, and fabulously funny. He, she discovered, when surrounded by the love and affection of his family, felt no inhibitions and was at ease in returning love, something she judged was an issue with him at times.

He playfully mentioned the series of boyfriends Emily had brought in over the years. "Hey, you guys, have you met Emily's new flavor of the month?"

He reminded Tess of his annual birthday present to her. "Jeez, Tess. For crying out loud, you're supposed to waft through the perfume, not douse yourself."

Before he continued, Lucy bushwhacked him. She turned and gave Ginny a mischievous smile and wink. "Ginny, it might interest you to know that when Mattie was little he had quite a fascination . . ." She leaned down low and whispered just enough to be heard, "With Mr. Peeper."

Matt's face turned crimson. "Oh, you wouldn't." He looked with dismay at Ginny. "Ginny, whatever they're about to tell you is not true. They're making it up, believe me."

Ginny looked confused and asked, "Who is Mr. Peeper?"

Tess was first to explain, "Whenever Mom had a particularly busy day, she'd ask if we wouldn't mind giving Mattie a bath."

Emily interrupted, "When he was really little, that is."

Lucy turned to Ginny. "Since he was the only child with different, hmm, how shall I say this? Oh, I know, genitalia."

Tess added, "We told him it was called, Mr. Peeper. Mom and Dad were a little confused at the beginning, they thought Mattie just had an imaginary friend, so they didn't think anything of it. Until little Mattie tried to make Mr. Peeper his entry for show-and-tell one day at school."

Mattie was horrified. "Ginny, I swear they've made this entire urban legend up."

Katie chimed in, "Oh, but it's true. It caused such a sensation that his teacher had to call Mom and Dad. He just couldn't keep his little hands away from his little, well, you know, Mr. Peeper."

Emily laughed. "After that day, Mr. Peeper was given a proper funeral, and Mom never asked any of us to bathe Mattie again."

Ginny laughed hysterically and looked at his sisters. "You just thank your lucky stars that Lorry isn't in here!" By now, all five of the women were laughing so hard their sides ached.

Tess stood and wrapped her arms around Matt's shoulders. "We're sorry, Mattie. It was just too good to pass up. Besides, don't dish it out if you can't take it." She leaned down lower. "So now, will you sing a song just for us tonight? Your loving sisters who have traveled so long and far."

"No way," Matt answered with a whimsical smile. "Not after that. Besides, the song list is already set."

Suddenly, all four sisters collapsed on top of him, mercilessly tickling him into submission. "Okay, okay," Matt cried, struggling to breathe. "But you have to check with the boss."

Ginny wiped the tears of laughter from her eyes and declared in between breaths, "Why, Mattie, I think it's a perfect idea!"

*　　*　　*

Outside, Lionel and his friend Carrie were enjoying the birthday cake during the intermission, when Lorry quick-stepped to them, wide-eyed and excited.

She spoke to Carrie, "Oh, I hope you liked the first set. We've had Mattie's birthday surprise planned for months. He started to cry, I saw it myself. The oldest sister, Katie, came all the way from Boston, Tess came from Denver, and Lucy came from the Bay Area. They all kidded me that all they really wanted was a break from the husbands and children for a bit! They're so excited to be together and to see Mattie tonight. I can't wait for you to meet them, they're all so nice."

Lionel asked sarcastically, "Was that part of your business plan too, Lorry?"

Lorry ignored him as she had been doing so for the past few days.

She asked Carrie, "Would you like to go backstage to meet him, I mean, them? All of them, before the second set begins?"

Lionel waved her off. "Jeez, Lorry. Let him rest up a bit. You know, to catch his second wind?"

Lorry sharply replied, "Well, I'm not asking you, Lionel, am I?"

Carry laughed at the altercation. "Maybe he's right, Lorry," she smoothly said. "Maybe after they're done for the night. Would that be fine?"

Lorry thoughtfully reconsidered, "You're right, Carrie, of course. But don't let Lionel hustle you out of here without first saying hello. Promise?"

Carrie's smile was dazzling. "We wouldn't think of it. I promise." Somehow her smile grew even larger. "They're very talented. I'm looking forward to meeting both Ginny and Matt."

At that moment, a police car abruptly stopped in front of the bistro, and they watched as Raul escorted an inebriated young man, who had insisted on using a fake ID, swiftly into the squad car.

"Well," Lorry lightheartedly said, "looks like we'll have room for one more for the second set." She quick-stepped away and called over his shoulder, "See you later, Carrie, Lionel."

Carrie poked Lionel in the ribs. "If I didn't know better, neighbor. I'd say you and Lorry are trying to do a little matchmaking tonight, hmm?"

Lionel said, "I've been nagging Mattie to ask you out for two and a half years, but he always comes up with one lame excuse after another."

"Well, it's quite obvious, Lionel," Carrie replied. "Can't you see it?"

"See what?" Lionel asked.

Carrie knowingly smiled and shook her head in astonishment. "Can't you see that Ginny is crazy about him?"

Lionel was shocked. "Wait, what? You think? But he's never said anything to me, and I'm his best friend. Besides, Ginny goes out with lots of guys, even Ty and Marty."

Carrie contemplated for a moment. "I can tell by the way he's acted tonight that he's not the kind of guy who would say anything, anything at all. I mean, just by watching him, anybody can tell he has too much respect for others to brag about such things. Either that or he's just chicken."

Lionel shook his head. "There's nothing chicken about Matt Jensen. And by the way, he has girls trying to crawl over him all the time."

Carrie smiled wisely. "But he doesn't let them, I bet."

Lionel agreed and softly said, "No, no, he doesn't, You're right about that." He grinned. "Although he is kind of clueless when it comes to women."

Carrie thought, *He's not clueless, he's considerate.*

Lionel checked his watch and ate the rest of Carrie's cake, which she had just nibbled around. "We should head back inside. If you thought the first set was great, wait until you hear the second."

\*   \*   \*

Lorry went bug-eyed when she entered the rehearsal room to find five women in hysterical laughter and Matt on his back struggling to catch his breath. She put a hand on her hip and, in a seductive voice, asked, "Are you ready, Matthew?"

Matt quickly found his feet. "Yes, ma'am." He turned to his sisters. "Well, I have to go now. See you after?"

Lucy answered, "Heck yes, you'll see us, Mattie. We're never leaving. Ever."

One by one, his sisters kissed their little brother on the cheek and made their way back to their seats for the second set.

Ginny took the stage and spoke to the enthusiastic audience, "Well, unless you've just arrived, you know the band, right? Mattie, will you come up, please?"

Amid the clapping and cheering, her barefooted partner, with a guitar pick pinched between his lips, shyly waved to the crowd and joined Ginny at center stage. He received his customary hug and kiss on the cheek.

Matt took a quick look through the crowd and found Lionel sitting at one of the back tables. His friend, Carrie, had her face turned to the side and was engaged in what appeared to be happy and lively conversation with Lorry. Lionel, sitting between the two, swung his head from side to side, trying to keep up. Matt smiled when he saw Lorry kiss Lionel before she quick-stepped about the bistro and figured they were back together, again.

Lionel whispered to Carrie, "Ginny always greets Mattie like that before the second set, but it's nothing serious." Carrie didn't hear him; her full attention was fixated on Matt. It was Lionel's turn to smile.

Ginny and Matt had been practicing the first song, "Seven Bridges Road," for nearly three years, and tonight as they sat side by side in front of a single mic was the first time they performed it in front of an audience. The lengthy practice sessions had paid off as their voices layered magically in two-part harmony. It was difficult to distinctly hear one dominant voice over the other. Matt had strapped a capo around the second fret of his guitar to allow Ginny's voice to be heard in the best key for the song. The audience had never before heard the two of them present music with such perfection, and as the song ended, their foreheads met and they smiled at each other, knowing they had done their very best. The ovation lasted at least three minutes, during which time, Matt searched the audience once more and froze in place, the breath knocked out of him when he first saw the glorious smile of Carrie Hardesty, her hands raised high with applause. It was so unlike him that his sisters turned around and around in vain attempts to find out who could have made such an impact on their little brother. It was nothing they or Ginny had seen from him before.

Ginny asked, "Are you all right, partner? You look like you've seen a ghost."

He looked down at his sisters, now in the front row and glowing with pride. After a wispy smile toward Carrie, he whispered to Ginny, "Yeah, I think so."

He stepped over to the amp and plugged in his electric guitar for the second number, Leonard Cohen's "Bird on the Wire." The song was originally written as a country tune, but Matt had arranged it as a blues folk song that featured a lengthy guitar solo. In slow ¾ time, he picked the notes through the introduction and nodded to Ginny for her cue. She sang with gritty determination and patiently allowed the melody to crescendo until the bridge, when she let Matt loose to play an exhilarating lead guitar solo. Tess screamed out, "You rock, little brother! You rock!" The audience stomped their feet and cheered in agreement. Matt broke into a self-conscious smile and, with a gentle push from Ginny, took his first solo bow in over three years.

Matt made a quick transition to the piano for a meticulous and snappy arrangement of Ella Fitzgerald's "Them There Eyes," then the audience hushed when the stage lights dimmed to a single beam on Ginny. Performing soft and emotional "While My Guitar Gently Weeps" by the Beatles, she stared up into the empty space above the crowd, then into her audience's exhilarated faces, and finally to Matt, who remained, as ever, unaware of her focus as the number came to an end. She was singing only to him. Fixated only on the set, Matt immediately pounded out the introductory notes to Steve Winwood's "Gimme Some Lovin'." Ginny unhooked her microphone, held it in her left hand, and with her right hand, bounced a tambourine off her hip and then high into the air. She waited until the entire audience was involved in the beat and rhythm before she cued Matt with a nod and started singing the song. The Jensen sisters danced in front of the stage and sang the backup along with their brother, energetically urging the crowd to participate. It was, as Katie was now fond of saying, wicked, good fun. After the commotion following the song's ending died down, Ginny sat down next to Matt at the piano, wrapped her arm around his shoulders, and they performed the doo-wop classic "In the Still of the Night" by the Five Satins. The Jensen sisters, having lost all track of how many bottles of wine they had gone through, sang along.

When the song ended, Ginny ruffled Matt's hair, "Time for your dedication, buddy boy. What do you have in mind?" Matt shook his head as Ginny led him by the hand to center stage. He wasn't sure what song to play, and Ginny had to pry her hand out of Matt's firm grip. She gently shoved him in front of the mic and, with a sly smile, said, "Don't make me tickle you, Mattie."

He cleared his throat. "Thank you all for the birthday wishes." Ginny saw his hesitancy and went to his side. She knew he wasn't nervous, but he was anxious over the attention that he tried so hard to avoid.

She whispered in his ear, "We can always talk about Mr. Peeper."

Matt smiled shyly, relaxed his shoulders, and spoke to the restless audience. "I'd like to thank Ginny and Lorry and all of you for the birthday surprise tonight. I'd also like to introduce you to four beautiful ladies who have given me the best present I could've hoped for." The crowd roared their approval when Matt looked down at his beloved sisters. "They are, and if you would please stand when your name is called, Katie, Tess, Emily, and Lucy. My big sisters, ladies and gentlemen!" Matt clapped and bowed to his siblings. "I'm afraid they've coerced me into dedicating a song for them tonight, but I . . ." He looked into their warm eyes brimming with pride, and the perfect song came to mind; he remembered it as one of their favorites. "Well, with Ginny's help, we'd like to sing this for them . . . and for all of you too."

He looked at Ginny, his eyes pleading for help. "Will you please carry me on this?" He whispered the song to her. She smiled and then replied, "Absolutely."

Matt returned to the piano, and Ginny picked up a tambourine. He waited for a minute to allow the excitement to build, and they ran the keys with his thumb ending at middle C. He held it for a ¼ note and then powerfully pounded out the first four measures of "Mony Mony" by Tommy James. After emptying yet another bottle of wine, the Jensen sisters screamed their delight and once again gathered in front of the stage to dance to Matt and Ginny's vigorous rendition. They played off each other with perfect timing, dust fell from the ceiling, dishes crashed in the kitchen, and Lorry quickstepped around the bistro, hoping the walls would remain standing. Outside people danced on the streets, even Raul. Matt looked up from the piano and found that Lionel and Carrie had moved next to his sisters and were jumping up and down in rhythm with the song. For a split second, Carrie caught Matt looking at her, and she smiled at him. Embarrassed, Matt lowered his head and continued to pound the keys and sing, his face inches from the mic. He gave Ginny a slight nod, and they abruptly ended the song even though the crowed kept dancing. Matt handed Ginny a towel to dab away her perspiration and then handed her a glass of water from which she took a small sip. He then used the towel himself and gulped down the rest of the water.

With the walls still standing and the dust settling, Ginny stepped back to the center of the small stage for her final number, the Disney classic "When You Wish upon a Star." As always, Matt had arranged the chart to bring out the best of Ginny's voice, and afterward, she beckoned him to join her onstage, where they stood hand in hand and bowed to the audience's wild, generous applause and approval.

The Jensen sisters, who by now had totally lost count of the number of bottles of wine they had consumed, ordered one more and screamed for an encore. They made it very clear they would not leave without being satisfied, but Matt wasn't sure if it was the wine talking or if they really wanted to hear him and Ginny sing one more song. Regardless, he knew they were serious, probably about both. A brief conference ended with Ginny nodding her head with enthusiasm, and while he tuned his guitar, Ginny made the announcement. "Do you folks want to hear from the birthday boy again?" The crowd began chanting his name, the Jensen sisters the most vocal. "All right then," Ginny said. "We have a really special song for you. Mattie?"

Matt looked around the room and asked, "Where's Lorry? Oh, there you are, good, because this includes you too. None of you probably know this, I mean, how could you? But I'm the only blue-eyed member of our family, as well as being the only blue-eyed performer. So we'd like to play this for the most amazing girls I've ever known. Um, it's a Van Morrison song called "Brown Eyed Girl" or, in this case, girls."

He whispered to Ginny, "Will you carry me again, please?"

She answered him with a warm embrace, "It's about time, don't you think?"

It was Matt's tribute, his serenade to the most important women in his life. They had given him what he couldn't discover or give himself. Without their knowing, they had brought him out from the dominance of his entanglements, depression, and his fears of failure. How he wished all the brothers were there tonight because he knew they were part of this revelation as well, much more than they knew. As he played his guitar, as he sang the song, as he listened to the crowd's response, he felt the uplifting and boundless joy and triumph of making others happy. An antagonizing reoccurring memory of Randy Holloway flashed through his mind, trying to deny him of his joy, but he fought it off, concentrating on the moment. He and Ginny shared a single mic, and she was glowing, fresh, and full of life. Her voice was like no other, and he felt such a privilege to share a stage with her. His sisters screamed their delight, as did the rest of the audience. He took his eyes off Ginny for a moment to look over the crowded room once more and found the face of Carrie Hardesty. Their eyes met and locked on each other; she smiled and stole his breath away. He felt his awakening grow and his soul soar beyond heights he had never imagined.

# Carrie

The four Jensen sisters remained firmly planted in their seats after the performance ended, visiting with Lorry and Ginny and exceeding their wine-drinking capacity far beyond their normal measure. But they figured the effects would lessen with the more bread sticks they ate.

"That brother of yours is really something special," Lorry said with a genuinely satisfied smile.

Ginny was quick to agree and then asked, "But where did he go? He was supposed to meet Lionel's friend tonight, right?"

Lucy pointed across the room. "There he is, sitting on the edge of the stage. Oh, look. Lionel and that girl are headed his way. Oh my, isn't she darling? Mattie's never had a girlfriend. Of course, he'd never tell us one way or the other." She looked at Lorry and Ginny. "Mattie tends to see the world a little differently from the rest of us."

Emily laughed. "That's exactly what I told them over three years ago."

Matt sat with his legs dangling over the edge of the stage and instantly stood when he saw Lionel and Carrie headed his way. He was nervous and fidgety, unable to control his body from even the most subtle of movements. He glanced up into Lionel's smiling eyes and relaxed although he could hear his sisters' running commentary from across the room.

He stuck out his hand to Carrie and bashfully said, "Hi. I'm Mattie, um, I mean, Matt. Matt Jensen."

Lionel rolled his still smiling eyes in disappointment. He had so wanted to make this introduction that he'd been planning for the past two and half years.

Carrie firmly took Matt's hand and delivered a sensational smile that made his knees buckle. "I'm happy to meet you, Matt. I'm Carrie Hardesty. Happy birthday!"

Still rather annoyed, Lionel spoke up, "Yeah, and I'm Lionel. Remember me?" He suddenly found Lorry at his side and felt her tiny hand grab on to his.

Lorry said, "Excuse me, Lionel dear." She pointed across the room. "We're all wondering if you'd join us, over there." Matt's sisters waved and shouted for Lionel to join them. Nobody noticed that Ginny sadly stared down at her folded hands.

"Maybe you can tell us some of your stories of life on the farm?" Lorry insisted.

"What?" Lionel sourly replied. "Who'd want to hear any . . ."

Lorry pinched hard into his hand. "Ouch!" Lionel winced. "Stop that, Lorry. Can't you see we're trying to get acquainted here?"

Lorry gave Lionel a look that guaranteed he might experience some paranormal activity that evening if he didn't obey her, and he finally got the message.

"Oh, right," Lionel quipped. "Farming stories. Or maybe the time Mattie took us cow tipping." He looked at Matt and Carrie, his eyes twinkling. "It was hilarious. So we'll see you later?" Lorry towed him away before he could get an answer.

With Lionel disposed of, Matt asked Carrie if she'd like to sit down. She answered that she'd love to and noticed with some interest that Matt had his back turned away from his sisters.

He uneasily asked, "Um, can I get you something, Carrie? We have soda and water or maybe a glass of wine?"

Carrie's dazzling smile reappeared. "I'd love a glass of wine. I bet you can use something too after tonight's performance?"

Matt blushed, which seemed to please her, and told her he'd be right back. No sooner had he stood than when he saw Tasha walking toward them with a carafe of red wine and a tall glass of ice water.

Tasha explained, "Lorry asked me to bring these to you on my way out." She gave Matt a little wink. "Here's to you, tiger." Matt thanked her, and Carrie noticed that Matt's sisters were all watching with amusement, but they quickly turned their heads away when they saw Carrie smiling at them.

"Well," she said brightly and raised her glass, "here's to an amazing show." They clinked their glasses together, and Carrie continued, "I mean, you and Ginny are fantastic together, Matt. You're truly gifted. And I loved the dedications to your sisters. Those are two of my favorite songs."

"Oh, thanks very much," Matt shyly replied. "Um, so what other songs do you like, Carrie? I mean, what kind of music?" He tried to think of something clever, he tried to be witty and entertaining, but his thoughts were swimming, and he remembered what he'd always known about himself: a head full of words but no useful expressions. The only thing he knew for sure was that he'd never been attracted to any girl like he was to Carrie Hardesty.

Carrie thought, *Okay, I guess we need to establish some common ground. At least he hasn't asked what I'm majoring in.* She explained that she liked all kinds of music. She also thought that she had never been attracted to any boy like she was to Matt Jensen.

Desperate to come up with something to talk about, Matt asked, "What's your favorite song?"

Carrie considered, "Well, I love 'American Pie,' but who doesn't?" She thought carefully and said, "I think my favorite song is 'While My Guitar Gently Weeps.' And by the way, you played it so beautifully. Did you know it's my favorite?"

"Oh, just lucky, I guess," Matt replied. He gazed at her narrow, straight nose, faint with freckles, which washed away from her cheeks, her naturally long eyelashes, soft brown eyes flecked with green, and how her lips puckered when she smiled and laughed. Suddenly he blurted out, "I think you're really pretty." His face turned crimson, and he put his hand to his forehead. "I'm sorry. That must have been totally embarrassing for you."

"Well, thank you, kind sir," Carrie replied with her dazzling smile. "But I don't think I'm nearly as embarrassed as you!"

"I don't think I've ever said that to anyone before, unless I'm related."

Carry asked, "Not even to Ginny?"

Matt answered evenly, "Yes, I've told Ginny that she's pretty. A couple of times, probably."

Carrie laughed. "I should hope so, Matt. She's breathtakingly beautiful."

Matt smiled weakly and whispered, "Yes, she is, inside and out."

Carrie thought, *Thoroughly honest. I'll give him that.*

Every sensation Matt felt was new to him. He was light-headed, his palms were sweating, and his heart was pounding. Just an hour before, he was confident enough to accomplish anything, now it seemed his lungs were compressing into his chest, his heart jolted to a state of euphoria. In these first few minutes with Carrie, he felt awkward and so inept he was afraid to even try to put a coherent sentence together. Carrie sensed his uneasiness and also sensed his reluctance to talk about himself. She gathered her hair and tossed it over her left shoulder. To Carrie it was a routine habit, but to Matt it was rather seductive and delightful to watch. She suggested he introduce her to Ginny and his sisters. He brightened up and agreed. She finished her glass of wine, declined a refill, and allowed Matt to take her empty glass. The spirited conversation from the other side of the room hushed as Matt and Carrie made their way over. One by one he introduced Carrie to his sisters, all of whom kindly greeted her. Ginny stood when it became her turn, and she eagerly took both Carrie's hands.

"Oh my," Carrie gushed, "it's wonderful to finally meet you, Ginny. I think you're amazing, absolutely amazing. Thank you for such a wonderful evening. I can't remember when I've had so much fun." She was so warm and authentic and totally without guile that Ginny instantly liked her. Matt's sisters felt the same.

Carrie spoke to Matt's sisters, "Thank you so much for including me in your reunion. You're a close-knit family, I can just tell." She looked over to Lionel. "How about that ride home, neighbor?"

Lorry nodded to Lionel that it was all right to give Carrie a ride home now, and he shot back a look that told everybody he sure as hell didn't need her permission. Ginny and Matt's sisters laughed as did everyone else, except Lionel. Matt walked them to the front door and mustered the courage to ask Carrie if she had any plans for the next day.

Carrie smiled her dazzling smile. "I run the track every morning at six o'clock a.m. You're welcome to join me." She poked Lionel in his ribs. "You're invited too, neighbor."

Lionel checked his watch; it was already 1:00 a.m. "Thanks, but I think I'll pass."

She smiled at Matt. "Maybe I'll see you then?"

"You will," Matt answered, and blushed in a way that totally delighted Carrie. "My life depends on it."

Katie, Tess, Emily and Lucy struggled to their feet, as much as they could, when Matt returned and applauded him with their warmest approval.

"Woo-hoo, Mattie. Way to go," Katie said.

Tess added, "Oh, Mattie, you big stud."

Lucy piped in, "She's a keeper, Mattie. Don't screw this up."

Emily let out a heavy sigh. "Oh my, he's grown up so fast."

Matt sat down with an embarrassed smiled, stretched out his legs, and casually placed his hands on top of his head. "I suppose you're all staying with me tonight?"

"Indeed we are, Mattie," Lucy beamed. "I told you, we're not leaving. We're never leaving."

Katie laughed. "It seems that, um, Emily has no vacancy. Imagine that? Anyway, Lionel's volunteered to stay at Lorry's for the night. He even changed his sheets or, at least, turned them inside out. Isn't that sweet of him?"

Matt grinned. "Yeah, I think it's called Stockholm syndrome. Well, what do you all say we go home and get you settled? So which one of you has a car? I usually walk home, but none of you seem to be in much condition for that."

Tess yawned and, with Emily's help, took a few wobbly steps. "It's been an awfully long day, Mattie. We're all sleeping in, if you don't mind." She wobbled a little more but steadied herself on a chair. "And we'd like our breakfast at ten o'clock sharp. Chocolate chip pancakes would be nice. And coffee, Mattie, lots of coffee."

The internal alarm in Matt's head woke him at 5:45 a.m. He had slept on the couch to allow Katie, Tess, and Lucy the privacy of the two bedrooms, and he was now recklessly tearing through the house, looking for his tennis shoes, socks, shorts, and a shirt. He made no effort respecting Tess's sweet slumber as she quietly snored in his bed and he went frantically through his drawers and closet until he found everything he needed for running around the track. He actually hoped Carrie was more of a jogger than a runner but would discover that would not be the case.

He quickly dressed and rushed to leave when he heard Tess drowsily call out, "Hey, lover boy." With her head buried in pillows, she held up the keys to her rental car. "Take the car, or you'll be late."

"Thanks, Tessie," Matt said, and deftly snatched the keys from her hand. "You're the best."

Tess yawned and rolled over. "Yes, I am the best, aren't I? And remember, Mattie: breakfast at ten o'clock, with coffee, lots of coffee." She was back asleep before he left the room.

Even the most slovenly of creatures could walk from one end of the NSU campus to the other in about twenty minutes, so Matt was able to drive to the track in about three. He spotted Carrie stretching out before her run at the far side of the infield. She had graceful long legs that supported a slim, athletic body. Her light-brown eyes danced with flecks of green surrounded by beautiful long lashes. Her auburn hair was tied in a ponytail that swished back and forth when she ran. Matt found it wonderfully captivating.

She smiled and talked while they ran, her back straight and chin held high. On the first lap, she said, "Last night was so much fun. I can't believe Ginny's voice. She amazing." She poked Matt in the ribs. "And you're pretty good too."

Matt gasped for air alongside Carrie, who ran effortlessly. During the fourth lap, she told Matt, "Lionel always talked about Ginny's Bistro whenever we'd bump into each other on campus. He's pestered me to go with him for as long as I can remember. I wish I would have taken up his offer a long time ago."

On the sixth lap, Matt stopped and bent to his knees; his side ached. He fell to the infield grass with a thud and panted for air. He apologized in between gasps. "I'm sorry, Carrie. But I'm gassed. You, you have great stamina, and I think I may be a little out of shape . . . way out of shape. Out of your league anyway."

"Well, I do this every day," Carrie said, her eyes sympathetic. "When was the last time you had any real exercise?"

As his breath slowly returned, he answered, "Maybe four years ago."

Carrie laughed. "Four years, seriously? I'm impressed you made six laps or five and a half, really."

Matt stared into her face. "I want to keep up with you."

Carrie flashed a sparkling smile and offered her hand to help him up. "Why don't we walk awhile, hmm?"

Grateful for the offer, Matt replied, "I like that idea." He hesitantly reached up to meet her hand. Carrie took a sturdy grip and pulled him to his feet, and they faced each other, motionless, staring into each other's eyes. Matt continued to hold her hand as they walked around the track, and they did not speak for some time.

"Is it true you broke Marty Nevin's nose?" Carrie suddenly asked.

The question stunned Matt, and he stammered, "H-how do you know about that?"

"Oh," Carrie replied, matter-of-factly. "Ty Keller told me."

Now he was downright bewildered. "You know Ty?"

Carrie showed a sunbeam of a smile. "I know all the brothers, Matt. Until last night, you're the only one I'd yet to meet, even though you're easily the one most talked about."

Still puzzled, he looked at Carrie, then straight ahead, and back to Carrie again, whose smile had not diminished. He figured she already knew of his blinding bout of fury that had resulted with him rearranging Marty's nose.

He sighed and quietly explained, "Marty said something that questioned Ginny's, um, honor."

"Oh my," Carrie mused, "and I assume then that you defended her honor?"

Matt stopped walking; he was quite embarrassed. "All I remember is what Marty said. The next thing, I knew he was laying on his back, holding his bloody nose. I was, and still am, very ashamed of myself. I scooped him up, borrowed Ty's car, and drove him to the hospital. I was in tears apologizing to him. Of course, wouldn't you know that Emily was on duty, right? I was helping Marty out of the car, and she rushed up asking what I'd done to him. Marty managed a smile and told her it was nothing he didn't deserve. He's forgiven me, but I can't seem to forgive myself."

Carrie giggled. "So you're gallant and honest?"

Matt shrugged. "It's nothing I'm proud about. I still regret the whole thing. It was just reflex."

Carrie thought, *Yes, a reflex of integrity.* Her next sensation defied all logic and was nothing she had never before experienced. A delightful feeling that led her to believe that there really is love at first sight.

They rounded the final lap and ended up in front of Tess's car. "Would you like a ride home, Carrie?" he asked.

"Thanks for the offer," she replied and kidded him, "but I think I'll run. I need to make up for lost time."

Matt said, "Oh right. I'm sorry about that. I'll do better next time." Then he had a bright idea. "I'm making breakfast this morning. Maybe you'd like to join us?"

He was so sincere and full of hope that she couldn't resist. She spread her arms wide and exclaimed, "Even looking like this?"

Matt took her hands and stared into her face. She was absolutely taken by his dark-blue eyes. "I think you look beautiful." With an impulse of sublimity, he bent down and kissed her, and to his unbelievable surprise, she kissed him back.

When their lips parted, she nuzzled his ear and softly said, "How can I turn down an offer like that?" Her smile overpowered him as it would continue to do for many years to come.

"I have to get a few things at the store before we can go home," Matt said and, in respect of Carrie's attire, added, "But I'll go in by myself. It won't take too long."

Carrie teased him, "Are you afraid of being seen in public with me, Mattie?" It was the first time she'd used his nickname.

He immediately became conscious. "Oh no. I'm sorry. It's not that at all. I'm not trying to offend, but what you said back at the track, you, um, sounded a little self-conscious, you know, about being in your running clothes and all."

"Me?" Carrie retorted with her dazzling smile. "Never. I was just kind of testing you. And maybe teasing you a little."

Matt felt a puzzled look come over his face. "Testing me? Um, okay. So how did I do?"

With a burst of delightful laughter, she put her hand on his knee. "You passed with flying colors."

Still a little befuddled, he replied with a sigh of relief, "That's good, I guess. I mean, I'm generally not very good at tests." He looked at his watch; it was 9:30 a.m. "Oh gosh," he said, "I'm running a little late." They rushed through the market aisles, and Matt haphazardly tossed items over his shoulders, underhand, and overhand for Carrie to catch, now laughing and oblivious to the slow-moving elderly men and women who disapproved of such behavior. Matt bought pancake mix, eggs, orange juice, chocolate chips, and bacon. He explained, "It's what Dad made for breakfast every Saturday morning."

Katie and Lucy were slouched over the kitchen table, their heads buried deep in their arms when Matt and Carrie arrived. Carrie poured them each a glass of orange juice, gingerly set the glasses down in front of them, and backed away while Matt brewed coffee. He quickly whisked the pancake batter, carefully folded in the chocolate chips, and began to fry bacon before he said anything to his sisters, who were now roused to the smell of breakfast being cooked.

"Do a little barkin' at the moon last night, girls?" he innocently asked.

Neither Katie nor Lucy moved, but both managed to simultaneously present their middle fingers high over their heads in reply.

"Oh my," Matt responded, "now what would your children think?" He placed a cup of coffee in front of each of them. "Wake up, I brought a guest."

Lucy slowly raised her head, her hair in her eyes a fallen tangle that she blew away in a single breath. "Oh, don't tell me Lionel decided to . . ." She saw Carrie standing a good distance away. She gave her a little wave.

Lucy tapped Katie on the top of her head until she sharply said, "Stop that, dammit." She moaned then looked up, rubbed her eyes, and noticed Carrie. "Oh, hi there, sweetie. Joining us this morning?"

Very amused, Carrie answered with a lightening smile, "If I'm not intruding."

Katie looked at Matt, still busy at the stove, and sighed, "Lord knows we can use one clear thinker around here. Hey, Mattie, where's the cream?"

Matt pointed to a small pitcher directly in front of her. "Oh," she said, slowly coming to life. "Thanks."

When the pancakes and bacon were ready, Matt looked around the kitchen and asked, "Where's Tess and Emily?"

Lucy said, "Um, Emily doesn't seem to be answering her phone." She pointed a lazy finger toward Matt's bedroom. "Tess won't get out of bed." She smiled conspiratorially at her brother, "I guess it's up to you, hmm?"

Carrie's eyes darted back and forth. Matt had obviously been given a subtle cue, but she was unsure what it meant. Matt smiled at her with elfish eyes and slyly replied, "I'll see what I can do."

Katie cautioned him, "Oh, Mattie, no. Don't do it."

Matt answered with a gunslinger's voice, "But I must."

"Do what?" Carrie curiously asked.

Lucy held a finger to her lips and winked, alerting Carrie to just watch and wait. Matt disappeared from the kitchen, made a quick stop in the bathroom, and then entered his bedroom to rouse Tess out of bed.

"Breakfast is ready, princess," he cheerfully sang out. He opened the curtains, allowing a searing beam of sunlight to shine directly on her eyes.

Tess buried her head in the pillow and testily replied, "Okay, Mattie, okay. Now get out of here."

Matt returned to the kitchen with an impish grin. "Wait for it," he said with a fair amount of satisfaction.

"Wait for what?" Carrie innocently asked. She then jumped in surprise, jolted by a hair-raising, bloodcurdling scream from the bathroom.

"Splashdown," Matt proudly said.

Tess screamed from the bathroom, "Goddammit, Mattie. I'm going to kill you! Someone come and pry me out of this cesspool."

Katie hurried, in between spurts of laughter, to help Tess while Lucy casually explained to Carrie, "He left the seat up."

"Really," Carrie answered, and looked at Matt's whimsical smile. "That's sure to wake her up." Matt shrugged his shoulders and grinned.

Tess fumed her way into the kitchen only to be handed a cup of coffee from her little brother. "Breakfast is served, my queen." He bowed reverently and thought how much she was starting to look like Mom.

Tess arched a single indignant eyebrow in a poor attempt to keep from smiling. She took a big sip of coffee, closed her eyes in contentment, and turned to Carrie, "Welcome to the Wild Bunch, dear. Now, where are my pancakes?"

# Last Duet

I t took not less than two weeks for Ginny Simmons and Lorry Cullen to develop a close, lifelong friendship with Carrie Hardesty. They were happy for Mattie that he had found such an enchanting young woman. The fact that Matt had fallen in love with Carrie did not surprise him as much as the fact that Carrie had fallen in love with him. He found that she was the only person, besides Mom, Dad, Kate, and to a small degree, Ginny, who could made him feel safe enough to pay enough attention to care for himself. His deeply entrenched inhibitors and entanglements vanished.

Rivalry or jealousy, which could have so easily appeared, never did. Carrie had the foresight to recognize the powerful emotional and tender feelings Ginny held for Matt and the inner conflict that she must be struggling with, especially when she saw them together, which was often. From the first time she saw them perform, Carrie realized that Ginny's feelings for Matt extended well beyond their relationship on the stage. She discussed with Matt that he would eventually need to confront this delicate issue. Neither of them dreamed of toying with Ginny's emotions. And certainly not Lorry's.

So in the same way that Ginny Simmons displayed musical brilliance, Carrie Hardesty displayed the genuine, intuitive brilliance of sound judgment. She loved people; she loved meeting new acquaintances and making new friends. She had a natural gift of coaxing the very best out of the paths that life led her down. It was unanimously agreed by everyone who knew her that Carrie Hardesty possessed the kindest, sweetest soul that anyone had the privilege of knowing. She was in love with Matthew Jensen and had an inherent acumen for bringing out the best in him, not on the stage, but in his life.

Ginny often contemplated, examined, and evaluated her special onstage relationship with Mattie and often wondered if he shared the same wonderful attraction she held for him and was at least to be willing to reciprocate. Could he duplicate the feelings, the love she had for him away from the rehearsal room and the bistro stage? Their common bond and their intimacy onstage were not hidden, and most thought the same level of intensity existed between them away from the bistro as well. Except for Marty Nevin, who knew better. But from Matt's perspective, their relationship was strictly platonic, like brother and sister, sort of.

Lorry Cullen had at times become adversarial with Matt, unsuccessful to her dismay, in her attempts to force him into the realization that the rapport he and Ginny shared as musical partners extended well beyond the rehearsal room and the stage. She went as far as telling Matt that Ginny had strong feelings for him, that perhaps she was in love with him and not as an honorary member of the Wild Bunch.

Matt's reaction was predictably perceptive and wise. He knew Ginny's feelings for him were legitimate but also knew these were a result of their devotion to each other as musicians, something restricted to performances. If meeting each other had been left to chance, it probably never would have happened.

He smiled tenderly but wittingly at Lorry, "She doesn't need me, Lorry. She needs you." Deep down, Lorry knew he was right. He was always right.

During her fourth and final year of law school, Lorry had recorded and made videos of every performance and had mailed demos out to a dozen studios, all of which were piqued with competitive interest to sign the brilliant, beautiful singer to a lucrative contract. By spring, Lorry and Ginny, but mainly Lorry, had decided on a small independent label who called themselves Barking Cat Records. She liked the name, not to mention the ten-thousand-dollar advance. The owner, Mr. Sedenfeld, had advised, even warned,

Lorry to contact an attorney before signing a contract whether if it was with him or anybody else. Lorry unwaveringly informed him, "I am an attorney, Mr. Sedenfeld. Both Ms. Simmons and I think your contract is very fair." She then added with great conviction and hand gestures that Mr. Sedenfeld could not see over the phone, "And we're going to make you famous." Mr. Sedenfeld was impressed.

"Can you imagine, Lorry?" Matt exclaimed upon hearing the news. "Can you imagine how Ginny will sound with full instrumentation behind her? With real producers and original music? She'll be phenomenal. She knows the power of what a song can do to an audience or just a single listener. She's going to change people's lives." He gently grabbed Lorry by her tiny shoulders and drew her to him. "How could I possibly keep her, and you, from this opportunity? Besides, I don't think there's a contingency in your business plan for someone like me, whose only job is to tag along." He drew her closer and whispered in her ear, "I will always love her, and I will always love you. But I know my limitations, Lorry, and I know I would limit Ginny. I would fail her."

He knew Lorry's interventions were intercessory, and perhaps she was trying to prime him. But he also knew he would have to meet Ginny, eye to eye, without Lorry and without Carrie, for how could he do anything less? He tried to figure out a way to master the art of gentle confrontation because the last thing he wanted was to hurt Ginny, but he knew she would be hurt. Logical approaches rarely apply to matters of the heart and soul, especially with someone as special to him as Ginny. He couldn't see how there could possibly be a happy ending.

*   *   *

Unlikely as it seemed, it was Owen, the perennially cheerful flower child with the large ball of frizzy red hair, who offered Ginny the finest counsel. They met by chance, although Owen didn't believe in chance, at Harley's Family Market. Owen was pushing a cart full of frozen chicken pot pies.

"They're on sale," he excitedly told Ginny. "Ten for a dollar. These will get me through the summer."

Ginny said, "I thought you were graduating, Owen. Have you had a change of plans?"

He gave her a sheepish grin. "Well, I'm going to walk with everybody at commencement, you know, but I have a few summer school classes to take. Somehow I got a little behind." His face brightened with an idea. "Hey, do want to get an ice cream with me? Across the street, at the Dairy Freeze?"

Ginny smiled; she could hardly refuse this refreshing young man with the cherubic smile. "Sounds great, Owen. I'd like that."

"Cool," Owen replied. "Um, do you have any money?"

They settled in the shade outside the drive-in, casually licking their ice cream. Owen chatted nonstop about his plans. "I'm going to attend a Bible school this fall, in Iowa. I want to be an evangelist or maybe a pastor someday."

"That's a lofty goal, Owen," Ginny said. "I sure wish you the best."

Owen replied, "From what I've heard, I'm not the only one with lofty goals. Congratulations on your recording deal, dear Ginny."

Ginny fidgeted. "Well, thank you. But I'm pretty nervous, afraid, really, to move away, to be without Mattie. Such a big change, you know?"

Owen didn't reply for several minutes. Finally, he gently said, "Look at me."

He had soft, charismatic green eyes that glowed with kindness. "I know what you and Mattie have is special, maybe even unique. I don't have any answers for you except to know that the Lord is taking you in different directions, at least for right now." He finished his ice cream and wiped his chin with the back of his hand. "I suppose we should all be a little nervous about the future. But don't you think it's something to embrace rather than fear? I mean, I can't wait to find out what's going to happen next. We have to look ahead, Ginny, there's no turning back the clock." He dug deep into his pocket, retrieved a packet of little cards that looked like matchbook covers.

He shuffled through them until he found the exact card he wanted and gave it to Ginny. He asked her to read it out loud.

She read:, "'For I know the plans I have for you,' declares the Lord, 'plans to prosper you and not to harm you, plans to give you a hope and a future.'"

Owen explained in a soft yet confident voice, "It's from Jeremiah. Chapter 29, verse 11. You can keep it."

Ginny folded the card in her hand and made a fist around it. "Thank you, Owen," she whispered. "Thank you."

Matt and Carrie announced their engagement during Christmas vacation of their senior year. They would be married in June at the Pine City First Congregational Church. Matt wondered why it was called First Congregational since it was the only Congregational church in the town where Carrie and Lionel had grown up together on neighboring farms, but he kept such questions to himself. Carrie asked Ginny to be her maid of honor, and she accepted. The confrontation between Ginny and Matt never surfaced, although they did share an emotionally intense time together before their final performance, which would mark their end and the closing of Ginny's Bistro.

Matt entered the bistro early in the afternoon to get ready for their final performance and was surprised to find Ginny sitting at the piano, tinkling out random notes. He laid down a folder he was carrying, sat down next to her, and put his arm around her waist. Ginny buried her head into Matt's shoulder and cried. After a while, Matt offered a tissue he just happened to have handy, wrapped both arms around her, and gently rocked her back and forth. He would be lying if he told her that he held no feelings for her, but they were not romantic feelings. He could play with her emotions, but that would be insidious, self-serving, and cruel.

"Thank you, Ginny," he softly said, and then kissed her forehead. "Thank you for letting me grow up here."

Ginny straightened. "You're the one who made all this possible, Mattie. I should be thanking you." She broke down and once again collapsed into him. "You're my hope, Mattie. My inspiration. I'm afraid to go on without you. I love you, Mattie. I love you so much."

He whispered back, trying to hold back his own tears, "I have true feelings for you too, Ginny. And I'll always be your biggest fan. You know that, right?" He continued, his voice comforting and soothing, "You're going to have an amazing career, Ginny, and an amazing life. You're just not going to change music, you're going to change the world. But we're on different journeys, and I say, Ms. Virginia Alison Simmons, that we begin our journeys tonight. Okay?"

She pulled away from him and smiled through her tears. "You mean, go out with a bang?"

Matt confidently replied, "Yes, ma'am. With a bang, not a whimper." He handed her the folder he had brought with him. "I'd like you to have this. It's the only copy."

Ginny opened the folder. It held the music to the unnamed melody he wrote to help him cope with Randy Holloway's addictions and death.

"It's yours," he told her. "I'm hoping you'll write the lyric someday."

She held it to her chest and whispered, "You can count on it, Mattie. You can count on it."

She suddenly changed the subject. "You know, that Owen is really quite the counselor, isn't he?"

"Yeah?" Matt replied with a chuckle. "He's good at that." He winked at her. "He must have given you one of his little cards."

"He did," Ginny replied with a grin. "He really helped me put all this into perspective."

"I'm really glad about that, Ginny," Matt sincerely replied.

Lorry Cullen had petitioned for Main to be barricaded and traffic rerouted for their final night before Ginny's Bistro closed its doors for the final time. The Downtown Merchants Association had given their quick consent, figuring it would be cheaper than hiring off-duty police officers to try to maintain any kind of order. Besides, they knew Raul would be there. Closed-circuit televisions had been strategically placed outside on the street so those unlucky to be allowed inside could at least watch the last show. Even so, the occupation code was strictly unenforced and ignored.

Lorry, Ginny and Matt sat rather subdued in the rehearsal room, just minutes away from when the first set was to begin. Ginny had put the playlist together without collaboration. It carried a theme of remembrance and love. It reminded Matt of a Lawrence Welk theme show, but he didn't say anything. For him, this evening should be all about Ginny.

Lorry suddenly stood and kissed Matt on the cheek. "Time for me to make my last run through. You know, to make sure everything is ready." She quick-stepped away with tears in her eyes.

Matt and Ginny stared at each other until Matt finally found his voice. "You know, my first piano teacher, Mrs. Winkleman, taught me for a few months then gave me a hug and told me I needed to find someone better. That's what you need too, Ginny. Someone to make you better. But we have a special connection, don't we? I don't know how else to describe it."

"Yes," Ginny whispered. "We do." She stood, offered to help him to his feet, and hugged him tight. "I'm going to miss you, Mattie. I'm going to miss you so much. I know I've told you already, but I want to say this one last time. I love you, Mattie. And I hope you and Carrie have the most wonderful life together."

Matt pulled away and stared down at her with his brilliant midnight-blue eyes. "Just promise me you'll remember one thing, Ginny: you're perfect."

The planter box that had hidden Matt from the audience for the past four years had been removed. Tonight, everyone would see him through the entire performance. He was a little surprised but did nothing to change the situation, especially since Raul was standing in the empty spot with his arms folded across his massive chest. He grinned. "Orders from Ms. Cullen, Mattie."

His obscure perch on the unlighted, dark portion of the stage was also missing, moved to center stage, and placed next to Ginny's. Resigned to the new arrangement, he sighed and kicked off his shoes and socks. He patiently waited offstage during Ginny's ovation and found himself clapping and shouting with the rest of the audience. He did love her, he concluded at that moment, but it was a love of friendship, a love without romance. The brothers were bewildered by their bond; how could Mattie possibly resist this beautiful woman who was in love with him? Tonight they finally understood that, had there been a physical relationship, splitting up and parting ways would undeniably be devastating for both of them. Their admiration for Matt Jensen was at that moment fully recognized and understood, solidified for life.

Ginny smiled like a sunbeam at her audience and acknowledged those who had gathered outside. "Our last night, folks. We hope you will enjoy it as much as we will." She turned and waved at Matt. "Mattie? Will you come up, please?" The crowd cheered, and Matt blushed. Ginny embraced him and gave him a gentle kiss on the lips then continued addressing the audience, "I want to remind all of you that this guy is the reason we've been so successful these past four years, although I doubt he'd ever admit to it."

From somewhere in the audience they heard Dr. Emily Jensen shout, "He won't, that's for sure!" The crowd laughed and raised their glasses in a toast to Ginny and Matt.

They sat side by side before a single microphone and played their first song dedicated to the brothers. Matt gently picked his guitar, and Ginny sang "One Bourbon, One Scotch, One Beer" by John Lee Hooker. The brothers, at their usual back table, stood on their chairs and cheered. Raul quickly inspired them to climb back down to the floor. Matt then moved to the conspicuously placed piano and played "I Wished on the Moon," a song he arranged for Ginny to sing in a slow, swing rhythm. Once again she allowed the music to work in her, to take over her body and soul; her happy spirit and freedom descended upon the audience. Matt stayed with the piano and played the introduction to "The Object of My Affection" in an upbeat tempo. The crowed instantly realized that Ginny's attention had been diverted from them to Mattie, who, in unusual fashion, stared right back at her. He smiled at her when the song ended, waited for the crowd to quiet down a little, and began the next song, "Across the Universe" by the Beatles. He always enjoyed it when Ginny sang a Beatles number, and he enthusiastically sang the harmony. It was estimated that at least five hundred people had gathered outside, and they became strangely silent when Matt sang the lead of James

Taylor's "Long Ago and Far Away" on his guitar. Ginny accompanied on the piano and sang the backup vocal. They immediately followed with "Ripple" by the Grateful Dead, with Ginny accompanying on the rhythm guitar.

Matt returned to the piano, and Ginny spoke for the first time during the set. "I'd like to dedicate this next song to my best friend, Lorry Cullen, and to a another friend, who gave me some very good advice earlier today, Mr. Owen Johannsen."

Owen cried out, "Really? For me? Cool."

Ginny smiled at Lorry, who was dabbing her eyes, and then blew a kiss to Owen. She sang "I Can See Clearly Now" by Johnny Nash. It was the last number of the first set, but Ginny lingered onstage and urged Matt to join her, hand in hand. It was their way of thanking the audience for their support during the past four years.

They turned to leave for the intermission, and Matt suddenly spoke into the mic, "Thanks, you guys, we'll be back. You know that, right?"

He heard Emily shout, perhaps a bit inebriated, "You better, ya big goof!"

Matt ducked into the kitchen for a glass of water and then went to visit the brothers, whom he found outside, smoking cigarettes. They congratulated him on his performance.

Matt shook his head. "It's not me, really. It's all Ginny, all of it. She's one in a million."

He wasn't being coy, and the brothers knew it. There was nothing condescending or insolent about Matt Jensen. He left the brothers and made his way through the crowd to the rehearsal room, only to find Ginny in a stage of undress.

"Oh my," he cried out, and quickly spun around. "I'm so sorry."

Ginny laughed and continued changing her clothes. "I've been doing this for four years, and you've just now noticed? I don't know whether to be embarrassed or outraged. Nevertheless, Matthew, I do appreciate your respect."

"You're welcome. Now are you finished, for crying out loud?"

"Yes, Mattie. You can look now."

He turned and gasped. Somehow, beyond Matt's comprehension, Ginny had taken strikingly beautiful to an entire new level. Her hair was tied back with a yellow ribbon. She wore a string of pearls around her elegant neck, which seemed to heighten her already-high cheekbones and round brown eyes. She wore no makeup because she just didn't need to. She had changed from blue jeans into a flimsy almost-chiffon-pink sundress with long, narrow straps that revealed just enough cleavage to make most men deliriously happy. The dress hemmed just above her knees, and on this night, for their last set, she would join her beloved Mattie in performing barefoot.

Ginny swished the dress back and forth. "What do you think?"

Matt's blue eyes twinkled, and he smiled. "You're beautiful, Ginny, as always. I just hope you're actually heard and simply not stared at. Ready?"

She went to him and crushed her body against his. "Yes." She softly kissed his lips. "And remember, Mattie. You're perfect."

They climbed up to the stage hand in hand to boisterous, raucous, and happy applause from inside the bistro and from outside too. Dan, Stan Jr., and Harley had managed to procure a front-row table for themselves and their families. Bobby served them, and Dan beamed with pride. The second set began with the haunting yet tranquil Irish traditional "Gartan's Mother Lullaby." Matt stayed with the piano for the next three songs, "Since I Fell for You," "Come Rain or Come Shine," and finished with "Every Time We Say Goodbye," which Ginny sang slow and painfully. She bowed to the audience and dabbed at her tearing eyes before she asked one last time, "Mattie, would you come up, please?"

He came into her embrace and simply held her. Carrie had moved to the front of the stage, borrowed Harley's chair, and stood up tall, clapping her hands high above her head. The rest of the audience, and the crowd outside jumped up and down, whistled, and cheered.

Finally, Ginny gave Matt a pat on his backside and moved away from him. She apologized to her audience, "I'm so sorry, but I'm a bit emotional. It's just that these past four years have gone by so fast for all of us, except for Owen, of course." The crowd laughed.

"But here we are, our last duet."

# U-Turn

att picked up his acoustic guitar, his family heirloom, and sat down on Ginny's left. They shared a single mic and sang "If I Needed You" by Townes Van Zandt. They turned from the audience and faced each other. Ginny patted Matt's knee in time as they tenderly sang one to each other, their last duet. As the song came to an end, they smiled at each other and pressed their foreheads together, knowing once again that they had done their very best.

The audience roared their approval and appreciation. Matt slowly retreated to respectfully allow Ginny to own the stage. She motioned for Lorry to join her, and together they cried, smiled, bowed, cried, and smiled again. Ginny grabbed Mattie's hand to join them. She and Lorry embraced him, and together the three joined hands and bowed to the audience one last time.

At last, Ginny spoke into the microphone. "I'd like to sing a special encore for two very special people, Matthew Jensen and Carolyn Hardesty, who are to be married two weeks from today. Mattie, would you please join your bride-to-be on the dance floor?"

The crowd parted to make room for Matt to take Carrie in his arms. Ginny sang the Disney classic "Once upon a Dream." Carrie's sparkling, dazzling smile lit up the bistro as she and Matt slowly waltzed around the tiny dance floor to everyone's delight. Carrie looked up to Ginny, her maid of honor, and thanked her. Matt said something that made Carrie laugh, but no one could hear exactly what. She embraced her future husband and kissed him deeply as Ginny's song came to a teary conclusion.

Matt made an unannounced final trip to the piano and started the introduction for "Go Now" by the Moody Blues. He knew Ginny needed closure, and he looked up to her, his eyes asking her to go ahead. She nodded that she would sing it as her final song in Ginny's Bistro.

Two weeks later, with the bistro closed and her bags packed and waiting for her move to California, Ginny made the four-hour drive alone to Pine City for Mattie and Carrie's wedding. She stopped in the parking lot at the First Congregational Church, turned off the engine, and sat motionless in her car. Her bottom lip quivered as she contemplated the upcoming wedding ceremony. She gripped the steering wheel and pressed her forehead against it. Brutal thoughts and emotions swarmed and spun through her head as she closed her eyes and dreamed it was she being escorted down the aisle by her father toward Mattie.

She decided that could not stay. She would risk the humiliation of leaving, the commotion it would cause, and the long-lasting malevolence. Worst of all, she would risk losing Mattie forever, even as a friend.

A gentle rap on the hood of her car startled her, and she screamed. A man approached and motioned for her to roll down her window so they could speak.

"Excuse me, miss. I'm so sorry to have startled you." The man was young but very formal. "My name is Bob. I'm the pastor of this church. Are you all right, miss? Can I be of any help?"

Relieved, Ginny rolled the window down about halfway. "I'm fine, thank you. I was, um, passing through and pulled in here to rest awhile."

Rather puzzled, Pastor Bob stared at her beautiful face. "So you're okay then, no troubles?"

Ginny thought, *No, I'm not okay.*

She started up the engine and began to put the car in gear when Pastor Bob asked, "Have you come for the big wedding?"

Ginny stared straight ahead. "Why do you ask?"

Pastor Bob raked his fingers through his hair. "Well, folks are coming in from all over, and you look to be about the same age as the bride and groom, that's all."

Ginny turned and smiled sadly. "No, I'm not staying. Um, would there happen to be a payphone nearby?"

Bob pointed toward the Richfield station across the street. "There's one at the gas station. Or you can use the phone in the church if it's an emergency."

"Thanks, but a payphone will do. It was nice meeting you," Ginny said as she pulled away, leaving Pastor Bob in a cloud of dust, scratching his head.

Ginny called Lorry and told her that she was too disturbed, too emotional to attend Mattie's wedding, let alone be Carrie's maid of honor. She had considered the implications and was driving back to Three Forks, where she would meet up with Lorry to drive to California.

For the first time in her life, Lorraine Cullen was stunned speechless.

It was far beyond the realm of possibility that Ginny turned around and left in an act of vengeance, but some did think that way. Matt and Carrie knew better, and they made every effort to assure Ginny they held no grudge toward her. They desperately wanted Ginny to forgive herself, to live her life without regrets, and to embrace the amazing career that awaited her with happiness and joy. And although she indeed become famous throughout the world, she could never forgive herself for leaving Mattie and Carrie's wedding.

# PART 2

*The weak can never forgive. Forgiveness is the attribute of the strong.*

—Mahatma Gandhi

# The Singer

Virginia Simmons gives her voice to an audience with extraordinary and unrivaled skill, spirited and passionate. She allows the power of her voice, the music, and the lyrics to fully consume and possess her, luring and molding her listeners into the same state of being. No wild gestures, no theatrics, Virginia Simmons sings as if she were the only person alive, regardless if she's in a theater or concert hall or any venue chosen for her.

She enthusiastically begins her pursuit to excellence as a complete unknown, perfecting her craft regardless of genre with such drive and integrity that she has no critics, only admirers. There are no gimmicks, no insecure self-promotions, and no one-hit wonders. Virginia is an overnight sensation that has lasted for ten years and has become the most recognizable voice on earth. She simply loves to sing, and the world loves to listen to her as she has no failings, only devotion. She sings to millions of people, travels millions of miles, and sells millions of records. She sings the national anthem before the World Series and entertains at Super Bowls. She performs before heads of state. She has, as Matthew Jensen predicted, put her voice into the heads of millions. There was never that descent into mediocrity that befell many singers. Her sound, her songs were always inventive, refreshing, and no pun intended, noteworthy. But she wonders, often of late, how long her success will continue. She knows in her heart and in her body that her gift is beginning to wane from the strain and grind of her relentless schedule.

Listening to the silence of her dressing room, she is distressed when looking at her reflection in the mirror. It's like staring at a stranger, an intruder. Her face is painfully thin, her cheeks shallow and concave. The makeup artist does a nice job hiding the gray circles beneath her eyes. She wonders where the years have gone and concludes that, while she may be getting an A in her career, she is getting a F in life.

Virginia Simmons knows that the solitude of standing alone on center stage is experienced by very few. But she will soon be there, alone as always. She has a peculiar sensation that tonight will be her last concert, her last performance for a long time hence. She is tired and needs time off to rest yet continues a frenetic schedule, one that crushes her, and regardless of the retinue of people that surround her, she feels the stress of being constantly lonely. Except for Lorraine Cullen, the gift of companionship is nonexistent.

As is her custom, Virginia peeks from behind the curtains to view her audience for tonight, a habit she has continued since her college days when she first gained the confidence to face a crowd without fear and stage fright.

"Just lose yourself in your song," her beloved Mattie would tell her, then he would whisper in her ear, "And remember, you're perfect." Sometimes he gave her a little peck on the cheek, but never more than that.

She walks past a grand piano toward the isolated microphone at center stage. The houselights turn down and the stage lights turn up; the curtain rises. She stands alone, in a magnificently luminescent pool of light. The audience instantly rises to their feet to acknowledge her, and the applause lasts for several minutes. She graciously receives the ovation as she learned to do long ago. At age thirty-six, she is being honored tonight as the one of youngest entertainers to receive the Kennedy Center Award for the Performing Arts. Virginia waves and smiles at the president and his wife. The president's wife waves back. The president blows her a kiss and sits down, which cues the audience to take their seats, and they become silent in anticipation. She gives the conductor a slight nod, the orchestra begins, and

Virginia Simmons sings. Her voice is like a pleasant scent that falls over the audience like a tingling fog.

She has been born with the gift of voice but taught the discipline of delivering a song long ago from her first accompanist, and she sings as if Mattie is the only person in front of her, the only man she has loved. She sees his face in the audience; she sees his face in the orchestra, on the streets, and always in her dreams.

Virginia will sing to the Kennedy Center audience for eighty minutes, stopping only to take an infrequent sip of water. And although her voice, the voice that penetrates the soul of anyone who hears it, is strong and stirs the crowd into sublime tranquility, it is evident to Virginia that a slight, unknown peculiarity emerges in her delivery.

The concert ends, and Virginia Simmons bows. She turns to salute her conductor and her orchestra. But rather than exiting offstage only to return for the obligatory encore, she stands frozen and rigid at the microphone. Uneasiness swells throughout the crowd, who honestly cannot understand what she is doing. The orchestra remains expectant but silent, not even tuning.

A hush now, and Virginia speaks into the microphone, her voice just above a whisper. She is encouraged to speak up as she cannot be heard or understood. She remains stock-still, crossing her arms, as if she were trying to protect herself, a diminutive figure standing alone under a single spotlight. She steps back from the microphone but, with a sudden burst of energy, catches herself and steps up to the mic. She gulps for air; her words are forced, showing the despair that has consumed her over the past three months.

"I have to stop now," she says, her voice hoarse. "I need to be away from this."

No press conference, no drama, no machination that only those with less confidence, but with much more vanity, would demand.

"I've had an amazing but nonstop career, and I end it here tonight with no regrets. I thank you all so very much, but I can't continue this anymore. I'm just so tired."

The audience blurs, the Kennedy Center spins around, and she rushes offstage amid murmurs and shouts that it cannot be possible, but it is. She reaches backstage and collapses into the arms of her road manager, Raul. She loses consciousness and wakes up in a hospital room, alone as always, she reminds herself.

The official story reads that Virginia Simmons is suffering from acute exhaustion and will be just fine with a few months' rest. But Virginia knows this is not true. She knows her voice, the greatness of her gift, is in decline, that she can no longer competently deliver a song. If she can hear it, her audience can hear it too. Her body is failing. Complete rest becomes her only hope for revival and renewal.

Released from the hospital after two days, she returns to her seldom-used ocean-front home in Carmel overlooking the Pacific Ocean. She leaves only once during her convalescence to attend the funeral of a college friend who has died far too young. It is a tortuous event that she cannot endure. She leaves in the middle of the memorial service.

Virginia is amused by the countless media reports of her whereabouts. Just like Elvis, she thinks. To her great relief, the impetuous press tires of her inactivity and moves on to find other celebrities to ambush. One report rings true: she is crushed by the death of her college friend Carrie Jensen.

# The Abyss

*F*iguring *her patient has drifted into her final and devastating coma, the nurse jumps back in surprise as Carrie Jensen's eyes suddenly flash open. She looks up to the nurse and displays a radiant smile.*

*Her husband is driving to the hospice home for the last time, and he hears her voice softly calling to him, pleading, "Hurry, baby. Come to me." He presses down on the accelerator and weaves in and out of traffic. Two little girls, firmly buckled up in the back seat, look at each other wide-eyed. They reach out and take each other's hands.*

Twelve-year old Shelly Jensen and her ten-year old sister Claire Jensen stand on the deck overlooking their backyard in suburban Seattle. They cling to Lorraine Cullen, unofficially Auntie Lorry, their eyes now empty of tears, their faces stunned in disbelief. They stare blank-faced at a group of men and women below them surrounding their dad. Except for Pastor Owen Johannsen, they are complete strangers. The girls return their waves and smile with uncertainty, wondering why such close attention is being paid to them. They slide out of view behind Auntie Lorry.

Claire points to them and asks, "Auntie Lorry? Who are those people?"

Lorry studies the group with a fond expression and then turns toward the girls with a sad smile. "They are your father's—and your mother's—best friends from college, a long time ago. They've all come a long way to be here at your mom's service. They love your dad—and your mommy too."

"But Mommy's dead," Shelly says flatly. "How come we've never seen them before, 'cept Pastor Owen? Shouldn't best friends stick together? I think I've seen that man with the cane before, though."

Lorry has moved back to Seattle after Ginny's retirement and has opened a high-end restaurant downtown. She looks down to the group once more and explains, "Well, sweetie, we all live far away from each other now, and that makes getting together very hard." Lorry glances to another group and points to Kate, Tess, Emily, and Lucy. "Just like your aunts and your cousins." Lorry's voice drops to a whisper, "We're scattered like leaves in the wind. And now your daddy is all alone."

"He still has us," Claire replies matter-of-factly.

Lorry hugs her. "Yes, sweetie, he sure does."

"Who was that lady who kind of screamed during church and left when she saw Claire and me with Daddy?" Shelly asks.

Lorry frowns. "Her name is Ginny." She offers no further explanation.

*   *   *

Nighttime is the worst part of Matthew Jensen's day. His perfect life, his perfect partnership, has corroded by Carrie's slow and untimely death. She had the sweetest and most generous disposition, which often left him in absolute wonder. How he wishes he had that beautiful gift, her wonderful outlook on life, and the capacity to give love back unconditionally to his daughters, but he feels helpless to do so. He lies in bed and watches the clock flip from minutes to hours. When exhausted sleep finally falls upon him, he wakes up sweating and screaming.

One month later, Claire rushes into her older sister's bedroom. Tears are streaming down her cheeks. She jumps into Shelly's bed, so afraid she is shaking, and clings tight to Shelly's protective embrace.

"Daddy's screaming in his sleep again," Claire whispers to her sister. "It scares me."

Shelly whispers back, "It scares me too. I don't know what's wrong with him. And he doesn't talk. Ever."

Shelly tries to be confident as she comforts her little sister. She tells her that everything will be all right but secretly wonders if this is true. The hope within her begs that Dad will be the way he used to be: funny, warm, and caring. The way he was before their mother died. Lorraine Cullen, Auntie Lorry, is with them more than their dad is. She picks them up from school and takes them to their piano lessons. She takes them for ice cream and then drives them home, where the nanny has made dinner. Auntie Lorry tells them that their dad is working late, again, so they eat alone. She tells them stories about their father: that he is a brilliant musician and a wonderful man, but they have become dubious of this. Shelly and Claire wish their dad would sing to them again, that they can sit next to him at the piano and watch his fingers magically dance over the keys. They want to sing to him too, all the songs he taught them, and to be cradled in his arms, where he would tell them how much he loves them. But he is disconnected and has created an emotional distance from them. He is rarely home and has abandoned their care to others

"I miss Mommy," Claire whispers.

\*     \*     \*

Ty Keller sits facing Marty Nevin at Hazel's in Kinneysville's lone diner, quite mystified by the news his friend and business partner has just delivered; perhaps stupefied and disturbed would be more appropriate.

"Shouldn't she be on a slow steamer to Paris or Greece or someplace . . . exotic?"

Marty takes off his hat, drags his hand through his hair, and pushes the letter across the tabletop. "Read for yourself," he asks for the waitress to bring them each a slice of whatever pie is handy. Apple would be good.

"Let me borrow those reading glasses of yours, would you?" Ty asks, trying to focus on the small print.

Marty sighs, "Why don't you go to the drugstore and buy yourself a pair?" He slides the half-moon reading glasses across the table.

"Why would I do that when I can borrow yours?" Ty replies.

"Well, I'm not always around, what do you do then?"

But Ty doesn't seem to hear him; he is firmly immersed in the letter, which, in brief, explains that Virginia Simmons has asked to come and stay on their ranch. Finally, after reading it twice through, he puts the letter back into the envelope and looks up at Marty. "I use Betty's glasses when you're not around."

Marty laughs. "I bet that's a good look on you." But Ty, preoccupied, doesn't seem to hear.

"Do our wives know about this?" Ty asks.

Marty brightly answers, "They do, and they're both on board."

Ty shakes his head. "So as usual, I'm the last to know, yeah?"

"Well," Marty judges, "we all figure you're the deal breaker on the entire success of this affair."

"My wife idolizes her, don't ya know? And so does yours."

"Hell, who doesn't?" Marty exclaims. "Including the two of us, as you recall."

Ty rubs his chin. "That was a long time ago, my friend. Besides, everybody knows she still pines away for Mattie. Why doesn't she stay with him?" He pauses thoughtfully. "Although that was quite a stunt she pulled at their wedding, just leaving like that, wasn't it? She did the same thing at Carrie's funeral."

Marty purses his lips. "Don't you think Mattie's a little overwhelmed with life at the moment? I mean, Carrie's passed away, and he has those two girls. Not to mention a high-profile job."

Ty's voice drifts away. "Yeah. I suppose you're right." He relives the sadness of Mattie's situation and recalls how just a few short years ago Carrie and Mattie had saved his life.

Marty knew what he was thinking and let Ty dwell on his near-death accident and his difficult recovery. He breaks the silence and softly offers, "I think she's looking for a quiet place to write a new album. A piano is being sent to the house. She wants a little solitude, maybe."

Ty straightens and brings himself back to the present. "She's sure picked the best place for that, huh? Not the end of the road, but you can see it from here." He chuckles. "Just think, Ginny Simmons is coming to Kinneysville."

"I think she's goes by Virginia these days," Marty informs him.

"Whatever."

\*     \*     \*

Matthew Jensen sits facing his therapist, staring at her feet; an unnamed melody drifts through his head. She wants him to open up and talk about his grief, his mourning. She tells him that it's natural to grieve over his loss and there is no timetable for recovery. Life continues, and it is imperative that he accept this reality as it is crucial to the healing process. But he is bottled up. He conceals everything from his family and his friends.

The psychiatrist snaps her fingers and points to her eyes. "Hey, I'm up here. Where are you?"

It became so natural for Matthew to embrace the joys in life, but it took no time at all for life to viciously purge and rip his joy away. In a rapid descent, he has vanished and withdrawn into a safety net of old entanglements from decades ago, the pit of his stomach in a perpetual knot. His daughters have Carrie's smile. It is painful for him to see them as they are just like she was, bright and vivacious. It haunts him. He sleeps fitfully, sweating and gasping for breath. He can see Carrie's face, her smile in his dreams. She seems so real that he's not sure if he is sleeping or not. He wakes up screaming, frightening his daughters to the point that he locks himself in the downstairs study, hoping he cannot be heard. But they do hear him. He knows they're thinking that what is happening to him is their fault. His emaciated gray face shows the stress from chronic, blinding migraines. The perennial bashful smile is replaced by a permanent frown. His hands shake, and creases dig deep into his forehead. The once-warm, penetrating midnight-blue eyes are distant, cold, and empty of hope. He feels he has ruined Carrie's zest for loving life and betrayed her ability to give love and affection and how she could so thoughtfully return the love and care from others. Matthew feels his inability to receive the love his daughters want to offer him, and he feels the shame and guilt. He wonders if he will ever emerge from his melancholy and embrace his children's love and their desire to care for him. He glances at a vase full of fading cut flowers and feels a kinship with them.

Matthew looks up an into the doctor's expectant eyes. "I'm not sure where I am at the moment. I-I can't explain what's happening to me." He bows his head. "I just don't know what to do, especially with my kids, so I don't do anything. I'm afraid I've failed in any effort to carry on my wife's legacy of love. And I'm failing my children. I mean, I'm the one person they should trust the most, and I've vanished before their eyes. I've shut them out. It's unforgivable."

The doctor knows his mind is spinning like a gale-force wind, that deep-rooted anxieties are tugging him away from the reality of the moment. She softly tells him, "But we're right here, right now. What's frightening about this? Why don't you feel safe? Right here, in this office? Don't you feel safe?"

"Yes, it's safe," he answers with the hint of a seldom-seen smile, "but it's not very relaxing."

The doctor treats dozens of grieving parents and needs Matthew to uncover the new pathway before him, one that is foreign to him at the moment but a pathway he must discover and hold on to nonetheless. But he's stalled in misery, and he cannot move forward. He cannot change until he truly wants to disentangle himself from old inhibitions that have taken control of him. The doctor knows he prefers to talk about others rather than about himself. He believes paying attention to himself will turn him into a selfish bastard like the late Vernon Holloway. He clings to diversions, which keep him from remembering who he is, what he wants, and the person whom he needs to again become. His spirit is broken, and all the time, he wants to feel worse. His emotions are fluid, showing his fear, guilt, and shame. His friends can see it, but he refuses their help.

The doctor points to her eyes again, urging him to focus on the fact that just the two of them reside in the safe confines of her office. "You're using the past to keep from seeing yourself and from paying attention to yourself." Like she was reading his mind, a skill Matthew concludes she has possessed for some time. The doctor adds, "You're not a selfish man, Matthew, and I'm sure you've been told that many times during your life, haven't you?"

Matthew shuts his eyes and shakes his head. "Yes," he answers. He takes a deep breath. "But it just seems that, anytime my character is challenged, I fail."

The doctor makes a few notes and eyes him suspiciously. "Are you taking the meds I've prescribed, Matthew?"

Matthew lowers his head. "No."

She writes a few more notes. "Well, I think we need to settle this issue right now. You've been coming here once a week for nearly nine years. That tells me you're willing to change, that you're willing to be healed, but you're also showing me that you're not interested in the treatment. You have major depression disorder, Matthew. You're manic-depressive, and you can't simply suppress or wish it away. But I can't help you until you decide to participate with me. Do you want therapy? Do you want to get better? Do you want your family back?" The doctor is very smart and knows precisely what she's doing by challenging him with such rhetoric.

Matthew looks at her; his face reveals his pain. "I'm not purposefully trying to be this way. I mean, it's not deliberate. I'd never do anything to hurt my children, but I know I am. I feel like I'm circling an abyss of desperation, just waiting to be sucked down without any hope of finding the surface. I don't know how I could have been so devoted to them one moment and how I've totally abandoned them in the next. It used to be that I could never get enough of them. Now I doubt they will ever forgive me. I don't deserve them, and I don't deserve to be happy." He pauses for a moment. "I'm so sorry," he whispers. "I think off and on I've probably been like this my entire life: when my sisters left home, when my parents passed away. When my best friend in college died. I tend to internalize my issues, keep them private. But it's conflicting: I used to find it so easy to care for others and, now I disappear, especially when someone tries to care for me. And I'm useless when it comes to caring for Shelly and Claire.

I've lost their trust. I just hope they don't hate me as much as I hate myself.

"But Carrie was able to see that. She made all my fears disappear and totally freed me. She showed me how to truly appreciate the joy of love and to know what it feels like to be cared for by another."

The doctor quits taking notes and stares at him with tears in her eyes. She knows that this is much more than simple self-pity and mourning. He is in a dark, dark place, and she wonders how much time it will take before he is drawn back to the light. When in the grip of depression, he realizes, he cannot recognize or imagine truth and honesty. It is a desperate mood within him that occurs randomly and without warning.

"I see Carrie's face in my dreams. I see her face in the evening sky and in the stars at night. I see her features in my daughters. I can feel her on my skin. I think by keeping my daughters at a distance deflects how much I miss her and how much I needed her." He shakes his head and whispers as if he were thinking out loud, "I know Shelly and Claire want to care for me, but for some reason, I just run away from them. My god, what a terrible, shameful thing I'm doing to them. I wish I would have died instead of Carrie."

He fidgets in his chair. "I think about the day we lost her. Chemo and radiation had eaten and burned her body away, she couldn't have weighed more than ninety pounds. Her hair had fallen out months before." He stops and swallows hard; his eyes glisten with tears. "She suffered through so much pain but was always positive, almost peaceful about it all. She had such great faith. I let the girls see her about an hour before she passed, and they gasped in horror at the sight of her. She kissed them and whispered to them, asking them to take care of each other and to take care of me. I stayed until the end. One last blink of her eyes, one last smile that faded away, and she was gone. I just sat there, holding her hand. Finally, the hospice nurse told me she had to be moved to the morgue. I tried to be as gentle with the girls as I could, and we had a few friends that helped us. But every time I enter our bedroom, memories of her flood back. All of her things, her clothes, and her makeup. I haven't touched anything of hers. Everything is just as it was, as if she will walk through the door, singing as always, and our lives will be happy and perfect again. I can still remember the smell of her hair after a shower." I can still feel her tenderness." He sighs. "But I suppose sometimes life doesn't turn out, it just turns."

The doctor folds her arms; she has never heard him talk so intimately of his late wife. "Those memories won't go away, Matthew. You can't forget them any more than you can forget her. But they're festering within you to the point that you're living your life in total paralysis. The success you're having with your work is no substitute. You have to determine how to live with your memories because, even though you feel they're a safe haven to hide in, they are not. We all handle loss in different ways, but your way is harming your recovery and your relationship with your daughters. I have a hard time believing you want to continue living this way. Do you?"

Matthew nods that he does not. He wants the darkness of his depression to simply leave his mind and body. He had never wanted to lose himself to grief, and he certainly never wished to hide and isolate himself from his children. He wants to gather Shelly and Claire in his arms, to kiss them and comfort them, to be there for them, other than the one night a year they were together in memory of Carrie's death. He wants to return to the light. He wonders if reconciliation is possible. Time rolls on for Shelly and Claire, but for Matthew, each day is a reenactment of the day before.

The doctor continues, "Your girls are smart, Matthew. They love you, and someday I know they will understand. But Matthew, Mattie, you must make an effort. Give yourself a chance. Go and talk to your girls, give them an opportunity to care for you."

He stares at his hands, his reply tentative and without confidence. "I'll try."

It does not go well, but he figures that he doesn't deserve much. His head is full of words he wants to share with them: how much he misses them, how much he cares for them, and how much he needs them. But nothing of use or purpose comes out. He speaks to them quietly, without making eye contact. They reply in rough, staccato monotones, their faces frozen, refusing to make eye contact with him.

"How are you?" he asks in a friendly tone.

"Fine."

"How's school?"

"Fine."

"Is there anything you need?"

"No."

"Well, please let me know if you do. If you need anything, anything at all."

"Yeah, we'll do that."

The doctor encourages him. "Don't give up, Matthew, keep trying. Listen to me, your entanglements will always be there, and like I've told you many times, you think they'll keep you safe, but they won't. I have a homework assignment for you, Matthew. I want you to think of one positive thought a day and remember how it makes you physically feel. Try to define it and to hold on to it. If you can do this and add to it, step by small step, you'll discover a new pathway."

"Okay."

"And, Matthew, there is one more thing: You are a gracious man. You've given everybody you know at least one second chance, haven't you? A chance at forgiveness and the opportunity for redemption?"

He sits up in his chair, his conviction apparent. "Well, sure. Everybody deserves a second chance."

"Then, Mattie, perhaps you should give yourself a second chance. Forgive yourself."

# Country Roads

"There ought to be a law against anybody wearing spandex if their butt is broader than their shoulders."

The irreverent observation is made by Ty Keller, sitting in his usual booth at the diner, across from his ranching partner, Marty Nevin. The remark is made as Hazel, the owner of the restaurant and tubby possessor of tight, ill-fitting pants, walks by, offering refills on coffee. She hears the comment and makes a point to spill hot coffee over Ty's hand. "Oops," she declares, "care for a refill there, hombre?"

Marty grins and tells Ty that he most likely deserves the retaliation and asks if he would please refrain from making comments about Hazel's choice of dress since, besides the few bars in town, this was the only place in Kinneysville where you don't have to eat in your car.

"Oh, she knows I'm just kidding," Ty replies as he fishes ice cubes from his water to cool off his burned fingers. "But I suppose I should've kept that to myself."

"Ya think?" Marty laughs.

"Well, this place could benefit from my many charms. So what brings you to town on this fine spring morning? Shouldn't you be chasing cows or breakin' broncs? Or do you want to take another look at the books?"

Marty and his wife, Donna, live on the ranch about thirty miles southwest of Kinneysville. He and Ty own all the land in between.

"We have some things to discuss. First off, she's coming tomorrow, you'll have to pick her up."

Ty looks perplexed. "What do you mean pick her up?"

Marty leans back, places his hands on top of his head, and smiles, "She's riding the dog."

"Are you shittin' me?" Ty cries with disbelief. "Ginny Simmons is coming here on the bus? She must own a dozen cars, for crying out loud." He looks suspiciously at Marty. "Where's she going to live, and what in the hell does she plan on doing once she gets here?"

Marty shakes his head and shrugs. "I don't know what she's going to do except maybe rest up for a while without anybody bothering her." He clears his throat uncomfortably. "She's, um, going to stay in my old trailer on the ranch."

Ty's head jerks back, and he laughs himself to tears. "Well now, that's something, I have to say. From penthouse to outhouse. I hope you've taken down all of your cow pictures."

"Yes, I have," Marty replies rather indignantly. "And it's not that bad. Besides, the girls are fixing it up."

"Well, it was fine for you, sure, but you have to admit it lacks a certain feminine appeal. And which girls are you speaking of, partner?" Ty asks. "Betty's been working full-time at the hospital, she hasn't had any time."

Marty leans forward on his elbows as if trying to keep a secret. "Lorry Cullen's been here for a week. She and Donna are making a few upgrades. New kitchen appliances, new carpet and wallpaper. They even replaced the grout in the shower. You wouldn't recognize the place.

"Betty's been out there a couple of times as well. They're all best buddies. I think they drink wine."

Now this is news to Ty. He has no idea his wife has been out to the ranch. He leans close to Marty, parroting his position. "So Lorry's here, huh? Always the last to know, I am."

"Yeah," Marty answers. "Keeping in mind your past, um, relationship with her, I felt it best to keep it a secret."

"There was no relationship," Ty replies, not quite irritated. "We've just never liked each other, that's all. And by the way, who's paying for all of these renovations to Martin's manor?"

"Don't worry, bean counter," Marty assures him. "Lorry and Ginny have paid for everything, no ranch money has been used. They insisted on that."

Marty tosses a twenty-dollar bill on the counter and retrieves Ty's walking cane. He waits for him to slide to the edge of the booth and then helps his best friend and partner to his feet. "Steady there, cowboy, you okay?" Marty asks.

"Yeah, I'm good," Ty replies. As he regains his balance, his body groans in protest. He makes his familiar gesture when asking a question he feels is of great importance. He raises his right hand to his chin and wags a single finger in a circle. "So. Just to clarify. I pick her up at the bus stop and then do what with her?"

Marty pats him on the back. "Drive her out to the ranch, man. That's all you have to do."

"I still can't believe it. Ginny Simmons is moving to Kinneysville."

"Virginia," Marty corrects him. "I think she wants to be called Virginia."

"Whatever. I'm just wondering if she'll remember me."

"Oh, come on now, Ty. Who could ever forget you?"

Hazel gives him a hug and a peck the cheek as he leaves. "You take care now, Mayor," she kindly says.

Ty Keller is such popular figure in Kinneysville that people call him Mayor, although it is an official position he routinely declines. His friendly manor and casual smile made him immensely popular when he first arrived in Kinneysville with his intention of partnering up with the homegrown Marty Nevin. It was a partnership that flourished. Officially charted as T/M Ranch and Farms, locals simply referred to the enterprise as the TIM. Ty Keller, with his recently earned MBA in hand, manages the finances of the TIM from the Kinneysville offices. Marty Nevin, who lives right on the ranch in a house he and his wife, Donna, have recently built on the canyon rim, manages the ranch and farm operations.

Little attention is paid to Ty as he casually slouches against the brick wall outside the bus stop, his hands thrust deep within his pockets. He is wearing sunglasses; a toothpick dangles from his mouth. His cane is planted firmly in front of him with his left foot curled up behind his right foot.

"Expecting a package, Mayor?" someone asks in passing.

"Something like that." Ty smiles in return.

He thinks anybody riding the dog is running either away from something or toward something. He wonders which one it is for Ginny, when he hears the bus gear down, pull off the highway, and slowly cruise into town. Except for the brief sighting at Carrie Jensen's memorial service, he has not seen Ginny since college. That was what? Eighteen, nineteen years ago? He wonders who has changed the most. It has to be him. The bus jolts to a stop, and a few passengers disembark, clutching and protecting their belongings as if bandits were lying in wait.

Ginny steps off last; she is wearing sunglasses, and her hair is tucked under a scarf. She pulls a small Louis Vuitton suitcase behind her.

*Hmm,* Ty thinks, *very incognito, she's not even wearing makeup, as if she needs any.* Ginny furtively looks around, hoping not to be noticed, when she hears Ty call out, "Hey, lady. You look just like Jackie Kennedy."

Ginny turns and smiles brilliantly. "And you, Tyler Keller, look just like Mr. Peanut!"

They laugh and embrace; he is alarmed by how thin and fragile she feels. "Well, lady," he lightly says with a little wave, "welcome to the happiest place on earth."

Ginny takes off her sunglasses and carefully looks him up and down. She is aware of his physical issues. "You look good, buddy," she cautiously says.

Ty sighs and shrugs his shoulders. He taps his cane on the sidewalk a couple of times. "Oh, I get around all right. Just a little slow sometimes. Lots of pins and needles, especially down my legs." Ginny hugs him again, this time gently, as if he were frail and fragile.

"But anyway," Ty said, changing the subject, "we're glad you're here, Ginny. We hope you can find whatever you're looking for."

"We?" Ginny replies, somewhat disturbed.

"There's quite a welcoming committee waiting for you at the trai—um, at your new place."

Ginny looks concerned. "Who else knows I'm here?"

"Don't worry, your hideout is a well-kept secret. Hell, they only told me last week. Apparently, they didn't want me to know that Ms. Cullen was skulking around. I can't figure that out, for the life of me."

Ginny laughs. "What was it you said about her? Oh, I remember, that she had a shortage of sympathy but a surplus of words."

Ty smiles. "Yeah, I suppose I should have kept that to myself. Then there was the time I congratulated her on finally discovering the cure for happiness. As I recall, she didn't think much of that one either."

Ginny laughs. "No, I don't believe she did."

He stops his reminiscing. He does not want to embarrass Ginny should the subject turn to Mattie and his issues. He quickly changes the subject. "Where's all your luggage?"

Ginny points to the small suitcase and forces a smile. "This is all I brought. The rest is arriving tomorrow."

"You might not need much more than that," Ty observes. "Well, let's get you out of here before someone sees me with another beautiful woman." He motions with his cane the direction to his car. Ginny steadfastly takes his arm, quick to notice that walking seems painful to him.

"From what I'm hearing, that's not too unusual," Ginny teases.

"And you've heard that from whom, might I ask?"

Ginny giggles. "Oh, you know."

"Yeah, your little terrorist friend, I'm sure. My god, she must have spies everywhere."

"Lorraine is very thorough, Ty, you've always known that."

"Ha! If that's what you want to call it, she is that, for sure."

The street is busy with cattle and grain trucks and school buses. Cars are waiting in line at the new drive-through espresso stand next to the post office. All the kids shout and wave at the mayor.

Two pickups with the T/M logo pass; the drivers honk and wave. As Ginny has hoped, nobody pays her any attention. She and Ty walk arm in arm up Kinney Street with only the occasional "Hi, Mayor" or "Hey there, Mayor."

"Looks like you've passed the test, Ginny. Either that or nobody would ever think to see your pretty face around here," Ty says lightly. She smiles and grips his arm a little harder.

Suddenly she shrieks in astonishment. "You still have this car? I can't believe it!" Ginny stares at a vintage 1962 light-blue Plymouth Valiant.

"Hell yes," Ty replies. "She's a classic, just like you."

Ginny smiles impudently. "Well, thank you, kind sir." She kisses the stubble of Ty's three-day-old beard, climbs into the passenger's seat, and gives the interior a good look. "Why, it hasn't changed a bit," she exclaims. "Not one bit."

Ty turns a little gloomy. "Well, it wasn't driven for a long time. Mattie took care of it for me."

It is Ginny who now turns a little gloomy, both at Ty's sudden mood change and the mention of Mattie's name. "Ty, I'm so sorry about what happened. To Carrie. And to you. It must have been terrible to go through."

Ty brightens. "I'm doing fine now. That's all that counts, yeah?"

She clears her throat uncomfortably and asks in a low voice, "What do you hear about Mattie?"

Ty glances out the side of his eyes. "Not much. I know he's in a bad way. He's hard to get hold of, he won't write or return calls. It must be tough, losing someone you love so much."

"Yes, it is," Ginny whispers. "He tried to call me about three years ago, but I wasn't home." She lifts her head high and smiles. "So when do I meet Donna and Betty?"

Grateful for a change in the subject, Ty jokes, "You mean Laverne and Shirley? Like I told you, everybody's waiting for you."

Ginny studies his face, noticing the faint scars. The skin grafts on his arms and hands have healed nicely. He knew what she was thinking but, at least this time, decides to not say anything.

"Will you tell me about it, Ty? Someday, when you're ready?"

He raises his knees to hold the steering wheel, takes her hand, and nuzzles it. "Sure. As much as I can remember." He lets her hand go and clears his throat. "What do you say we get you home, okay?"

"Yes, I'm ready."

Ty gives her another sly glance. "Well, I hope so."

He turns the key, and the Valiant cranks to a violent start. He checks the rearview mirror, pulls onto Kinney Street, and drives slowly past the grain elevators, the International Harvester store, and into the country. "I'd take the shortcut." He chuckles. "But there isn't one."

Ginny gazes out the window and takes in this country she hopes will bring her recovery, revival, and renewal. Ty notices a slight tremor in her hands and studies her from the corner of his eye. She is sickly pale and thin.

She guesses his thoughts. "I know, Ty. I'm quite a mess right now."

Ty replies with a warm smile, "Well, lady, I believe we can help with that."

"Oh, c'mon," Ginny says with a dubious tone, "no special treatment. Please."

"Well, you know you won't get any special treatment from me, or Marty either." They both laugh. "We figure on leaving you alone. You'll know when it's time for some company. Just let us know, yeah?" Ginny nods in thanks.

It is about twenty-five miles from Kinneysville to the trailer and another four winding miles to Marty and Donna's house on the canyon rim. Neither of them speaks. Ginny stares out the window, flush with memories of Northern State from twenty years ago. The rolling hills of the prairie are checkered with emerging wheat fields, green as felt, and with the browns of fields left fallow. She doesn't ask how the ranching business is going, and Ty offers nothing in return. Despite the chill of early spring, she rolls down her window to catch the fresh country air. She pulls off her scarf and lets the wind blow her long blond hair into tangles. It is a remarkable feeling for her, one she has dreamed of for years. She is instantly rejuvenated.

Finally, Ty breaks the reverie. "Look familiar?"

185

"Yes, sir," Ginny says. She rolls up the window, sighs with deep content, and sinks deep into the vinyl seat. "It's beautiful."

She looks at Ty. "I'm a little nervous meeting Betty and Donna."

"Don't be, they're just as nervous to meet you," he assures her. "They'll fawn over you a little, but you'll soon discover they're both phenomenal."

She teases him, "They must be something special to get along with the two of you."

"And how is Marty?" she suddenly asks.

Ty mocks astonishment. "Wait. What? You mean Lorry hasn't filled you in?"

Ginny laughs. "I believe he moves too far under the radar, even for her."

"Well, he's not a hermit, if that's what you're thinking," Ty lightly replies. "Why, he was just in town last week with, you know, Lorry's letter."

"Quite the shock, I bet," she teases.

Ty loses himself in thought for moment and finally looks at her. He raises his knees to catch the steering wheel, reaches for her hand again. "None of us are surprised that you want to get away from it all for a while. But coming here? Yeah, it's a bit of a surprise, I'll admit that. But when you think the situation through, it makes perfect sense. Nobody will bother you out here, Ginny. At least with the four of us around." He hesitates and ponders if he should continue with the obvious. *Oh, what the hell,* he thinks. "But it does bring up the elephant in the room, don't you think?"

Ginny purses her lips. "Mattie," she softly says.

"Yeah, Mattie. He's all alone. Kind of like you, yeah?"

Ginny's eyes glisten with tears, and she looks out the window. "Yes, Ty. Kind of like me. He called me a few years ago. I-I wasn't home. I guess I told you that. He said he was on some kind of therapeutic exercise. Sounded like his old usual self, mostly. I didn't call him back. Ty, I'm still embarrassed and ashamed of what I did at Mattie and Carrie's wedding. Do you think he forgives me?"

Ty rests his hand on her shoulder. "Of course he forgives you. You, of all people, must know that."

It is worth the awkward silence that follows, although he's glad nobody else is present.

He turns on his left signal indicator even though there is not another car or truck in sight and turns onto a road where a single mailbox stands along the highway with a single name: Nevin.

"Just a few more miles," he cheerfully tells her. Ginny sits up with anticipation; her solemn mood over Mattie has retreated, for now.

The country road turns from asphalt to crushed gravel with a few potholes that Ty deftly avoids. Narrowing down now to the width of a semitractor, the shoulder is bulldozed into the wheat fields every couple of miles for another vehicle to pull into on the rare chance somebody might approach from the opposite direction. Ginny hears meadowlarks and magpies offensively chatting at each other, and she smiles at the sound.

The narrow road continues to split through the prairie's hills until Ty slows down and turns onto a seldom-used track. He stops on a small rise that looks down onto a twelve-foot-wide-by-forty-eight-foot-long mobile home settled securely under four ancient cotton-wood trees. Three dusty pickup trucks and a shiny Buick are parked by a wrought-iron porch as if they have been randomly dropped from the sky.

"Well, lady," Ty says. "Welcome home. Shall we?"

Ginny looks down to the trailer and gently puts her hand on his knee. "Home," she whispers. "Yes, let's do it."

Gravel crunches under the Valiant and bounces off the undercarriage.

Marty Nevin hears their approach. He whispers, "They're here." He looks to Betty and Donna. "Are you two ready for this?"

Both ladies rush to the bathroom for last-minute adjustments to their hair and makeup.

Marty chuckles. "She's not going to care how you look, for crying out loud. Besides, I'm sure she's just as nervous as you two."

He nods to Lorraine. "Let's go meet her, proper like."

Lorry gives a simple nod and reaches for his hand. "She's changed, Martin. Try not to stare, okay?"

Marty casts her a bemused look. "Hell, Lorry, who hasn't changed? Except for you, maybe. Just take it easy on old Ty, would you? If anyone has changed, it's him."

She smiles and slaps his wrist. "Don't worry, Martin. I'll be gentle—if he is."

Ginny quickly jumps out of the Valiant with the intention of helping Ty up and out, but he waves her off. "No worries, lady. I've had a lot of practice at this. But thanks just the same."

She steps back, not fully convinced, and then watches Ty swing both feet out of the car, firmly plant his cane on the ground, and stand up with little effort.

He grins. "See? Nothin' to it."

"You are a wonder, Ty Keller," Ginny tells him with adoring eyes.

"Yeah, I know. But we should probably keep that to ourselves."

From twenty yards away, Ginny hears another familiar voice. "Aw, don't give him any special attention, Ginny. He's just showin' off. It's what he does, don't ya know?"

She turns and sees Marty Nevin facing her with a wide smile. She rushes to his expectant embrace, and like Ty, he is shocked by her frailty. He gently rocks her back and forth and whispers, "Welcome, miss."

"Thank you, Marty. You're a lifesaver."

Marty chuckles. "Well, I doubt that. But I promise to be a good landlord." He glances up to the porch where Donna and Betty are standing in starstruck amazement. Marty calls to them, "Well, c'mon down, you two. She's not gonna bite."

Ty mutters just loud enough to be heard when he spies Lorry Cullen poke her head outside. "No, she won't. But I can't vouch for that little one up there."

Ginny smiles and extends her arms in greeting to Donna and Betty. "Hello. I'm Ginny Simmons."

Neither speak as they descend the porch stairs arm in arm, as if protecting themselves from some form of aberration. Ginny reaches for Betty's hand and pulls her into a hug. "You must be Betty."

"Yes, ma'am," she manages to say, and immediately joins her husband's side.

"And you're Donna. Right?" Ginny asks cheerfully. She reaches out and pulls Donna into a similar embrace. She whispers to her, "Thank you so much for offering this place. I can't begin to tell you how much this means to me."

Donna manages to reply, "You're welcome, Ms. Simmons. It's an honor."

"Please, call me Ginny. Okay?"

Donna bows her head, still not quite believing the Virginia Simmons is moving to their ranch and to beat all things, is moving into their trailer. "Um, all right, Ginny. May we help you inside?"

Ty holds up the small suitcase. "This is all she brought. Not exactly digging in for the winter, is she?"

Ginny turns to Ty and tries her best to scowl, an unnatural mood for her, and Ty knows it. "I told you, Tyler Eisenhower Keller, oh yes, I know your middle name: the rest of my luggage comes tomorrow. Savvy?"

She winks at Betty. "Sometimes you have to talk to him like that."

Betty rolls her eyes and hooks Ginny's arm around hers. "Don't I know it! Let's get you inside and settled. Shall we?" She turns to Ty and Marty. "You two stay out here. There's crud on your boots . . . and you smell like cows."

A loud crash is heard from inside, startling Ginny, and she hears Lorry laugh. "That's just Marty's *Hereford Journal* collection falling off the table. He thinks you'll find them fascinating."

Donna shakes her head and gathers the magazines off the floor. "I told him to get rid of these." She shouts to Marty, "Take those boots off, and come in here to pick these up. For crying out loud, Marty, Ms. Simmons doesn't want to look through these."

Ginny smiles. "It's all right, Donna. Leave them here. And please, it's Ginny. Okay?"

Lorry gathers her belongings and announces that it's time for her to be on her way.

"So soon, Lorry?" Donna asks. "We were hoping you'll all join us for dinner at the ranch tonight. The piano you ordered for Ginny was just delivered. We put it next to Marty's office."

Lorry shakes her head and looks at Ginny. "No, it's time."

She hugs Donna and Betty and unveils a case of her favorite Spanish Garnacha. "A gift for all your help. It's been such a pleasure getting to know you both, really."

Ginny follows Lorry outside and smiles to herself as she advances toward Ty, who immediately takes a cautious step back. "Oh, would you relax?" she hisses. "I'm not going to bite you."

She wraps her tiny arms around his waist. "You take care of yourself, Tyler. You know how I worry."

"I will, Ms. Cullen. You take care too. Please say hello to Mattie for us." He looks at Ginny. "For all of us, yeah?"

"I'll do that, Ty."

Ginny and Lorry walk to her Buick arm in arm. They embrace and whisper words to each other before Lorry guns the engine and speeds away, leaving gravel and dust in her wake. Ginny stares after her until she's out if view.

Ty joins her. "It must be a little strange to be left alone like this, yeah? I mean, we'll be around whenever need be, but it's been what? Since college that you've been friends?"

"Before even then, Ty," Ginny absently replies. "Way before. But you're right, it's been a long time." She reaches for his hand and smiles. "But I think it's time I renew old friendships."

Changing the subject, Ginny asks, "Is there a way to pick up the rest of my belongings tomorrow?"

Marty digs into his pocket and retrieves a single key. He tosses to it to her. "It's for that blue pickup. It's yours to use anytime. Now, it's hard to get lost around here, and we don't have cell phone service, so you'll have to use the CB radio. Donna and I are on channel 11, and you can get Ty on channel 19, if you can find him, that is. Otherwise, use the landline."

Ginny clutches the key like a lost puppy. "Thank you, Marty. Thank you all, for everything."

Ty said, "Betty and I can meet you in town to help load up your stuff, okay? It's, um, hard to get lost in Kinneysville, no matter how much you try."

"Thanks, you two, I really appreciate that."

Ty looks at Betty. "Let's head for home, shall we?" Betty nods.

Donna puts her arm around Ginny. "Are you sure you won't join us for dinner tonight, Ginny? We'd love to have you." Ginny hesitantly shifts.

Marty's eyes narrow. "Why don't we let her relax into the place for the night, huh?" He raises his head and sniffs the air. "Besides, there's a storm movin' in."

Ginny nods her appreciation. "How about tomorrow night, Donna? Will that be all right?"

"Sure, Ms. Simmons—Ginny—we look forward to it."

Marty begins to walk away and suddenly spins around on his heels. "Hey, Ginny. You're not some kind of vegetarian or anything like that, are you?"

Ginny throws him a beguiling smile. "Not while I'm living on the TIM!"

# Ghosts

I t is three o'clock in the afternoon, already a long and exhausting day for Ginny. Finding herself alone again, she brews a cup of tea and walks catlike through the trailer. She inspects the nooks and crannies and smiles at the Remington and Russell prints that line the narrow hallway from the living room to the bedroom. The place is rarely occupied since Marty and Donna built their house on the canyon rim, just the occasional summer intern from nearby Northern State University. She reminds herself to buy a few groceries while in town tomorrow.

She opens a few windows, allowing in the sweet aroma of recently tilled earth and the pleasant, perfumed fragrance of black-eyed Susans, now in full bloom and smothering the surrounding hills. The bedroom is light and cheery, as are the bathroom and shower. Clearly the work of Lorraine, Betty, and Donna.

Sitting down on the living room sofa, she laughs at Marty's stack of *Hereford Journals* and intends to stow them in the spare bedroom that Marty used as his office when he lived here. She reminds herself of the real purpose in coming to the little trailer, besides a change of scenery, which is to find the inspiration to write the songs for her first album in nearly ten years. She could have stayed in Carmel. She could have gone anywhere in the world, but this country is familiar, and she hopes the prairie hills will not only revive her health but also help her career begin anew. She still has much to accomplish.

The sweet herbal tea has its effects, and she soon dozes off. Visions of the bistro flood her dreams, and images emerge from her past. She dreams how Mattie had given her the courage and confidence to discover the full scope of her voice, how he was able to gently draw out her talent by challenging her with different genres of music.

"It's your voice, Ms. Simmons," he had told her in his bashful way. "It's your face. It's everything about you. You're perfect."

She has never stopped loving him and wonders if he has forgiven her. Ty Keller's words from earlier that day pass by, "Of course he forgives you. You, of all people, must know that."

Ty is right; Mattie has always had a forgiving spirit. He even forgave Vernon Holloway. Even so, she worries about him because, of all people, she also knows how hard Mattie can be on himself, even with the most innocent of things. She dreams about Carrie. How lovely she was, how full of life. They had become so close to each other. She dreams about the frantic moments that led up to her sudden departure the day before their wedding. She wakes up and whispers out loud, "How will I ever get over that?"

She wants to go to Mattie after Carrie dies, but discovers she cannot even make it through her memorial service without falling apart. Lorry assures her that, since she's decided to move back home to the coast, she will be there for Mattie and especially his children, Shelly and Claire. It is a promise Lorry holds to this very day, almost ten years now. The new restaurant she has opened is extraordinary, but Ginny figures no less.

Five o'clock in the afternoon finds the sun low; its long rays stretch over the hills. Dust mites float through the air, and fluffy cottonwood seeds are casually carried by gentle breezes. She listens to the meadowlarks' final call of the day and watches deer timidly appear. She puts on a light sweater, pours a chilled glass of chardonnay from the refrigerator, and walks outside to enjoy the sunset. Despite the chilly morning, the afternoon has turned unseasonably warm. Low-lying sunbeams momentarily blind her. She shields her eyes and turns away; the warmth feels good on her neck and back. She recalls Marty predicting a big storm to blow in but pays it no mind as the placid early evening feels so comfortable. She looks up to a big blue-black sky transitioning into twilight, washed by the evening's emerging stars. Her memories of this empty vast land are nearly triumphant, so unlike the confinement of the city. She climbs the hill behind the trailer and turns around just in time to see the outside lights illuminate the four ancient cottonwoods, whose branches, still empty of leaves, look like skeletal fingers clawing at her new home, just beyond their grasp. Keeping the lights in sight so she will not lose her way back, she summits the deceptively steep hill, sits down on the grass to enjoy the end of the day and drink the rest of her wine. The sun sets before her, and moon rises behind her. Both are the same pink-orange color. Standing now, she gets goose bumps as the temperature suddenly drops, and she thrusts her hands deep into her pockets; her light sweater offers little protection. She wonders why the deer have mysteriously disappeared and why the songbirds are mute since there is a little daylight left. She's frightened when she notices the rising moon turn bloodred then fade to black when the first lightning bolt bursts from the sky and scorches the earth. She screams from the suddenness of an incendiary surge of wind that drags her to the ground. A swirling pillar of dust blasts her face and eyes, blinding any sense of direction. She stumbles to her feet and frantically searches for the lights elevated around the trailer, but all is dark. After she makes a few tentative steps downhill, a second gust of wind from behind pushes her to her knees. Her face and legs are scratched and bleeding. She screams again when a second lightning bolt strikes the ground fifty yards from her, but it lights up the sky long enough for her to find home. She covers her ears when thunder claps overhead and feels electricity in her hair and fingertips. Walnut-size hailstones spill out of black clouds and pound her head and shoulders. She loses a shoe in the mud and slips on the wrought-iron porch, scraping both knees and bumping her head before falling into the trailer, panting for her breath.

"Oh my," she says in relief. "I'll never doubt Marty Nevin again."

She urgently flicks light switches up and down, but the power is off. She leans against the wall, making tentative steps toward the bedroom in the rear of the trailer so she can change out of her wet clothes. She can't believe how dark it is. Passing by the empty spare bedroom, she spots a single picture on an otherwise-bare wall illuminated by a lightning strike. She stares at it in disbelief. Another shock of lightning pierces the sky and lights up the room, plainly revealing the faces on the photograph before turning to dark. They are all there: Lionel Henslaw, Ty Keller in his full navy dress blues, Marty Nevin, in a suit, and the unmistakable, cherub-faced Owen Johannsen. They're standing with their arms around each other's shoulders, their faces in varying degrees of delight. Standing in their midst, in her wedding dress, is Carrie Jensen, her head held up high in laughter, which now rings in Ginny's ears. She reaches out and clutches the picture to her chest, soaking it with her tears until exhaustion takes her into a fitful sleep. Violent gusts of wind bucks the trailer back and forth on its footings and wakes her. She opens her eyes in time to catch the last lightning bolt of the slow-moving storm and screams when she sees the faces in the photograph come to life, standing above her like ghosts. But a sudden peace, however, such as she's never experienced, comforts her like a warm blanket. She looks up to see Carrie Jensen float past, her face as brilliant as the sun. She smiles her brilliant smile, radiant and phosphorescent. It looks like a thousand sparkling gems are spilling out of her mouth, and she speaks. "We've always forgiven you, Ginny. Now forgive yourself. Go to him. Go to Mattie, he needs you."

The warm and peaceful sensation continues to flow throughout her mind and body.

*I'm forgiven,* she thinks, and she repeats out loud, "I'm forgiven." Despite her confusion, it becomes a defining moment in her life.

As quickly as the peaceful feeling falls upon her, it departs, and the fear returns. She follows a light bouncing off the walls and hears someone desperately calling her name from the shadows. "Ginny, it's me, it's me! Are you all right? Where are you?"

She looks up to see the figure of a woman rushing toward her holding a flashlight, but the roaring wind drowns her voice. Ginny speaks out, her voice just above a quiver, "Carrie?"

"No, Ginny. It's Donna. Marty's working on the generator. It'll be okay, Ginny. You're okay. We're here now. Do you understand?"

The lights flicker on; the refrigerator motor begins to hum. Ginny watches in confusion as Donna rushes around, turning on all the lights. That done, she finds a blanket to wrap around Ginny, who is shivering in her wet clothes, and then sits down next to her. Ginny remains disoriented until she recognizes Marty coming in out of the storm and kicking off his boots. She remembers where she is now and clings to Donna with one hand, the other hand holding the picture. Donna has heard the story and gently pries the picture away from Ginny, who releases it without thought.

"Whew!" Marty exclaims while shaking rain and hailstones off his hat and jacket. "Quite the slammer out there tonight. We lost our power and figured the same thing happened here. I'm just glad we had that old generator gassed up. Did you hear that thunder as it rolled through?" He sees Donna with an arm wrapped around Ginny, who is whimpering gibberish about Carrie being there in the dark and something about forgiving herself.

Marty gives Donna a puzzling glance and holds his hands up as if saying "What the hell?" He asks, "Did she bang her head or something? And look at her, she's all cut up. Ginny, what happened to you?"

Donna nods to the photo and hands it to him. "You didn't leave this behind on purpose, did you?"

Marty quickly snatches it away and puts it out of sight. "Course not."

He squats down in front of Ginny to inspect her bleeding face and legs. "That's quite a bump on your head, miss." He is so affected by Ginny's condition that his eyes swell with tears. He reaches out and gently pushes a strand of hair out of her eyes and softly says, "Well, how 'bout I get some ice for your noggin, then we'll get you cleaned up. You're safe now, Ginny. Understand?"

Ginny nods that she's all right. She's embarrassed. "I'm sorry. I got caught outside in the storm. Thanks for coming. Thanks." She finally releases a sad smile. "I guess I'll take your weather forecasts more seriously in the future, Martin."

Donna asks, "Ginny, how about I spend the night here, hmm? I can sleep on the couch. And I'll go into town with you tomorrow too. We can have breakfast at Hazel's. Would you like that?"

"Thanks, Donna," Ginny replies. "I'd like that. I'd like that very much."

Marty shuffles for the door. "Well, okay. Um, guess I'll be goin' then, huh?"

Donna flashes him a smile and raises her eyebrows. She nods toward the door and motions for him to leave. Now.

He winks at Ginny and grins. "I know that look, miss, and it's not to be trifled with. See you all tomorrow. G'night."

"Good night, baby," Donna replies. "Don't worry. We'll be fine."

He stomps down the wrought-iron porch, starts up his truck, and is soon swallowed up by the night.

Finally regaining her bearings, Ginny playfully pokes Donna in the ribs. "He's still quite a looker, isn't he?"

Donna laughs and stands up. She helps Ginny to her feet and then pulls a bottle of Jack Daniel's from her purse. "Yes, he sure is." She giggles. "But just like the rest of his little band of brothers, he definitely marches to the beat of his own drum."

Ginny is surprised that Donna knows all the brothers. "That's what made them so special," Ginny informs. "Back in the day, that is. Have you ever seen them when they're all together? It's mass hysteria!"

Donna, her reply dull, answers, "Just once, but it wasn't a very happy occasion." She's referring to Carrie Jensen's funeral and memorial.

Donna lightens the moment and holds up the bottle and, with a sly grin, adds, "My sweetie will just have to go without tonight. Why don't you get changed, okay? I'll get the first-aid kit and then make us both a nightcap."

The following morning finds Ty Keller leaning against a pile of boxes and suitcases freshly unloaded from the UPS truck outside the post office. He saw the truck pass by from his office window and tries to raise Marty on his CB channel. To his surprise, Donna's voice comes back with a simple "Ten-four, we'll be there in a minute."

Five minutes later, they pull up next to Ty, who motions Donna to roll down her window. He smiles wide and exclaims, "Two girls in a pickup. I'm telling ya, this is the sexiest thing I've ever seen."

Donna laughs and says, "Quit your sweet talk, sailor, help load this stuff on board." She turns to Ginny and winks. "He's not as helpless as he wants you to think."

Ty raps his cane on the sideboard. "Hey, I'm right here, you know?"

With all Ginny's belongings loaded up, Donna wraps her arm around Ty. "We're going to the diner for breakfast, Mr. Bean Counter. How 'bout you join us?"

Ty laughs and gives Donna a peck on her cheek. "Now, I how can I resist an invitation like that?"

The trio walks into Hazel's Diner, and heads turn. Ginny is immediately recognized. To her pleasant surprise, however, after receiving a few smiles and nods, everyone returns to minding their own business. She feels safe and as confident as ever about her purpose for coming to Kinneysville. She orders an egg-white omelet. Already thinking of material for her new album, she makes a mental note of Ty's observation. The third track on the album is titled "Silly Boys, Trucks Are for Girls." Eighteen months later, she plays the song to a packed house at Hazel's and receives a standing ovation.

# Prairie Town

Visiting the nation's capital, Lorraine Cullen is thoroughly amused as her longtime boyfriend, a very disturbed and frustrated Lionel Henslaw, stirs at least twelve packages of Sweet'N Low into his iced tea. They're in a quaint Georgetown restaurant, and he's stalling what he knows is a futile attempt to dissuade Lorry out of her latest assault of meddling in another person's personal affairs.

"Lorry, this is apocryphal, it's catastrophic. It's lunacy. A train wreck just waiting to happen. Why can't you just leave him alone, for once in your life?" He lowers his head and shakes it back and forth, incredulous. "You're going to drive me to drink. You know that, right?"

Lorraine knows this is a weak maneuver. It is well-known that Lionel can't consume even the smallest amount of liquor without becoming violently sick. He is helpless, as is often the case with Lorry, to stop her from proceeding with what he considers an inauspicious and conspiratorial tactic of reuniting Mattie with his daughters and with Ginny.

She casually sips her vodka martini. "He needs us, Lionel. Owen will be there."

"Of course Owen will be there," Lionel acerbically retorts. "He wouldn't dream of turning down a free meal."

"Lionel! You know that's unfair." She leans forward; her tiny hands turn into two tiny fists that pound on the table. "Now you listen to me, Mr. Secretary of Agriculture. If it wasn't for Mattie, you'd be back in Pine City, squatting in the dirt, pulling weeds, and you know that better than anybody!"

Lionel loves the way her little nose twitches when she gets angry. But once again, his smiling eyes betray him.

Lorraine slams two tiny palms on the table. "You jerk!" she exclaims, not hiding her disgust. "You've been playing me all along, haven't you? Well, just for that, you're sleeping on the couch tonight."

"It's my house, Lorry," he replies, fully satisfied with his feint. "Exactly."

*   *   *

Three thousand miles away, Marty Nevin rides his mount, old Peasley, along the ridgeline that separates the ranch house and the trailer. It's four miles by road, but he covers the distance easily cross-country on horseback during his early morning rounds. He brings his horse, Peasley, to a halt, reaches back into his saddlebags, pulls out his thermos, and pours himself a cup of black coffee. He spies Ginny jogging up the road, coming into view, on the way to her little studio at the house. Beyond her he sees two objects moving fast and directly toward her. He fetches his binoculars from the saddlebag and zooms in on a coyote pursuing a small deer. They're on a collision course with Ginny. Even from a mile away, Marty knows his voice will carry, but she doesn't hear his warning. He trains the binoculars on her and notices she's wearing headphones.

"Oh boy," he says out loud. "This can't be good." He retrieves his 12-gauge shotgun from its scabbard, loads a single shell, and fires the one round into the air. His normally passive mount, Peasley, had dozed off and was startled awake by the shotgun blast. Marty finds himself soaring through the air and landing firmly on his butt with the open thermos close behind. Old Peasley looks rather satisfied. Marty stands up, dusts himself off, and finds that the shot has frightened off the two animals and that Ginny was hightailing it back toward the trailer. Pleased to sink his heels into Peasley's flank, Marty forces him into a hard gallop for the first time in years. He quickly catches up with Ginny and explains what has just happened.

"Climb up here, miss. I'll give you a ride up to the house."

It takes eighteen months for Ginny to return to good health, and it has given her the creativity to compose the songs for her new album. A better diet, exercise, and plenty of rest in between have been the answer, although Marty claims it was eating red meat for the first time in years.

She loves the country and loves living in the trailer on the ranch. She jogs and goes on horseback rides with Donna. She shovels snow in the winter, plants a garden in the spring, and gathers wildflowers in the summer. She buys a dozen French Marans chicks from the feed store just because she likes their color. She rides fence with Marty. She even buys a chocolate labrador puppy who sleeps with her every night.

Talk between them is casual. She gives Marty a little squeeze, rests her head on his back shoulders, and thanks him for the thousandth time for all they've done for her. Donna has become a great friend, and she enjoys all the time she spends with Betty. It is a reconnection of friendship she thought forever lost to her. Donna converted a downstairs bedroom into a small studio where Ginny works on her new songs. It is bliss for her to sit upstairs and listen to Ginny compose and sing, but whenever Marty is in his office next door, he will often bang on the wall, telling her to keep it down; after all, he was doing real work. Ginny always stays for dinner and a glass of wine or sometimes two. She enjoys listening to many the facets of managing the ranch, the emerging grain markets, and the next time Owen and his ever-expanding brood will make their yearly visit. And the view is phenomenal. From her studio, she looks out from large double-pane windows to watch the sun rise in the Rockies and set over the distant Cascades. She finds it hugely inspirational.

As they start down the ridge toward the house, Ginny gasps again at the view up and down the canyon. It just never wears out. Marty reaches for his binoculars and spots Ty's car in the driveway and wonders why he's driven out so early in the morning. Ty is a night person. He lets Ginny slide off of Old Peasley at the front door and walks him to the stables, where he removes the saddle and lets him have a well-deserved drink of water. As he enters the mudroom to remove his boots, he hears excited chatter from the kitchen and figures that Ginny is telling them about the near collision between the deer, the coyote, and the jogger. *Hmm,* he thinks, *sounds like a country song.* He peeks around the door and discovers that Betty has come as well. Donna and Ginny are busy making breakfast as Marty gives Betty a little peck on the cheek and asks her why they deserve her fine presence this morning.

Donna takes one look at Marty and exclaims, "What in the world happened to you?"

Marty points toward Ginny. "What? She hasn't told you?"

"No, told me what?"

Marty explains the circumstance that resulted in him getting thrown off his horse.

Donna laughs until she cries. "You got tossed off old Peasley? I thought he always just walks in his sleep!"

Marty replies amid the laughter and rather indignantly, "Well, it kind of hurt. Besides, I had a damsel in potential distress." He spies them suspiciously. "So what you are all talking about in here, anyway?"

Ty hands Marty a letter and his reading glasses. "You should read this, maybe twice. It's from Lorry."

Marty blinks in surprise, puts on his glasses, and begins to read.

My dear friends,

Years ago, for reasons never made known to me, you referred to yourselves simply as the brothers. A facetious cognomen, I came to realize, but brothers of some sort you were nonetheless. I must admit to being quite jealous of your little group, your witty antics, and your incomparable spirit of friendship and camaraderie, which even to this day remain a mystery to me. I hope the passage to time has not weakened your special bond of friendship, and I appeal to that and to your kindness for what might possibly be a final effort to save a man's relationship with his family and, indeed, that same man's very existence. The man I am bringing to your attention is Matthew Jensen. Mattie.

It has been ten years since the passing of our dear friend Carrie. Ten years, which, I am sure you will agree, have passed with lightning speed. For Mattie, however, it seems that time has been one excruciating day after another, full of pain that never dulls. He is a man—a brother—whom I fear is in the throes of insidious despair. Who among us would have thought this possible? Who among has considered that, if any one person could recover from the sting of tragedy, that person would be Mattie? Who among us has taken the time to care and search into his heart?

Yes, his life goes on. His many projects continue to prosper, but these are temporal and empty of the fulfillment one needs in life. He continues to respect those around him and extend the same simple courtesy and dignity that has always drawn so many to him over the years. He cannot be anything less than he ever was, but he is alone and cannot be anything more. As a result, he has withdrawn into himself, a seemingly self-imposed isolation. His life has become a languorous routine, and the relationships with his friends and, most importantly, with his daughters seem staunchly abandoned.

His daughters, Shelly and Claire, are amazing young women with the same zest for life as their mother's, but they seem poised to simply acquiesce to their father's grief, to his reticence, and move on with their lives without him.

Whether this is by Mattie's design or not, I do not know. I do know, however, that an irreparable and irreconcilable chasm is in the making, one I hope you will help to repair. At stake is the life of a man vanishing before our eyes, a man who, without any desire for adoration or recompense, has given so much to all of us.

So I am asking you, as brothers, for your help. I am asking that you to gather for a special evening of reunion at my restaurant, where I hope Shelly and Claire will discover for themselves the man we so affectionately call Mattie. I am asking that you share in an evening of awakening, encouragement, and restoration.

I am asking that, for one evening, we try to give back to Mattie what he has given to all of us.

All my love,
Lorraine

Marty lets the letter fall to the table, props up his elbows, closes his eyes, and massages his temples. *Hmm,* he thinks, *hardly the merry widower.*

He shakes his head and replaces the letter into its envelope and cheerlessly says, "I think they should go on *Oprah* or something."

Ty notices Donna's eyes burn into Marty. He clears his throat and motions to Ginny and Betty. "I think we should adjourn to the deck while these kids go at it." Betty looks at Marty with the same steaming expression while Ginny, eyes wide in astonishment, follows Ty outside.

Before they could reach the outside deck, they hear Donna scream, "What in the hell is the matter with you? You know as well as I do that without Mattie's help you'd still be living like a hermit in that trailer!" She picks up a nearby frying pan and wildly waves it in the air above her head before pointing it directly toward her husband. "You know it was Mattie who made all this possible. Don't you? Huh? Well, we're all going, Mr. Big-Time Rancher. You can just stay here and talk to your stupid cows all day long. Good luck."

Marty casually pours himself a cup of coffee. "I'm just not sure we should intrude, that's all. I didn't say that I'm not going, for crying out loud."

Donna stops waving the frying pan and holds it at bay. "Wait. What?"

"Well, it sounds like they need something. Maybe we can help, although I don't know how. I just know that I'm in, 100 percent."

Donna knows she's just been played, again. She smiles. "Sometimes you can be the biggest jerk in the world." She shouts to Ty, Betty, and Ginny, "You can come in now."

Ty, who has been watching and listening from a window, shouts back, "Not until you put down that frying pan, missus."

The three slowly walk inside with grins on their faces. Marty asks Ginny, "I hope to hell and high water that you're in on this too?"

Ginny coos, "From the beginning, kiddo. Owen will be there too."

"Oh, of course Owen will be there. He wouldn't dream of turning down a free meal."

\*     \*     \*

Lorry's plans instruct everyone to gather in two months at Owen Johannsen's home, which he shares with his wife, Rachael, and their five children. Marty insists they have at least six redheaded children, two boys and four girls, all of whom own a striking resemblance to the Farkle family. He determines he and Donna will stay in a local hotel. Lorry grudgingly relents; she hates it when her plans are changed. Lionel will stay with Lorry and is handed the difficult job of keeping Matthew's grown children, Shelly and Claire, entertained until the entire party is seated before Mattie's arrival. It is his annual evening out with his daughters, the tenth anniversary of Carrie's death.

\*     \*     \*

Matthew Jensen had recommended Owen Johannsen to his church's hiring committee, who, after going through two pastors in three years, were anxious to find anybody who wasn't likely to bolt for the greener pastures of Southern California or the Bible Belt. Owen was hired as soon as he; Rachael; their five-year-old daughter, Ruth; two-year-old son, MJ; and their infant son, Isaac, could be tracked down. That was nearly twenty years ago, and in the time since, Owen has built a vibrant ministry. One needs to understand, however, that Owen is very quick to give all the credit to God.

It has been ten years since Matthew has been inside the church, eight years since he has seen Owen, and four years since they have shared a conversation. Owen finally accepted Rachael's advice that Mattie will call or come when he is ready. Matthew is uncertain if this is the right time to try to reenter into his family's or his friends' lives, but he knows that Owen's church is a safe place to start. If he chooses, he can slip in and out before being noticed. He believes that, with the therapy he's received, his battle to gain the upper hand on his depression is mostly mitigated, although he knows the struggle may never be completely conquered. His new medications are so effective that he ponders their legality.

Church membership has grown from a few hundred to over one thousand during Matthew's absence. He quit receiving any updates about the congregation long ago, and he gawks at the size of Owen's flock. He is by no means surprised. Matthew finds a seat in the very back in the midst of people he does not know. He leans back in his chair when he spots Claire. She is walking down to the front row and sits next to Rachael and a handsome young man with red hair whom he supposes is Isaac. Matthew smiles when Isaac puts his arm around Claire and kisses her cheek. The two have grown up together, and he figures that Owen and especially Rachael have filled in admirably in his absence from Claire's life. In some odd fashion, this pleases him. Matthew becomes uncomfortable when, despite the one thousand or so people in the worship center, Owen passes over them all and narrows his gaze directly to him. Owen smiles at him. There will be no sneaking out this morning and no avoiding Owen.

Matthew is so busy intercepting the distress signals bouncing around his brain that he has no recollection of the service. He sits in his chair, and Owen stands at the elevated pulpit until the worship center is emptied. Owen does not want to bring any unnecessary attention to his friend. They meet in the center and embrace. Owen is crying but manages to whisper: "Welcome back, Mattie. Welcome back." Matthew does not speak; he simply hugs him back.

Once back in control, Owen firmly but gently tells him, "Mattie, you must talk with Rachael. And you must see Claire."

Mattie replies, "I have seen her, when she walked down and sat with your family."

Owen grins. "Yeah, dude, I know you did. I've had eyes on you since you walked inside. But you must know how desperate Claire is to see you, Mattie. C'mon, I'll go with you."

"Um, Owen," Mattie softly says, "I should probably go on my own."

Owen slaps his shoulder. "Of course you should. Why do you think I volunteered? But Rachael first, okay? And don't worry, Mattie, Claire is here for another hour. She teaches the high school kids."

\*　　\*　　\*

Satisfied that her goals have been met, Ginny packs up to leave the ranch and return to her home and recording studio in Carmel. She has accomplished beyond everything she had hoped in her eighteen-month stay on the ranch. Her health has recovered, and her renewed energy allows her to compose her first album in ten years. She's titled it *Prairie Town*. Except for the music to one song, with which she has penned only the lyrics, she has written all the music and lyrics as well as arrangements. She plays her new material, except for one song, before a packed house at Hazel's Diner the night before she leaves. It is her profound thanks to the entire community, who has accepted her in their midst without fuss or fanfare.

Virginia Simmons's return to the music industry is just as abrupt as her departure ten years before. Her new album is a sensation. At first, producers are concerned that the quality of her voice has been affected during her ten-year hiatus, which includes her eigh-teen-month disappearance to the ranch near Kinneysville. Is the tone still there? Can she still maintain perfect pitch? They insist she work with a voice coach, who promptly determines that Virginia Simmons's voice has not only recovered but has also somehow become stronger, as long as she properly warms up.

She is amazed at the advances made in the recording indus-try during her absence, especially digital recording. And even more amazed by something called social media. Such things have yet to reach Kinneysville, let alone the trailer at the ranch. *Prairie Town* goes platinum two weeks before its release just in preorders. Among those waiting for the album is Shelly Jensen, an ardent fan. Virginia will begin a five-city tour to promote the new album, and Shelly buys one ticket as soon as they are available. The tour will begin where everything started for her, back home and quite near Ms. Brown's fifth-grade class. *Prairie Town* becomes the biggest-selling album of its time.

# Attitude Adjustment

Twenty-year-old Claire Jensen and her twenty-two-year-old sister, Shelly, meet often, at least three times a week, usually for lattes. Both girls left home as soon as they graduated from high school and have never been back, even for holidays. Matthew meets their financial needs for tuition and all other expenses, although neither is careless with his money and is by no means frivolous. They have been emotionally disconnected from their father for years and now wish to be financially free from him as soon as possible. Shelly is close to realizing this dream; she will graduate from Northern University, where both girls are enrolled, in just a few weeks. She receives job offers from outsourcing firms, but the truth of the matter is that she cannot decide what she really wants to do or exactly where she really wants to go. She just needs something for right now, even part-time. Just enough so she can to be totally independent from her father, whom she wishes never to see again. She can look for a real job in the meantime.

Claire Jensen sips on her mocha frappuccino and winsomely smiles at her sister. "So I saw Dad. He asks how you're doing."

Shelly replies with the rueful expression she always shows when their father is mentioned. "Oh god. Really?"

Claire lightly chimes back, "Yes, really. It was actually kind of sweet. He was at church. Isaac and I heard Rachael scream and hurried to investigate, she was in a complete puddle. Anyway, she turned aside, and there he stood. We waved, but I had to leave. Isaac talked to him. He wants to make sure we're both going to be at Lorraine's tonight for dinner."

Shelly loathes any contact with their dad. "Yeah, I'll be there. I figure on just having a salad and then make up some lame excuse to leave early." She thinks, *That shouldn't bother him, he left us years ago.* She asks Claire, "Do you want me to pick you up? We can make the same quick retreat."

Claire laughs, mostly at the irony of their meeting for this once-a-year anniversary of honoring their mom's death, a woman of whom she has only fleeting memories. She casually tosses back her auburn hair and looks appealingly to her sister.

"Oh, no, thanks, but I'll meet you in the lobby. We can go upstairs together. How's that?"

Already disinterested, Shelly replies, "Well, fine then, but the offer stands."

Claire sits up in her chair and, with a touch of good humor in her voice, says, "You know, I have a good feeling about tonight. Like something exceptional is going to happen." Claire speaks quickly and animatedly. With her constant optimism toward life, she is considered bubbly, perky, and exceptionally charming.

Shelly agonizes over her sister's enthusiastic outlook and replies with lament, "I think you say that every year, don't you?"

Claire giggles and shrugs her shoulders. "Yes, but this is different. I can't explain it, but I really think there might be a break-through tonight. Don't ask me why or how." She stopped talking and held her head high as if she were silently solving a math problem. "It's odd though, Lorraine called me too." She looks sideways at her sister. "I wonder how she even found my number. Anyway, she's asked if we could both be there at four thirty. Will that work for you?"

Shelly finishes her latte and stands to leave. "Whatever, sis. I'm just glad he didn't call me. I've been disappointed enough." She hugs her sister and says with pain in her voice, "I'll see you then."

"Oh." Claire suddenly remembers; she produces a piece of paper and hands it to Shelly. "It's a lab report. Seems they've found cysts on both ovaries, but nothing to worry about. Take a look when you have a chance. I'm scheduled for a battery of tests over the next few weeks, but I expect nothing to come of it, just a little surgery. It's a quick and short procedure. But still, there's this voice in the back of my head reminding me how this turned out last time we went through this with Mother." Claire is confident that there is nothing to be worried about yet can't help but be marginally disturbed that what had happed to her mother can very well happen to her.

Shelly's eyes tear up, but she soon puts on a brave face. "Does he know?"

"Who, Dad? Yes, of course. He cried."

*   *   *

Lorry Cullen cradles a hot mug of orange spiced tea, contemplating the events she is determined to set into motion later in the day. She has made her plans with great attention to every detail and is sure they will be carried out to perfection, despite Lionel Henslaw's futile protestations.

*Well,* she thinks, *I can handle Lionel. After all, I've been handling him off and on for what seems my entire life. Of course, it might be that he's handling me.* She hears him stumble out of her bedroom and into the shower. She laughs when she considers their situation and wonders if they should do away with this awkward, coast-to-coast relationship and make their lives permanently together. She tears up thinking how nice life would be married to Lionel, but a coast-to-coast relationship is difficult. Owen would certainly approve, though.

Lionel appears from the kitchen, holding a cup of coffee, and stops short. "Lorry, are you crying?"

She wipes a tear away. "No, I am not crying, Lionel. Are you finally ready?"

Lionel shrugs. "Well, I'm dressed, if that's what you mean. I don't think anybody can be ready for what you have planned for tonight."

Lorry stands on her tiptoes, straightens his tie, and lightly kisses his lips. "Oh, you'll be just fine, Mr. Secretary. But remember, tonight's success depends entirely on you."

\*   \*   \*

Matthew Jensen enters the elevator and descends one floor from his corporate offices to Lorraine's Metropolitan Grill. He is excited to see his girls, if just for a few hours. He still struggles with his emotions when he's around them and with the guilt he has kept alive for the past ten years. Was he inert with self-pity? Does depression still have a firm grip around his throat? Regardless, he detests how he has treated Shelly and Claire and the way he has forsaken his friends. The only person who refuses to accept his detachment is the indomitable Lorraine Cullen. She would not allow Mattie to treat her that way. He is glad Lorry continues to be active in his life, but always wary of her machinations. Lorry Cullen can be quite complicit when she wants to be and at times provides Mathew with nothing less than total exhaustion. But tonight his tortured heart and beleaguered soul seek peace and solace, not the recalcitrant attitudes he will most likely receive from his daughters, and rightly so, he believes. He has lost any hope of reviving a loving relationship with his daughters.

The elevator door to Lorraine's opens, and Matthew is immediately met by the hulking figure of Raul, who is blocking not only Matthew's path but all light too.

He greets Matthew with a seldom-seen smile that reveals solid gold front teeth. "Hello, Mattie. Your table is not quite set up. Ms. Cullen asked that I meet you and keep you company until things are ready."

"What things, Raul?" Matthew asks. "Is Lorry planning one of her legendary theme events tonight?"

Raul embraces Matthew like he's a toy. "Something like that. I hope you enjoy. Your daughters are in the lounge with Secretary Henslaw."

"Lionel is here?" Matthew asks with surprise and then suspicion. "Official Department of Agriculture business or just a visit with Lorry?"

Raul releases Matthew, who takes a deep breath to recover from the big man's tight embrace. "Now, Mattie. I wouldn't know anything about that. Would I?"

"Hmm," Matthew muses. "I think you know everything, Raul."

Raul smiles, rests his two giant paws on Matthew's shoulders, and shrugs.

\* \* \*

One-half hour earlier, Lorry had met Shelly and Claire and introduced them to a well-dressed gentleman, Mr. Lionel Henslaw, secretary of agriculture and close personal friend.

"Lionel, dear?" she asked in a tone that could sweeten saccharine. "Will you please keep these lovely girls company until their table is ready?"

Lionel withdraws his handkerchief and lightly dabs his forehead. "Well, Ms. Cullen, I believe that's up to them, wouldn't you say? I'm not sure I'd be very good company in the midst of such striking young ladies."

Lorry scowls at him, grabs his elbow and escorts him to the lounge, and tells Claire and Shelly to follow, which they do but with great caution.

To the girls' relief, Lionel Henslaw is both witty and charming. They are greatly amused with stories of his life in DC, his travels, and his escapades, but especially tales of his college days and his roommate. A special young man, Lionel explains, who helped shape his life, saving him from an existence of backbreaking farm labor near the small town of Pine City.

"We know where Pine City is, Mr. Secretary," Claire excitedly pipes up. "Do you mean to tell us you're from this part of the country?"

"I am indeed, Claire. And I'm a proud graduate of *the* Northern State University."

"Humph," Shelly sourly retorts, "that's where our dad went too. We both go to Northern, but I bet you already knew that."

Studying his fingernails, Lionel lightly admits, "Well, yes. I have heard something to that effect. And who can blame you?" He sweeps his arm around. "Especially with the excitement of the big city and this lovely revolving restaurant Lorry has built for herself. She's something else, isn't she?"

"You know, Mr. Secretary," Claire says with a winsome grin, "you seem to be about our dad's age. Maybe you knew him. Matthew . . . oh, here he comes now. He doesn't look very happy though."

Shelly looks at him with angry and accusing eyes. She growls, "When does he ever look happy?"

Both girls allow their father to give them a cordial peck on their cheek. Shelly withdraws deep into her chair, slumps down, and tightly crosses her arms.

Matthew guardedly greets Lionel. "Good evening, Mr. Secretary. And to what do we owe the pleasure of your company tonight?"

Claire anxiously sits up. "Dad? Do you know the secretary? Were you at NSU together?"

"Well," Matthew replies, slowly and painstakingly, "Lorry introduced us. They're—"

"Yeah, we already know," Shelly interrupts. "Close personal friends. She told us too. The secretary is quite engaging, Dad. Maybe he could give you a few pointers."

"Ms. Jensen." Lionel leans toward Shelly and admonishes, "I find your attitude absolutely superfluous, wouldn't you agree?"

Shelly shrinks deeper into her chair like quicksand swallowing her up. She whispers, "Yes, Mr. Secretary. I apologize."

Lionel motions toward Mattie. "I think you should apologize to your father, not me."

Shelly makes a threatening gesture that she would get up and leave. Fortunately, Lorry had warned Lionel such a thing might occur, so he purposely sits to block any exit. She seems poised to simply run Lionel over in an attempt to escape but remains still. She does not, however, apologize to her father.

Matthew, in an uncharacteristically and warm way, wraps his arm around the secretary of agriculture's shoulder and lightheartedly says, "Oh, will you lighten up, Lionel? For crying out loud." The gesture and statement stun Matthew's daughters. They could never recall a time when he has been remotely waggish and lighthearted.

They notice a light in his eyes, a consciousness that they have no memory of seeing before.

Lionel grins and shrugs. "Yes, Mr. Jensen, of course." He glances at Shelly. "Maybe we should all lighten up, yes?"

Shelly purses her lips but decides to take Lionel's advice and adjusts her attitude, a little. "So, Dad. Did you know the secretary at NSU? He's been going on and on about this fabulous friend and roommate who shaped his life."

Lionel warmly smiles as he reminisces. "He was a shy young man but very breezy and easygoing. He was incredibly insightful, perceptive, and intuitive. I really do owe every success I've ever had to him." He comically arches his eyebrows that highlight his laughing eyes. "Even Lorraine!"

Once again, to the girls' complete surprise, they detect their father becoming playful and high-spirited. "You see, girls, Lionel and Lorry are a couple, sort of . . . sort of."

"Well, Mr. Secretary," Claire declares with an alluring, sunny smile, "and how long has this been going on, hmm? And how did you ever meet?"

Lionel once again studies his finger nails and shrugs. "Oh, for twenty-five years, give or take. What can I say? She's a force of nature. Lorry went to NSU too."

Claire laughs with delight. "Twenty-five years! So which of you has the commitment issue?"

"It's more of a logistical issue, I believe," Lionel sheepishly replies.

Claire pipes up, "Wait a second. Dad? You must have known Lorraine too. Did you?"

Matthew becomes impassive. "Yes, Claire. I've known her since college. I worked for her. That's how I paid for school." He thinks of elaborating but notices Shelly appears troubled.

She asks in a near whisper, her eyes downcast, "Mr. Secretary, Lionel. Did you know our mother?"

Lionel sits back, removes his glasses, and studies them. He has been expecting this. He glances at Matthew, who is staring straight ahead, stiff and circumspect.

Lionel answers kindly, "Yes, Shelly. I knew Carrie. Very well, actually. We grew up together in Pine City. We were neighbors. I knew her my entire life. She was a very special woman and very special to me."

Shelly persists, "Why didn't you hook up with her?"

Lionel, not really knowing what *hook up* means, puts his arm around Matthew in a brotherly hug and then ruffles his hair. "Because, girls, Carrie fell in love with my roommate."

Shelly and Claire stare at their father with all the incredulity they could muster. Finally, Claire sits back, gathers her auburn hair, and tosses it over her left shoulder. The motion is so reminiscent of Carrie that Lionel winces.

Shelly callously yet seductively asks, "Tell us, Mr. Secretary. Tell us about our dad."

"Yes, Mr. Secretary—Lionel," Claire asks, but with her usual effervescence. "Please tell us everything." She has a wonderful idea. "Wait, I know! Why don't you join us for dinner?"

Quick to realize this idea may save her from an abominable two hours with her dad, Shelly asks, "Please, Mr. Secretary, Lionel?" She tosses him her most dazzling smile, the one she knows cannot be resisted. "Please?"

Lionel raises his palms and replies, "Well, I wouldn't want to intrude. What do you say, Mattie?"

Claire pinches Shelly under the table, when she hears Lionel call her father Mattie. Neither can recall anybody ever using his nickname since their mother had passed away. Not even Lorraine.

# Reunion

Apparently, Owen forgets the evening's events are meant to be a surprise. His megaphone voice booms throughout the restaurant as he and Rachael greet Marty, Donna, Ty, and Betty.

Lorry rushes up to him with a rebuke. "Jeez, Owen. They can hear you in the kitchen. Mattie's sure to know you're here now. Jeez! Keep it down, will you?"

Owen grins. "Sorry, Lorry. I'm just so excited. Besides, he doesn't know about these two cowboys . . . and cowgirls yet."

She scolds Marty as well, "And, Martin, quit fussing with your tie, you look quite handsome."

Marty slowly replies, "Well, it's kind of a different look for me, Lorry. We usually don't wear ties back home. Just sayin'."

She turns and quick-steps toward the lounge but, over her shoulder, retorts, "I'm sure he knows you're here, Owen. Don't forget how observant he is, not to mention his insane power of hearing."

All three men start laughing, which causes Lorry to stop in her tracks and turn around with her tiny fists on her tiny hips. "Will you goofballs go to your table before I call for Raul?"

Owen, Ty, and Marty contritely duck their heads in false remorse and skulk toward their table in a slow shuffle. Lorry looks to Betty, Donna, and Rachael, who simultaneously raise their palms in surrender. Lorry smiles at them, shakes her head, and heads to the lounge, only to find Matthew suspiciously missing.

She slaps Lionel on the shoulder. "And where is Mattie?"

Lionel grabs her hand and kisses it. "He has excused himself to the gents', my love."

"Oh, honestly, Lionel. We talked about this," Lorry replies, plainly annoyed. She gives a surreptitious nod to the omnipresent Raul, who immediately rushes to the restaurant's exit.

Earlier in the day, Lorraine considered that Mattie might make a dash for the exit once he figures out how this evening is to unfold. Regardless of his mental condition, he still remains incredibly intuitive. She makes sure Raul, her longtime personal assistant, road manager, and sometime bodyguard, is standing at the exit to prevent Mattie from leaving.

Marty Nevin peeks around the corner from their hidden table and watches the entire affair open up. Careful not to be seen, he crouches behind a partition. He sneaks a look at Raul crossing his arms around his massive chest and waits for Mattie to come around the corner to the exit. An elderly couple who had just been served their entrées are a little concerned with Marty's proximity to their table. He raises a single finger to his lips. "Shush, it's all right. I'm just the health inspector." The couple instantly stand up and leave, their dinners left intact. Marty helps himself to one of their untouched bread sticks and watches the spectacle between Mattie and Raul unfold.

With his head down, Matthew rushes for the exit. He has all too soon figured out what is about to happen this evening and is sure that Owen, whose voice he heard, is in on everything. And after spotting two Royal Stetsons in the coat and hat check closet, he knows that Marty and Ty are also here. He instantly retreats to the renounced authority of decades-old entanglements. They physically attack him: his pulse races and his heart pounds; he breaks into a cold sweat and labors to breathe. He's afraid of the upcoming confrontation with Lionel and his daughters. Not to mention Lorry's interventions. He wants to run away from it all.

Not noticing that Raul has blocked his exit, he runs smack into him and bounces back about two feet. He recognizes Marty Nevin's laugh from somewhere to his right.

"Oh, hello, Raul. I see you're strategically placed, as always."

"Mattie," Raul says and points, "I believe the restrooms are the other way. You're not thinking of leaving, are you?"

Raul wraps a giant tattooed arm around Mattie, and he turns him around where Lorry is standing with her arms open and inviting. "Come here, Matthew."

Her tender embrace relaxes him. He looks into the lounge, where he spies his daughters, wide-eyed and wondering what is happening, their drinks suspended in midflight. Lionel's lips remain pursed, but once again, his laughing eyes give away his amusement. Lorry nods at him, the sign that it's time for Lionel to escort the two girls to their table where the Nevins, the Kellers, and the Johanssens are waiting.

"Matthew," Lorry whispers, "we're here to help you put the past to rest once and for all. Your children love you, Mattie, but you have to allow them to show it. I love you, your friends love you."

She tilts her head back; tears well in her eyes. "We're going to end this estranged relationship. We all want to help you tonight, Mattie. Will you let us? Please, Mattie? Please?"

Matthew manages a hint of a smile. "Well, I know Marty and Ty are here. And Lionel's presence is no coincidence, is it, Lorry?"

Lorry shakes her head that his assumption is correct.

"And I heard Owen the moment he came in. He wouldn't dream of turning down a free meal."

Lorry laughs. "I asked him to tone it down a little, but I don't think he's capable. So it's time, Mattie. Let me take you to your family."

\*　　\*　　\*

Lionel Henslaw stands and formally addresses Claire and Shelly, "Ladies, please allow me to escort you to our table?"

Shelly hesitates. "Mr. Secretary, what is happening here? What's going on? I mean, our dad has disappeared, thankfully, but this entire evening seems like a setup."

Claire interrupts her sister, "Oh, c'mon, Shelly. Maybe you're right, but so what? I say we make the best of it. It might be fun!"

Lionel smiles at Claire and shakes his head. "You are definitely your father's daughter, aren't you?"

Shelly wickedly rolls her eyes. "Just biologically. All other similarities end right there."

*Hmm,* Lionel thinks, *how can we possibly efface this dysfunctional family? This Shelly is a real pill and has a hardcore grudge against Mattie. I'd rather she would just go ahead and leave right now. But that would ruin what is sure to be her understanding that there's much more to her father than neither she nor Claire is aware of. Oh well, I'm hoping it all turns out well for Mattie and his kids.*

*   *   *

Except for Owen and Rachael, whom Claire affectionately hugs and Shelly guardedly greets, Secretary of Agriculture Lionel Henslaw makes very formal and ceremonious introductions.

Ty greets Shelly with enthusiasm, "Hi there, sunshine."

Shelly is annoyed by the amiable greeting but extends her hand and cautiously replies, "Hello there." He stirs up a memory from down deep, a slight but distant recognition. Maybe he reminds her of an old boyfriend, of whom she has had plenty in the past few years, none of whom seem to last very long.

Ty winks at Shelly. "How 'bout you girls join us tonight?"

Claire shrugs her shoulders in honest regret. "Oh, I'm so sorry, but we just made plans to join Secretary Henslaw."

Shelly adds rather maliciously. "Besides, we have to have dinner with our dad. Unless he's giving us a break by disappearing. Again."

Ty and Marty exchange glances, both thinking that, while Claire is irresistibly sweet and vivacious, Shelly is resistibly bitchy.

Marty says, "Well, that's why we're all here tonight too." He burns a no-nonsense stare into Shelly's eyes, the kind he gets before roping a steer. "Why don't you have a seat, miss? Right here, between my wife and me."

Taken aback by his mild, passive-aggressive rebuke, Shelly shrugs and whispers, "Okay, sure."

They all look up when Lorry arrives, arm and arm with Matthew. "Look who I found," she sings out.

Both Shelly and Claire watch in bewilderment as each person stands in a show of respect to their father. One by one, he is ardently embraced as if he is some kind of hero. Shelly is shocked when Ty, tears streaming down his face, rests a hand on her father's shoulder and gives him a brief kiss on the cheek. She has never seen a man kiss another man, not even in movies. She notices he uses a cane to stand and steady himself and wonders what happened to him.

Shelly and Claire exchange glances. Their expressions indicate they have no idea what's happening, and Owen is quick to pick up. He knows that, at the beginning anyway, he is the one whom the girls can trust. His soft, compassionate green eyes bore into Shelly and then into Claire. He leans forward, puts an elbow on the table, and rests his chin in the palm of his hand.

"We're all friends from NSU, and we've been close ever since. Brothers, actually. We can't explain our kinship to one another or our comradery, we just accept it." A passing server attracts his attention and he calls out, "Hey, can I get a beer, please?" Everyone looks at him in a total state of surprise. He lifts his head when Rachael kicks him under the table. "What?" he innocently asks.

Ty says, "First of all, you have to understand that this is all Lorry's idea. Not that we mind."

Claire throws him a teasing smile. "You mean, Lorraine. Right?"

"Yeah right, Lorraine," Ty replies, rolling his eyes and making Claire giggle.

Lionel now takes over as the designated speaker. "Like Owen told you, we're lifelong friends from college."

"Kindred spirits, really," Owen adds. He wraps his arm around Ty's shoulder. "We've had our share of tragedies, but we've all become stronger as a result. Blessed, if you will."

Marty speaks, "So when Lorry, um, I mean, Lorraine, sent for us to be here tonight, to meet you and see Mattie, well, we jumped at the chance."

Shelly recoils and makes a sour face. "Why? I mean, it sounds like you're good friends, but what's in it for you? We'll probably never see you again."

Marty raises a defensive voice toward Shelly. "Why? Because we love your dad, that's why. All of us, including our wives, and Lorry. Young lady, if you only knew what he's done for all of us, I'm sure you'd know why and would never ask a question like that again."

Donna rests her hand on her husband's in an attempt to calm him down. It works, and Marty relaxes a little. "Maybe you both need to look past his issues and realize for yourselves what kind of a man Matthew Jensen is. It's about damn time you did. That's what's in it for us." He nods toward Ty. "We owe him our ranch and our farms."

Owen says, "And I owe him my ministry."

Lionel says, "I owe him every good thing that's happened to me. Even Lorry."

Ty tears up, and Betty rests a hand on his. "He saved my life." Rather lightly now, he adds, "And you haven't seen the last of us. I guarantee you that."

Shelly is fuming. "What makes you say——"

Lionel interrupts, "You're wasting your time, Shelly, asking what's in it for us. Life is too short for that kind of an attitude. That's one thing Mattie taught us from his actions and his examples of how he treated others."

Shelly impertinently flips her head toward her dad. "He hasn't given anything to Claire or to me. And the only example he's shown is how to be an absent and irrelevant parent."

Owen slams his hand down on the table so hard that silverware bounces to the floor. "Then you're even more shortsighted than I ever thought possible." The outburst shocks the women, but the men cover their mouths to keep from laughing. Lionel's eyes are smiling.

Shelly casts her eyes down. "I'm sorry, Pastor. It's just that he disappeared from our lives, it was a difficult way to grow up."

Matthew twirls the hair behind his right ear. Except for Owen's poor attempt to come to his rescue, he sits quietly and seems unaffected by the conversation. He knows it is his time to speak, to confront the complications of abandonment. He studies his daughters and marvels how much they look like Carrie.

"You must know," he begins, his voice is low but fluid. "You must know that what's happened to me and how I've acted toward you is not your fault." He stares at them, the sparkle of his midnight-blue eyes returns, and he repeats, "It's not your fault."

He leans toward them and sighs. "When I was growing up, I'd never heard of depression, let alone recognize the symptoms, but I've had it off and on my entire life. My folks said I was just sad when there was a change or departure in my life and that at times it happens to everyone now and then. But my therapist says—"

Shelly exclaims, "Hold on. You see a therapist? How long has this been going on?"

Matthew looks at her evenly. "For ten years, sweetheart."

Her anger glowing and tears brimming, Shelly admonishes her father, "Why didn't you ever let us know? I don't understand. I just don't understand."

"Because," Matthew quietly replies, "because I was concerned, afraid, really, that you two would think that you were the cause. That my problems are your fault."

Claire silently weeps, but Shelly explodes, "Are you telling us that you disappeared from our lives to protect us? Because you think we wouldn't be able to handle it? Are you kidding me? You are hopeless, you know that? Absolutely hopeless."

All seven men and women try to come to his aid, but Mattie raises a palm to stop them. He replies, "Yes, I do know that. I know I've been a terrible father. In the beginning, it was grief over Mom passing away. But it became much more than grief and mourning. I have major depression disorder. The therapy has helped . . . and the meds. You see, I became obsessed with my failure as a father—and as a friend. I hated myself, not from self-pity but from remorse over mishandling every tragic event in my life. I knew you two would always have each other, and I'm sorry that I didn't let allow you the opportunity to show how much you wanted to care for me. I apologize for everything. I love you both so much. And I miss you." He gestures to everyone around the table. "I miss all of you. I don't like being alone, but I've built this shelter around me, and there it stays. I am alone."

He sits back and smiles, but there is sadness in his eyes. "I don't know how either of you will take this, but you must know how proud I am of you, for growing up under the circumstances I forced upon you, and for your successes at Northern. And please trust me, your mom would have been proud of you too. So proud."

Shelly and Claire are speechless and emotionally charged, not knowing what to think of this revelation. And did their father really just apologize? Did they hear him right? Owen comes to their aid. "We kind of knew how losing someone affects your dad. Especially after Randy..." He stops and clams up; perhaps he shouldn't have brought this up. Too late.

"Who is Randy?" Shelly asks. "Why isn't he at this little intervention?"

Lionel removes his glasses and sets them on the table, next to his untouched dinner. "Randy was one of our brothers, Shelly." He pauses, takes a deep breath, and slowly releases it. He stares at his shoes. "Long story short, he committed suicide and died in your dad's arms. Your aunt Emily was head resident at the Three Forks Hospital, but she couldn't save him. She knew how Mattie would take his death and tried to explain to me what to expect when he experiences loss. But just like Mattie, I didn't know anything about depression. And I couldn't believe that happy-go-lucky Mattie Jensen would be prone to such a devastating disease, that he could descend so low. None of us, all of us. We didn't know what to do, and we certainly weren't equipped to help him. So to our great regret, we didn't do anything."

Claire whispers, "Oh, Daddy. I'm so sorry."

Shelly stares at her father, crosses her arms and legs. She nervously kicks her foot up and down.

Lionel adds, "Only two people really knew how to pull Mattie out of his shell after Randy died and Emily left for her job in San Francisco. Your mom, of course, and Ginny."

Claire sits straight up and inquisitively asks, "And who is Ginny?"

Seven pairs of eyes look at Mattie, totally perplexed. How could they not know?

Ty shakes his head; he has rarely been a part of something so forlorn. "Are you kidding us? You've never told them? I mean, anything?"

Mattie shrugs a single shoulder and shakes his head. "No."

# It Was Complicated, Kind Of

Shelly stops her leg in midkick and contemptuously asks, "So who is Ginny? Was she an old girlfriend or something?"

Marty looks at Owen, who looks at Ty, who looks at Lionel, who blunders. "I don't even know how to start."

It is Donna who helps them out. "Better start at the beginning." She pulls a photograph from her purse and hands it to Shelly to share with her sister. "This is them. And look, Owen actually has hair!"

It is a picture of four young men with Lorraine and Carrie. They were all sitting on what appeared to be a small stage with their legs dangling freely. Their father was sitting on a piano.

"So why were you all laughing?" Claire asks.

Lionel replies, "It was something that Ty said. Tell them, flyboy."

Ty takes a deep breath and held it for a few seconds before exhaling. He grins a timorous grin. "I said to Carrie, 'Now don't you worry about your wedding night, Carolyn. I've seen him in the shower and there's nothing to be afraid of.'"

Laughter from their table fills the entire room. Heads turn around; amused expressions look in their direction. "I probably should have kept that to myself," Ty says.

"Oh, I don't know," Shelly gleefully replies. 'That's pretty funny stuff! And why isn't this Ginny person in the photo?"

Matthew smiles at his girls, glad that some tension has been released. "She took the picture."

With her interest climbing, Claire observes, "That doesn't explain who this Ginny is though." She is quick in sensing that her dad doesn't want to talk about her. The table grows silent, and expectant eyes all look to Mattie to explain. It is only right that the story should come from him.

"Ginny and Lorry owned the restaurant where I worked," he guardedly begins, "and Ginny was supposed to be at our wedding. In fact, she was actually the maid of honor but decided at the last minute not to come."

Shelly gives a confused look. "Wait a minute, she was Mom's good friend but bailed on your wedding? Some friend, huh?"

Lionel interrupts Matthew, who is beginning to struggle. "What happened is that she was and still is, I believe, in love with your dad."

Shelly and Claire both speak at the same time, "Wow. What did Mom think?"

Matthew tries his best to explain. "Well, they were great friends, and yes, Mom knew. Ginny and I, well, we had a complicated relationship, kind of, but not an intimate one, at least."

The cold sweat returns, his heart is furiously pounding, and he feels shortness of breath. Shelly seems to be enjoying her father's strain and stumbling for words. Regardless of her dad's mental illness, she feels that she is entitled to actually watch him suffer the physical effects of his depression.

"Ginny was a singer. I played in the band, so we had an onstage relationship that lasted four years," Matthew stammers.

Marty almost barks at him. "He didn't play in the band, he was the band. It was just the two of them, you know." He eagerly looks at Shelly and Claire. "They were great together. Really great, I mean, gifted in fact. And they sang together too. They were awesome. Just awesome."

"And you two were so close that she fell in love with you, is that what I'm hearing?" Shelly demands. "Well, this is all news to us." But for an unexplained reason, she softens a little and studies her father. "But it's been interesting news." She thinks, *Maybe I've selfishly misjudged him. I mean, he obviously has had issues to deal with. Maybe I've even been a little bit wrong about him. And after all, he has apologized even though it will take much more than that to convince me. He's going to have to show me.*

Ty makes with a gesture with his hand and rolls back in his chair. "So just to clarify: Marty and I kind of fought over her. We took her out sometimes. It was hard because they only worked the weekends, ya know?"

Lionel says, "And I can tell you young ladies that nothing ever inappropriate happened between Ginny and your dad. He treated her as if she were his sister, as much as he could. And he had plenty of experience with that. Your dad knew Ginny loved him, but he never used that to his advantage. He would never do that to anybody."

Shelly is quick to retort, "Except us." The comment draws such scorn that she almost melts into her chair.

"I'm sorry, Dad," Shelly whispers. "You didn't deserve that. We just never knew until now what you've been through." She folds her arms. "But you should have been more open, you should have shared your struggles with us. It's almost unforgivable."

Marty smiles. "Almost? Well, Shelly, we'll take that as a step in the right direction. And besides, you'll find throughout your life that an unforgiving spirit is nearly as damaging as that cancer that killed your mom. Believe me. I know."

Shelly slowly smiles and regards the expectant eyes all looking at her. "Yes, Mr. Nevin. Yes, it is."

"My friends call me Marty. You should too. And it's been my own experience that only those with strong character can truly forgive another. It's those with weak character who refuse to forgive. They'd rather feel sorry for themselves. You have the chance to decide who and what you want to be."

Claire speaks after trying to process all this new information, "So this Ginny lady was in love with you at the same time Mom was? And they were great friends? You said it, Daddy-o, it must have been complicated. So whatever happened to her?"

"She moved to California to start a career," Matthew replied. "I'm sure she's forgotten all about me."

"Oh, like hell," Owen exclaims, and smiles. "She'd be on a plane tonight if you'd just man up and call her."

"I did call her a few years ago—part of an exercise in my therapy. She never picked up the call and never called me back. I just figure she's forgotten me. Who would blame her?"

Claire echoes Owen, "And why haven't you called her since, Dad? I think you should."

Matthew looks as though the thought had never occurred to him. "I'm not sure I can do that."

Shelly smiles her most dazzling smile. She looks so much like Carrie that it makes everyone at the table hurt. "Yes, Dad, you should. You must! Snooze, you lose there, Pops." Shelly has not called him Pops for ten years. She thinks out loud, "Besides, don't you wonder what she's like today?"

# Listening to Silence
# (Ginny's Appeal)

Only Lionel Henslaw knows what will happen next for this little group, but unfortunately, the outcome is unpredictable, especially with the ungenerous Shelly. Although it seems to him that she is beginning to relax and lighten up just a bit. He sighs a noticeable sigh and thinks, *Poor old Mattie, I hope this won't be too much for him or his kids. After all the drama, there's no way he will be able to refuse Ginny's upcoming appeal. And his children, at least Claire, would never allow him to deny her.*

The conversation is so intense that nobody notices that a few tables on their right have been removed and replaced with a small stage. An older but sturdy Baldwin baby grand piano is pushed up. Microphones and lights are set up.

There is no fanfare, no introduction. Virginia Simmons appears on a stage for the first time in ten years like light emerging from a dense fog. It is rather comical as not one person in the restaurant notices her. She sits down on a stool and grins, taps the mic a couple of times, and simply says to the crowd, "Hello, everybody. I'm Virginia."

Shelly begins jumping up and down, sending napkins, forks, coffee cups, and Owen's dessert to the floor. She shouts, "Oh my god. Oh my god. Look! Look who's here! It's Virginia Simmons, and she's just ten feet from us!"

Matthew's chest aches with adrenaline. He labors to breathe, and the blood rushes from his face.

Shelly glances at her dad in alarm. "Whoa, Pops, are you all right? You're white as a sheet!"

"I'm pretty sure he's fine, sunshine," Ty replies. He nods toward Ginny. "I think she wants to talk to you."

Shelly turns and finds Virginia Simmons is looking straight toward her like they are old friends. Ginny smiles. "It seems there's at least one person who hasn't forgotten me."

Shelly grabs a menu with intentions of trying for an autograph. "A pen! Who's got a pen? Anybody? I need a . . . Lionel, surely *you* have a pen?"

Lionel nods and produces a pen from his suitcoat. "Keep it, kiddo. Something to remember me by."

A very courteous Shelly Jensen approaches the stage, holding up her new pen like the Olympic torch. "Ms. Simmons? Would you sign this, please?"

Ginny smiles down at her. "Sure, sweetie." She reaches over the piano and picks up a sheet of music. "But why don't I use this instead of one of Lorraine's menus?" She signs it. "To Shelly, I hope you're enjoying your evening. Love, Virginia Simmons." She reaches down, cups Shelly's face in her hands, and kisses her cheek. Claire is right behind her and is treated as graciously as her sister is. She is quick to notice and wonders how Virginia Simmons already knows their names. She instantly puts the puzzle together and is about to say something, but Owen, ostensibly reading her mind, holds a finger to his lips, shakes his head, and motions toward her dad. She understands.

Shelly is so delirious with joy that it doesn't dawn on her for several moments just how it is that Virginia Simmons knows her name. *It doesn't matter,* she thinks. "Oh, oh, quiet, everybody. Quiet. I think Virginia is going to sing. Oh my, isn't this amazing? She's so beautiful."

She hears Ty say, "Aw, you ain't seen nothin' yet, sunshine." But she has no idea what he is talking about.

Ginny addresses the starstruck restaurant patrons, "I'd like to play a couple of songs from my new album, my first in over ten years.

For most of the past two years, I was given the great fortune of reconnecting with some old friends. They gave me the strength, the conviction, and a home to write the words and music for *Prairie Town*. I've written these songs based on recent experiences, my journey through exhaustion, and understanding the glory of renewal and the peace forgiveness can bring to one's soul. These songs are my tribute to those who gave me courage to continue. I hope all of you enjoy them."

The first song is a ballad she has named "Chasing Sunsets." The second is country western, named "Silly Boys, Trucks Are for Girls." Both are met with standing ovations. The voice thought lost to the world has recovered and rediscovered.

Matthew is in complete distress and thinks to himself, *Lorraine, I should have known.*

He remembers what the doctor has been pushing him toward these past ten years, which is to live in the present. He decides to ignore the warning calls of past entanglements, tragedies, and bad decisions and to stay in the moment. "Nobody has a time machine, Matthew. We can't re-live, but we can live." He is determined to keep the abyss at bay.

He admits to himself that facing Ginny is exciting yet very dangerous, and he knows how dangerous this is for her too. He will let the evening take its own direction and follow wherever it leads: the new pathway he's been seeking all these years now lies before him.

Ginny speaks again; her entire focus is on Mattie. The music for this next song was actually given to me by my first and only true love. When we parted ways over twenty-years ago, he asked if I would someday write the lyrics to his unnamed melody. I've often considered that our years together at NSU were the most—

Shelly screams, "OH MY GOD!" She immediately clasps both hands over her mouth in wide-eyed embarrassment. Ginny is not in the least bit disturbed by the interruption. She smiles grandly at Shelly and then Claire. Claire points to Shelly's autographed sheet music. The previously unnamed melody is titled "Listening to Silence." Music by Matthew Jensen. Lyrics by Virginia Simmons.

Shelly slumps exhausted into her chair and fans herself with her autographed piece of sheet music.

Ginny holds out Mattie's guitar that Lorry has brought after breaking into his home earlier in the day. She speaks weakly, almost pleading. "I'm hoping that you need me as much as I need you. That you want me as much as I want you. Mattie? Will you please join me? Please? Play for us?"

He doesn't move, his eyes pleading with his daughters. *What should I do?*

Claire offers her reassurance, "Do it, Daddy. Do it!"

Shelly takes his hands in hers, leans over, and kisses her father. "Go for it, Pops."

Mattie looks up to Ginny, her arms extended in welcome. He stands, stiff and slow, and makes his way past his teary-eyed brothers and their wives, whose tears freely flow. Lionel stands and hugs his best friend. From across the room, Lorry claps her little hands; the rest of the restaurant follows suit. Raul begins to sob and darts into the kitchen.

Mattie climbs the small stage and tenderly takes Ginny in his arms. She tilts her head slightly and kisses him. She whispers, "Will you carry me on this, Mattie?"

"It will be an honor, Ms. Simmons. Thank you."

Ginny and Mattie embrace again, and then Mattie escorts her to the piano, where she prepares to play. Mattie sits on a nearby stool, ready to begin the opening chords that he will play, from memory, on his guitar. Ginny, stares at him and smiles, her eyes wide and eager with love. She enters on the piano. Mattie accompanies on his guitar, and Virginia Simmons begins to sing.

## "Listening to Silence"
Music by Matthew Jensen. Lyrics by Virginia Simmons.

Verse 1
I stare out my window at the deep blue sea.
Remembering all you said and all you've done for me.
You are my best kept secret.
I see your face in every dream.
But your life is such a lonely existence.
Afraid of the light. Listening to silence.

Verse 2
The rain beats steady on my old tin roof.
The lightning flashes, and thunder rolls through. Hear now my
voice because I'm all alone too. There's so much more time. Let
me mend your broken soul. My heart is bleeding, cut to the
marrow by your sacrifice, your disease. I beg you to come me.
But you're alone and miles away, always listening to silence.

Chorus
So please ask me now in that way you do.
I'll run from here and I'll come to you. I beg you to leave
your sadness, to leave your dark existence. Move to my
light and embrace the happiness I've kept for you.

Verse 3
So I ask you now, my dear, sweet man.
To leave your past and all the past demands. You've hidden away
for far too long; free yourself from the shadows of darkness.
I feel like a bursting star.
I'll give you peace we both can share.
I'll give you love to show I care.
Step into my light, hear my voice, stop listening to silence.

Chorus
So please ask me now in that way you do.
And I'll leave these hills and skies so blue.
I'll come running from anywhere.
I'm the only one to be with you. (Repeat.)

# PART 3

Above all, keep fervent in your
love for one another.
Because love covers a multitude of sins.

—Peter the apostle

# Frozen

It is not difficult to understand why, in a city bursting with coffee shops and espresso stands, Shelly Jensen chooses this particular little hole-in-the-wall. It is not a sterile, cookie-cutter franchise, the kind found on every corner and strip mall in this overcaffeinated part of the country. Her store is small and intimate, with no designs toward world domination.

The inconvenient locale appeals to an eccentric, yet loyal, clientele who does not come here to "catch up." Solitary tasks are performed within the deep shelter of self-imposed seclusion. They read or work or listen to music. The optimistic plan their futures with unblemished naïveté, while misanthropes, by the strictness of definition only, are stowed away in dark, private corners. Headphones are securely fitted over their ears. Those uncertain of their fates, in the company of scatterbrained conspirators, plot misguided schemes of revenge for wrongdoings, either real or imagined, and watch any newcomers with darting and suspicious eyes.

Shelly arrives every morning promptly at 7:30 a.m. A large black case hangs from her shoulder. This is her place. She loves the aroma of applewood brightly burning in the well-vented fireplace and the sweet, fertile aroma of coffee beans roasting. She loves the cozy yet mismatched couches and overstuffed arm chairs, the ancient dog-eared *National Geographic*s and *New Yorker*s. She loves the eclectic music offered by obscure indie musicians, nameless except to patrons. She loves the privacy.

She orders her drink, a venti americano with two pumps of hazelnut syrup, and buys the morning paper. The barista could have her coffee ready before she even walks through the door, but he loves to hear her delicate voice, so he waits. She lays the case on a small armchair close to the fire and rubs her shoulder. Glad to be relieved of its weight, she returns to the bar to retrieve her drink. She takes a slow, tentative sip and approves of the slight bitterness. Just the way she likes it. She nods to the barista and offers her approval with a hint of a smile, just enough to win him over for life. "Thanks, Cory," she says dismissively, and turns away.

Cory blushes at what he considers a compliment. His eyes follow her as she walks away, taking time to fully enjoy the scope and sway of her body. *Long and lean,* Cory thinks, *and that smile of hers, when she smiles, that is, lights up the room.*

Shelly settles comfortably into the soft armchair facing the fire and withdraws a big Toshiba laptop from the black case and plugs in the power cord. The computer is a gift from her father as she has recently graduated from Northern University, summa cum laude, with a degree in finance and business administration. The laptop is a sweet setup. She wonders if her dad listens to McCartney: *You can't buy love, Dad . . . but keep trying anyway.*

As she waits for the computer to boot up, she gingerly pulls a folded newspaper clipping from her wallet. It is limp and thin from being often read. It is her mother's obituary. She reads it every morning and has done so for the past ten years. She looks at the words and rewrites them in her mind, narratively, if for no one else than herself and her younger sister.

> Carolyn Hardesty Jensen is thirty-six years old when ovarian cancer claims her life. She leaves two daughters, Shelly, aged twelve, and Claire, aged ten. Her husband, Matthew, is so overwhelmed by grief that he descends into depression so deep that he emotionally abandons his children to everything but provision. To this he overcompensates, showering them with clothes,

music lessons, cars, trips abroad, etc. He gives them everything but himself. All his daughters want is for him to be a presence in their lives, normal, like he used to be. They crave his attention and affection. They miss his smile, his conversation, his gentle and warm personality, which has drawn so many to him.

But he is forsaken to his affliction, and his children are the victims. When family and friends offer help, he withdraws and hides. He knowingly and helplessly drifts away.

Perhaps he is beyond repair. Perhaps he is beyond hope. Can I ever forgive him?

Shelly reminds herself that the obituary cannot be rewritten any more than one can go back in time and rewrite their own life. She is conflicted because she is warming to her father's recent gestures of reconciliation and of others on his behalf. Regardless, she feels damaged and makes no attempt to feign her contempt of him. The rush of adolescence was the most difficult time. She was stung by his rejection and abandonment. She didn't understand and always wondered if she and Claire were to blame. By college, she no longer cared. Thus, she will not easily forgive, and to others the relationship seems bygone. In the reality of this day, however, she is willing to meet her dad's harmonious attempts to reconcile but decides to keep such information to herself, at least for a while longer. At least until she can decide if obstinacy can deliver her any kind of satisfaction. She remembers Pastor Owen saying that her mother had an extraordinary faith, strong enough to find beauty in all things, in all people, and in all the events of her life, including her own death. Shelly wonders how a faith can be so powerful but is cautious to discover this for herself.

In the ten years following her mother's death, Shelly Jensen sometimes suffers from inexplicable and random mood swings. Perhaps as a result, she creates and nurtures a spirit of glacial imprint: base, sanctimonious, and unforgiving. She is a pill: insidious, judgmental, and suspicious of everyone but her sister. And is as bitter toward life as the acrid taste of her americano. She is not mean-spirited, however, and can turn on the charm as easy as turning on a faucet. Unfortunately, it is rarely put on display as she knows it is fake and arbitrary. She examines herself today, as she has most days recently, and decides she no longer wants to live with the challenges such attitudes bring. This is no longer the impression she wishes to present. She knows first impressions can be selfish observations, and she should not be harshly judged, especially when considering how her dad has treated her. Through the years, she does not hesitate to blame him for the way she thinks and behaves and how her sour disposition is often put on display. She is in a desperate inner struggle against the perception she has created but is unsure how to reverse the effects of her conflict. She hates being miserable and, worse, trying to pass her misery along to others. She fiercely wants the intimacy of a relationship but is emotionally unavailable, wary, and suspicious. She wants to care for another without the constriction and fear of abandonment and doubt. Shelly wants to rid herself of her tortured heart and beleaguered soul. A sincere handshake or a hug would be bliss. Men are attracted by her beauty but repelled by her passive-aggressive and ever-present distrustful demeanor. She is weary of her presumption that life should be much more than the one she is experiencing. After everything she and her sister have been through, shouldn't they deserve a more positive life? A better life? And although deep down she knows she is a martyr of her own inventions, she remains remote and alone, close only to her sister and her now-distant relationship with Lorry Cullen. Shelly and Claire share the special bond that befalls two children who grow up on their own. Claire, however, is quite the opposite from her sister. She is fun to be around and has the ability to bring out the best of anyone around her. She is witty, upbeat, and captivating. She is also very confident that her renewed relationship with her dad and Ginny is genuine. Claire learned how to hide her pain, but after their recent dinner with her dad and his friends—and Ginny—she has embraced the strength, the astonishing peace and freedom that a forgiving spirit instills in the soul. She ardently wishes that Shelly will have the strength to abandon her enslavement to her acerbic personality and understand how pitiful and bitter one becomes when they are determined to resist the opportunity to forgive another, regardless of an ugly past, which cannot be changed. It is the present and the future that matter, that can be built upon. It is love that endures, not enmity. Claire unequivocally believes in giving others second and even third chances. She understands that, beyond all things, forgiveness is a blessing, a gift that frees the soul. But Shelly's soul feels frozen, and she will not easily forget the quantity and the cause of her pain. The notion that one can care more for another than one can care for one's own self is foreign to Shelly; she prefers the chaos of a victim's mentality. She chooses to believe that forgiveness cannot be manufactured or in any degree earned. Perhaps Claire will help her realize that forgiveness cannot be faked and show her how to grasp the difference between what is disguised and what is sincere. Her acrimonious internal agenda must be ripped apart from cloaked influences and be unconditionally dismissed. Shelly is glad that constant challenge to liberate the soul comes naturally to her sister, Claire, but acknowledges that it does not come naturally to her. She has to persuade herself to take the daunting journey of learning how to forgive.

Tucked inside the obituary is a photograph taken of her mom when just a few years older than Shelly is today. It was taken the day she was born. She studies the picture and searches for the similarities others swear she and her mom share. Folks say Shelly is a dead-ringer and gasp in disbelief. She is delighted with any comparison. Shelly has auburn hair like her mom's. The chin and the nose are the same, just prominent enough to be admired. They are the same height and weight, slender and tall. A friend of her dad has recently told Shelly that her mom's smile was so radiant it could eclipse the sun. Shelly has that smile too, but it is rarely offered. Her eyes are different though; they are not her mom's brown eyes flecked with green. Shelly's eyes are midnight blue and intense like her dad's. She struggles to discover within herself the incomparable disposition her mom owned, her passion for life, however short it was, and the immutable love she shared with her dad and gave unconditionally to her and Claire.

She sighs and carefully wraps the obituary around the snapshot and returns it to her wallet. She will repeat the routine tomorrow.

Graduating from college offers Shelly the opportunity to invent herself. She hopes a new person will emerge, one who is not aloof and self-absorbed. But she is afraid she cannot change and has concluded she is cursed by her own design, whether fabricated or not. She hesitantly probes an uncertain future in her uncertain world. She wonders if she worked so hard to achieve her many accomplishments, simply to please her father, to gain his praise and adoration. Although he seems impressed, he crushes her when neither was offered. She is alone now and on her own. There are no classmates with whom she can get together. There are no invitations to go out, and she realizes that loneliness is not part of her life; it is her life.

Cory, the barista, walks her way and stands across from Shelly, but she pretends not to notice him. "I'm on my break," he says. "I'd offer you a refill, but I see you're still good."

Shelly does not look up. "Yes, still good," she says, but as an afterthought, she looks up and adds, "But thanks all the same."

"You sure read a lot," Cory observes, just hoping to hear her voice.

She lowers her eyes. "Yes, because I can do it alone." She instantly regrets the curt reply and apologizes, "I'm sorry, Cory. I think I'm just preoccupied." She flashes him the seldom-seen, full-power Shelly Jensen smile that makes Cory melt into a puddle of ecstasy and motions to a chair across her. She asks if he'd mind joining her until his break was over. When recovered from the shock of this invitation, he sits down and points to the newspaper now opened to the classified section.

"How goes the job search?" Cory asks. "Any prospects?"

Shelly leans back, flips her long auburn hair over her shoulder, and absently twists the ends. She sighs and purses her lips. "Well, nothing is really jumping out at me, although I'm not too inspired." She takes a sip of her now-lukewarm americano. "I guess I can always move back home and teach piano lessons to the neighborhood kids." With a bitter laugh, she adds, "Now that would be a last resort."

Cory looks into her eyes, hoping for some indication that she's remotely interested in him. "I'm sure you've had some offers, right?"

Shelly stares down and studies her shoes. "A few, yes. The tech firm I interned for last summer made an offer, along with a few others. All here in town." She smirks. "Even my dad has offered to help. Apparently, he's well connected." The bitterness in her voice does not go undetected.

Cory's eyes dart around the café. He hesitates. "Well, you know, you can always make lattes for me. You can pick your own hours, and I'll even let you tend the fire."

She gives him an ungenerous smile. "What a remarkable, unattractive offer, Cory. I'm afraid I'll have to pass." She immediately regrets her response.

Cory's head jerks back, astonished by her mockery, and rises from his chair to leave.

Shelly quickly recovers, "Cory, wait. Please. I'm sorry, you didn't deserve that." She sighs in resignation. "I think," she pauses, "I think I'm just a little confused right now. I shouldn't take it out on you."

Cory sits back down, his face blank. Shelly sits up and wraps her arms protectively around her chest and purses her lips again. "I think what I need"—she pauses the way people do when considering an important decision—"what I really need is to go somewhere I've never been. A place where I can reinvent myself, where nothing will be handed to me because of my dad—or his new girlfriend."

Cory comfortably crosses his legs, leans back, and folds his hands on top of this head. He grins. "Well, good luck with that."

"What?" Shelly retorts, the persistent pique returning. "You don't think I can make it on my own, Cory? What the hell?"

Cory slaps his thighs and stands to leave, though lingering longer than was perhaps necessary. He winks at her. "No, that's not what I mean. What I mean is, I don't think you can go anyplace, and I do mean anyplace at all, that hasn't heard of your dad's new girlfriend. In fact, they were in here earlier this morning. I think they were looking for you. You just missed them."

She scoffs, "Hmm, well, that was good timing." She folds the newspaper and sets it aside without having read it, indicating to Cory that he can now leave her alone.

Shelly plunges deeply into the chair, trying to disappear. She sighs and whispers out loud, "I need to thaw out."

# Totally Importune

Shelly focuses on the laptop and logs on to check her email. She has been waiting to hear from a former classmate, a LinkedIn contact, through the alumni association. They are friendly but not friends, and Shelly is surprised how quickly the reply returns as she made the query only a week ago. *Well,* she thinks, *there's probably not too much to do in a small town, wherever it is.* The acquaintance had taken a job as a high school English teacher in a small town about six hundred miles away in the dry eastern part of the state. She may as well have been on the moon, but the area holds a certain interest for Shelly, and the town is not totally unfamiliar, although she's never been there.

She opens the email and is surprised by its length and depth. It is almost like reading *Wikipedia*, but with personal notes intertwined here and there. It appears to Shelly that the entire area is recruiting her. She begins to read the email that is smothering and dull yet seductive.

Hello Shelly:

This is a peculiar, wind-blown prairie of thick, sedimentary soil. It has an equally peculiar definition: loess. The early French Canadian traders called this land Perlouse. Roughly translated, "the land with short and thick grasses." Leave it

244

to the French to be concise and vague at the same time, right? Lost in translation, no disrespect to the early French Canadian traders, is the most extraordinary feature: the endless, empty hills. Two and one half million acres of hills covering parts of three states. A unique moonscape of grass. The soft, bald, undulating hills are deceptively steep, heaving up and down like a deep breath and caressed by ceaseless winds, which, eons ago, sculpted them into perfect rounded mounds, rolling like ocean waves. Too bad the early French Canadian traders discovered the Tetons first.

The great river that flows northwest from the Wyoming Rockies lacerates and divides the land with a deep, craggy canyon with towering rock formations, which the first overland immigrants claimed looked like castles, and from a distance they really do. The eight-thousand-foot-deep canyon reveals the composition of the earth and reveals why this is the finest wheat-producing area in the country, if not the world. On the surface lay topsoil, up to three hundred feet deep in places. How this was formed has been a matter of debate, and many theories abound. Some scholars insist it is decomposed volcanic ash, blown here by prevailing winds that never stop. Others theorize the soil was pushed south by Ice Age glaciers and left behind as the ice slowly retreated north. Still others postulate it is silt, washed in and deposited when, after a disastrous freak of nature, a massive glacial lake hundreds of miles away broke through its natural ice barrier, released the pent-up waters, and flooded the entire region over and over before finally receding into rivers and lakes, some of which remain and are so deep the bottoms have never been charted.

The second and most impermeable layer is a buried sea of basalt columns, proof of volcanic activity, probably from the Cascade Mountains some three hundred miles to the west. Trapped in the crevasses and cracks sits one of the world's largest aquifers, allowing the scant population an endless and rechargeable source of water. The third and thinnest layer is sandstone – soft, red rock, scratched and scarred by rivers that plowed through in ages past. Finally, with a grudging resistance to time and the relentless passage of the river current, is bedrock granite.

*Hmm,* Shelly wonders. *What's with the geology lesson?* She closes the email for the time being and makes an appointment with a local headhunter who insists Shelly can be placed in an entry-level position as an administrative assistant with a local software start-up. But last thing Shelly wants, besides moving back home with her father, is to be an administrative assistant to anybody.

Her attention returns to the email, and Shelly hopes the sender will describe what the town is like. Are there people their own age? Is there anything to do besides watching wheat grow and writing lengthy and boring emails? Going away becomes more appealing to her, but she won't move just for the sake of moving. Later that evening, not waiting for a reply, she reopens the email only to find more poop about the land with short and thick grasses.

The climate here is turbulent but not extreme, and every season is distinct but capricious. Winters are brutally cold, certainly not like the coast, where all it does is rain. The low sky turns blue gray with blinding ice storms and snows building twelve-foot drifts. As quickly as the snow and ice arrive though, they are frequently melted away by

Chinooks: fast-moving tropical winds from the South Pacific that can raise the temperature sixty degrees in hours, turning the snow to slush and the soil to thick, impassable black mud (some people call this a Pineapple Express, but personally I think that sounds more like a cocktail than weather event). Summers are equally cruel with temperatures so hot you can feel yourself helplessly being pushed into the ground. Fierce winds sting the eyes and carry dust high into the atmosphere, only to be dropped indiscriminately over everything. But there is a time, in the spring and again in autumn, however brief, when the temperature is just right, the wheat fields are an insane velvety green, and the wind offers a momentary and comfortable respite. Hardly a paradise, but nonetheless, it's a pretty nice break for a month or two; the place will grow on you.

If the region isn't distinct enough, years ago, the government drew state lines right through the center of this geographical oddity, dividing farms, families, and counties. A thoughtless move made by politicians who had never been west of the Appalachians. One thing I've learned is that folks around here like to make their own decisions. The first permanent settlers were either wheat farmers or ranchers or otherwise employed in their support. Their lives were slow, plodding, and as predictable as the seasons, but they were their own lives, independent, solitary, and much preferred over anything else.

Shelly has had enough of this rambling message as she can stand. She is poised to delete it into oblivion, when a reply to her earlier query suddenly pops up on her computer screen: "Shelly. I'm sorry for the lengthy email, but I strongly feel you should know as much as there can be known about our part of the country before you take the position with the TIM. Wouldn't you agree? And please keep in mind, you will not be the first person who comes to the Kinneysville prairie to find yourself."

"Find myself?" Shelly screams out loud. "Find myself! Just who in the hell does she think she is? Who does she think *I* am?"

She furiously replies that she does not understand but is willing to give her the benefit of the doubt if she will only explain what she's talking about and to please get to the point. "Oh, and by the way," she adds, "what position? What or who in the hell is the TIM? WTF?" She clicks Send without a sign-off, drinks a glass of merlot, and goes to bed.

An early-morning sunbeam leaks through a windowpane and lands rather rudely on Shelly's eyes waking her before she has any desire to wake up. She rapidly sits, feels a little dizzy, and flops right back into bed, her hand coming to rest on an empty bottle of merlot. She thinks that perhaps she sipped down more than one glass last night. She shuffles to the shower, the prospects of another aimless day awaiting her, and remembers the odd email and the appalling insinuations the writer makes. She dresses, casually looks at herself in the mirror with a shrug of acceptability, packs up the black case, and walks to the coffee shop. Along the way, she stews and fumes about the assumptions the writer has made; just the same, she is eager to reopen the email just to find out if any sense can be made of it.

Cory has her americano made and waiting for her when she walks through the door. Shelly slightly lifts her chin in gratitude, settles into a chair near the fire, boots up her laptop, and opens the email.

> Nestled deep within the land of short and thick grasses is the thriving town of Kinneysville, population: 2,361. Elevation: 2,043. Other than being the county seat, it is a place of little note for outsiders, but it is a hidden treasure for those of us who live here. Years ago, as county lines were first drawn up, a few farsighted individuals lobbied

for Kinneysville to become the location of the state's Land Grant College rather than the county seat, the reasoning being one of prestige and the certainty of growth. But the opposition, headed by old man Kinney himself, won the argument. After all, he owed the bank, the store, and the railroad. The Land Grant School, Northern State University, is located in the town of Three Forks, about sixty miles away, and has become the center of the universe for folks around here anyway.

As the county seat, Kinneysville is adorned with a remarkably plain brick courthouse and jail with absolutely no aesthetic appeal, something more likely found in Missouri or Minnesota, which makes sense because that's where everybody came from one hundred or so years ago. No tree-lined boulevards here, at least for now, just a few craggy old cottonwoods and willows clinging to the creek that zigzags along the edge of town. However, an anonymous benefactor, most likely the TIM, recently gifted the town an ungodly amount of money for city improvements and an effort to beautify Kinneysville is well under way.

Now, before I continue, and believe me there's more: I want you to know how warmly I was embraced when I first arrived here, everyone was so caring and friendly. You can experience this too. There is a true sense of community. I know you're going to love it here.

Shelly thinks, *How can I love a place I've barely heard of? I don't even know where Kinneysville is!* But her attitude shifts from adversarial to curious: "You're going to love it here."

The words ricochet in her head with cruelty. *Nobody seems to like me here, how can people whom I've never met, whom I've never heard of like, and accept me?* She looks around the coffee shop, hoping for something or someone to focus on, but finds nothing of interest, not even Cory's longing and less-than-furtive glances. Then it strikes her: she can go to Kinneysville to begin again, reinvent herself, to become the person she truly hopes to become. "And please keep in mind, you will not be the first person who comes to the prairie to find yourself." She Googles Kinneysville to at least find out where it is located and discovers that it is as far away from home as she can get and still be in the same state and time zone.

She blurts out loud, "What the hell is the TIM?" Distracted heads turn her way, but she pays no attention to those whose trains of thought she has derailed, pulls out her cell phone, and punches number 2 on her speed dial. It is not the person she particularly wants to call, and her insides are tied in knots, but she knows this is the one person who can feed her as much information as she wants. She almost hangs up before the other line picks up. Memories of the worst times of her life crowd her head. She thinks, *He should be ashamed of himself.*

Before she stops the call, a kind and inviting voice answers after two rings, "Hi, Shelly."

Shelly wonders, *How does he know it's me?*

She hears a gentle laugh, the one she has been desperate to hear for so many years now, and then the warm voice, "My new phone has caller ID."

She hesitates, and the caller asks, "Shelly? Are you all right?"

"Yes," Shelly answers very businesslike, as if she were talking to a stranger. She asks, "I'm wondering if you would help me with something."

"Of course, Shelly. Anything."

"Have you ever heard of something or someone called the TIM?" She envisions his kind smile, his eyes dancing with delight. The happiness and encouragement he has received simply by her calling him.

He laughs again, genuine and sincere. "Yes, I have. It's the name that locals use for T/M Farms and Ranches. They're in Kinneysville."

Shelly pauses in deep, perplexed thought after she is told, "I think they're expecting your call." *And please keep in mind, you will not be the first person who comes to the prairie to find yourself.*

Shelly speaks, her voice scratchy and low, "Okay, thanks. Um, say hi to Ginny for me."

"I'll do that, baby, and don't worry, you'll be great as always. I love you."

Shelly tentatively, almost forces her reply. She whispers, "Thank you. Bye, Pops."

She thinks about the freedom she might have if she just lets the past be the past and forgives her dad, especially after she has learned of his mental illness. But she's not sure she has the capacity for such decency. *Damn,* she thinks. *Just when our family looks like it has a chance of being happy and solid again, I'm receiving an invitation to move away. And to a place I know nothing about, except what the writer of this obnoxious email has told me. Not to mention, Claire's biopsy report has yet to come in. The timing of this is utterly inopportune. Damn.*

She opens an arbitrary browser and types Kinneysville. Several pages pop up, leading her to dozens of articles and outside links. One particular byline strikes her attention. She clicks on it and opens an article from Kinneysville's weekly newspaper about a man who believes that in a previous life he was responsible for the disappearance of Atlantis. His name is Bertram Butterfield. A link to Bertram Butterfield reveals that he's a grain operator for T/M Farms and Ranches.

Shelly thinks, *Oh, I can't wait to meet this guy. I mean, if I decide to go.*

*   *   *

"When is this kid going to get in touch with us, I wonder?" Ty Keller rhetorically asks. "I hope it's soon."

Donna Nevin smiles and replies, "Give her a little time, taskmaster. Maybe she just has to get used to the idea of working for you two yahoos. I know I'd think long and hard about it."

"So would I," Betty adds. "After all, she hardly knows us." She offers Donna a refill on her wine.

"She knows a lot more than she thinks she does," Ty says. "She just needs a reminder, that's all."

Marty sits up in his chair. "Oh, c'mon, Ty. She was just a little kid at the time. She didn't even recognize you when we met them."

Ty smiles and raises his finger to emphasize a point. "You guys are looking at this from entirely the wrong perspective."

Betty replies freely, "Oh, we are? Well, maybe you can enlighten us?"

"She'll remember me, in time," Ty answers distantly, "because some memories just aren't meant to be forgotten."

*   *   *

A week passes, and Shelly Jensen has yet to call T/M Farms and Ranches. She has serious reservations. How does this company she's just now heard about know who she is, let alone have any interest in her? And why do they want her? She finds no job opening or description on the internet or any other kind of media. She is still rather perplexed by her dad's comment that they are expecting her to call, whoever they are. She wonders what expectations they have for her. She specializes in international business, seeking out and developing new markets. To nurture businesses to succeed, especially new ventures started by women. And why would a cow outfit want someone like her? Shelly is an accomplished equestrian, but she can't see herself rounding up cows and, worse, castrating baby bulls. The biggest snag is that she knows nothing about these potential employers. Even though her dad insists that she has actually met them, Shelly has no recollection. Her internet search produces nothing of significance, with the exception that the small town of Kinneysville has recently embarked on an active and progressive campaign to improve the town in a way that will benefit the populace, regardless of who they are and what they do. Sidewalks have been built on every street, the high school has just opened a new gymnasium, and all school buildings have been completely renovated. The public library has been endowed with new computers. Even potholes are instantly filled. Flowering trees line both sides of Kinney Street. Local taxes have not risen in years. Extra funding for city and school improvements have come from anonymous donors. The crime rate is nonexistent, and local businesses thrive.

*Hmm,* Shelly thinks, *sounds just like Mayberry.*

# Hillbilly Hell

Shelly studies the telephone number for T/M Farms and Ranches. She doesn't recognize the area code and rolls her eyes, not quite believing what she's about to do.

"Oh, what the hell," she says out loud, and thinks, *It's only a phone call. I can listen to what they have to say and tell them thanks, but no, thanks. Besides, I hate the country.* But words from the email ring in her ears: *And please keep in mind, you will not be the first person who comes to the prairie to find yourself.*

She quickly dials, hoping no one will answer. But instead she's met with an affable greeting, "Good morning. T/M Farms. This is Ty. Can I help you?"

The voice seems so familiar that Shelly is too taken aback to reply.

The man on the other end sings out, "Hel-lo, you called me, remember? I can hear you breathing, so I know you're there."

*This voice,* Shelly thinks, *I know it from somewhere.*

Collecting her thoughts, Shelly manages, "Hello, sorry. Yes, I'm here. Um, my name is Shelly Jensen. I've been asked to give you a call about a—"

Ty interrupts with a happy voice, "Well, Shelly. Good mornin' there, sunshine. Glad you're calling. How goes it?"

A faraway memory grips her. She remembers, when she was very young, a man used to call her sunshine. But she can't retrieve the time or the man's name, just a flashback of a Cheshire cat–like smile.

Was he a visitor? No, she seems to recollect he may have stayed with them, before her mom died. Maybe the memory is not even real.

"Shelly, I can still hear you breathing. Are you okay, sunshine? Maybe I startled you. If so, I do apologize."

Shelly replies quickly, "Oh no, sir. I'm sorry, and yes, I'm all right. You just prompted a memory, that's all. I'm a little discombobulated at the moment." She becomes annoyed at Ty's silence and begins again. "I'm sorry. Your name is Ted?"

"No, ma'am. My name is Ty. Ty Keller, we had dinner together a few months back. Remember? At Lorraine's? I was the handsome one."

"Oh my god! I remember you now." She giggles. "But I believe your friend Marty claimed that he was the handsome one and that you just stand in front the mirror and admire yourself."

Ty replies, laughing, "Well now, it's a good thing he's not around at the moment, yeah?"

Shelly laughs too. "So I take it you two work together?"

"That's right, sunshine. I'm the T, and he's the M. We were originally going to name the operation M/T, but we figured that might send the wrong message."

Shelly is surprised that she's actually enjoying this conversation. She has an odd feeling that she's known Ty her whole life.

"May I ask you something, Ty?" Shelly says.

"Anything."

"Why do keep calling me sunshine? I mean, it seems like you know a lot more about me than I know of you."

Ty pauses; he doesn't want to have this conversation over the phone. "Why don't you come by the office, and I'll tell you all about it. Are you here in town?"

"No, sir. I'm calling from home. My dad said you might have a position open, but I can't find a job description, a website, or anything else. I'm looking for full-time work."

"Well, that's part of the problem, Shelly. We don't have a website—yet. You'll just have to come in for a face-to-face. We're kind hoping you'll guide us into the twenty-first century. Now, I can fly over and pick you up, but I really think you should drive, you know? You can get a better feel for the country."

Shelly is surprised. "You have your own airplane? Really?"

"Sure do," Ty replies. "And I'll tell you what, you drive yourself over here, and we'll go up for a spin. The view of this country from the air is amazing, especially the canyon. It'll change your life."

By now, Shelly is more intrigued than irritated. *After all,* she thinks, *it won't hurt to listen to what these cowpokes have to offer. I can always say no and drive away. Besides, a road trip may be just what I need.*

"How long of a drive is it to Kinneysville, Mr. Keller?" Shelly asks with some concern.

"Well," Ty slowly replies, "that depends on how many pit stops you have to make, but I'd figure seven to eight hours. You should probably buy a map."

"Should I make a motel reservation?" Shelly asks.

Ty responds, "I'm not sure I'd recommend staying at the local motel. It's, um, a little rundown at the moment. But you will be an honored guest at our home. We have plenty of room, and you can stay with us until you find something permanent." He chuckles. "Marty has an empty place out on the ranch, but you'll definitely want to check it out first. There are pictures of cows on the walls." More excited now, he continues, "So today is Tuesday. Do you think you can make it here by Friday? That's Marty and Donna's day in town. We're both really anxious for you to join us."

Shelly takes a deep breath and exhales. "I think Friday will work just fine. I suppose I'll drive over on Thursday."

"Excellent, sunshine, you'll be here in time for dinner, yeah?" Ty says, and gives her directions to his and Betty's house, along with the phone number. "I'll let Marty know. By the way, how's your dad? Are you and Claire starting to get along with him a little better these days?"

Shelly immediately flares up. This subject is none of his damn business, but she softens her anger. "Well, Claire seems to be, and I think he's doing just fine." And she sarcastically adds, "He and Ginny seem to be joined at the hip. I think it's disgusting." She regrets saying this as soon as the words come out of her mouth.

"Oh, Shelly sunshine," Ty gently replies like a favorite uncle would, "rancor is just not becoming on a beautiful girl like you. Lighten up a little, huh? It's not a crime to be happy."

Shelly thinks, *If he calls me sunshine one more time, I'm going to slam down this phone so hard his eardrum will burst.* But she doesn't think Ty's reprimand is pernicious; it's more like friendly advice. She reminds herself how desperately she wants to lose her crabby nature and put all contempt for her father behind her.

She sighs. "You're right, Mr. Keller. I'm working on it."

Ty smiles into the phone. "Call me Ty, sunshine. We're going to get along great, just like the old days."

Shelly thinks, *The old days? What old days? What's he talking about? I don't have old days. He's the one who's old. I'm only twenty-two, for crying out loud.*

Stopping only once for gas, the restroom, a large bag of peanut M&M's, and a Diet Pepsi, Shelly drives east toward distant blue-and-green mountains that never seem to get any closer. After descending the final hills and bends into Kinneysville, she is rewarded with the most fantastic view. Thousands of acres of velvet-green wheat, barley, and oats all rippling in the wind, waiting for the sun to burn them brown for harvest. It is too late in the day to go to the T/M offices, and she doesn't want to find Ty and Betty's house too early, so she parks on Kinney Street and walks around town. Colorfully painted flower boxes, complete with drip irrigation systems, are planted with annuals and wildflowers. Cherry trees, lilacs, and dogwoods, all in full bloom, line both sides of the street. Shelly thinks it's lovely, a pleasant oasis, after having passed through dozens of gray, despondent, and lifeless small towns on her long drive to the Kinneysville prairie. In fact, she thinks, it reminds her of a beachfront resort town, although she's eight hundred miles from any kind of a beach. Most of the businesses lining Kinny Street hoist awnings offering a pleasant and shady respite. A ladies' boutique, not exactly Nordstrom, she thinks, but it looks nice nonetheless. A bookstore that serves lattes and offers outdoor seating, a wonderful General Store that looks like it stocks everything, and even a specialty food store selling all non-GMO products. Exploring all she thinks she possibly can, she searches for a place to buy something cold to drink, and after passing a few bars that don't look especially inviting, she finds herself in a diner face-to-face with a woman who has squeezed her rather corpulent body into what Shelly believes must be the least comfortable pair of spandex pants imaginable. She sits at the counter and asks for a glass of lemonade. The diner's walls are crowded with framed and signed photos of whom Shelly figures are local celebrities: cowboys and cowgirls, hunters and fishermen all holding their trophies. Shelly thinks it's all rather foolish until she spies a photo of a woman, posing with a guitar, who is a dead-ringer for Virginia Simmons. *Impossible,* she thinks. Checking her watch, she feels it is probably about the right time to find Ty and Betty's place, so she walks to the register to pay her bill.

"Oh, it's on the house, honey," the lady announces with a friendly smile. "Any young gal who leaves the city to come and work for the TIM shouldn't have to pay for her first drink, even if it is just lemonade."

Shelly is paralyzed to thank her. She gives a hesitant smile, a quick nod, and walks toward her car, thinking, *This is how Alice must have felt when she walked through the looking glass.* She fishes out the address to the Kellers' house to enter into her phone's GPS, only to discover she has no service.

"Oh, great," she moans out loud. "I'm in hillbilly hell." She walks back into the diner to ask if anybody might give her directions to Ty and Betty Keller's house.

"You're back," the cashier declares. "Looking for directions, I'll bet. Lucky for me, though." She reaches under the counter and pulls out a dessert box. "Here, you should take this pie for dessert, okay?"

Shelly remembers the lengthy email writer describing how warm and welcoming the entire town made her feel, and now Shelly begins to understand, although she finds it a bit odd. She's directed to take a left on Prairie Street and drive until she sees a house with a big porch and a blue '62 Plymouth Valiant parked out front.

"It's not too far, sweetie. And thanks for taking the pie."

Shelly smiles a brilliant smile and thinks that she has been doing more of this lately. "It's my pleasure, miss. I hope to see you again."

"Oh, you will. I'm Hazel, and this is the only place in town where you don't have to eat in your car."

"Well, okay then, Hazel," Shelly reluctantly replies, a small amount of caution returning. "Thanks for the directions and the dessert. It smells great." She sets the pie down on the floor of the back seat of her car, turns left on Prairie Street, and looks out for the vintage Valiant.

Prairie Street winds up a steep hill east of town, and Shelly wonders if she hasn't been duped and is now driving into an ambush of desperados. She reaches the summit of the hill, and a ranch home with a wraparound porch comes into view. She spots the Valiant and pulls into the driveway, warily climbs out of her car, and picks up the pie, which she thinks by the smell is strawberry rhubarb. Nearing the house, she hears someone picking a banjo and then sees a man sitting on an Adirondack chair at the far end of the deck, revealing a far-reaching view of the Land with Short and Thick Grasses. There's a can of Coors Light on the deck next to the chair and a cane leaning against the wall. An unexpected memory floods her brain. She wonders what has prompted this vision and from how many years ago it comes. Shelly remembers she could not have been more than five or six years old, but just by looking at the back of the man's head, she knows who he is. *Oh my god! I recognize him now. He's Uncle T. Why didn't I see it before?*

Before Shelly speaks, the screen door slaps open, and a woman whom Shelly remembers as Ty's wife Betty screams with joy, "Oh, you're here. You're finally here!" She embraces Shelly and kisses her cheek. "Welcome, honey. We just knew you would come." She looks at Ty, who is smiling behind her. "Didn't we, baby?"

It's the Cheshire cat smile that slows Shelly's thinking and brings another spark of memory from her childhood. Ty appraises Shelly, "Shelly sunshine, you're a dream come true. Welcome to the happiest place on earth. Hey, is that pie?"

Betty releases her grip on Shelly and wipes her eyes dry. She pries away the pie box from Shelly's unknowingly careful grip. "You've been to Hazel's, I see. Why don't we go put this in the fridge and let this big goof fetch your luggage, okay?"

Still trying to find her bearings, Shelly replies, "Um, sure." She looks at Ty. "There's only one bag. Thanks, Mr. Keller."

Ty rolls his eyes. "You know, sunshine, you used to call me—"

Betty interrupts, "Just call him Ty. Or Tyler when you're mad at him. Not if, but when, I promise." She brings her into another embrace. "You're welcome to stay with us until you can get settled, all right, Shelly? We're just so happy you've come."

Shelly stares at the two in a confused trance, not able to make sense of the warm, friendly welcome and their familiarity with her. She is unable to answer.

"See there?" Ty pleasantly laughs. "She's so happy that she's speechless, yeah?"

The single-story, ranch-style home is obviously built for a person who has difficulty walking around, and Shelly realizes that it is built especially for Ty. The inside is decorated with eclectic art, from the western pictures and sculptures of Russell and Remington to Kate Cory and Jackson Pollock. One wall is dedicated to pictures of airplanes, in black and white and in color. She remembers Ty saying he owns and flies a plane of his own. She smells garlic, olive oil, and all things delicious coming from the kitchen and suddenly feels famished. She hears "Iris" by the Goo Goo Dolls playing in the background, and she isn't entirely sure why this doesn't surprise her. She feels her preconceived notions and postulations breaking down and realizes that she's melting, just a little. Warm and happy feelings surge through her, and when she sees Ty enter the house with her suitcase, she delivers her most radiant smile, which freezes Uncle T in his steps.

Ty says, "Now that's the smile I've been waiting for. My god, if you don't look just like your mom, except for your eyes, of course." He takes the single suitcase in their guest room at the opposite end of the house. It has its own entry. "Shelly," he calls out with a chuckle, "is this all you brought?"

"Just the one suitcase, yes."

"Not exactly digging in for the winter, are ya?" Ty mutters. Shelly doesn't know why he answers like this, and an uncomfortable sensation passes through her, appreciatively cut short, and disappears when Betty sings out that dinner is ready.

"I have a really tasty Grenache," Betty exclaims. "And I've been saving it for a special occasion like this. How 'bout we crack this baby open?"

"Sounds great," Shelly enthusiastically replies. She winks. "But I seem to remember *Uncle T* likes his Jack Daniel's—Black Label." She smiles her dazzling smile at Ty, who responds by embracing Shelly, almost squeezing the air out of her lungs.

He looks at Betty; all three of them have tears in their eyes. "I told you, baby. Didn't I tell you? Some memories just aren't meant to be forgotten."

Dinner proceeds in awkward silence, none of them really knowing how to begin. Shelly breaks the lull. "Exactly what kind of position are you and Marty offering, Ty?"

Ty stands up, rather easily, walks to the wet bar, and pours himself three fingers of Jack. "Anybody else?" he asks. Both Betty and Shelly reply that a shot sounded pretty good—but just a shot.

Ty asks, "Why don't we adjourn to the porch?" He glanced at Shelly. "Let's get caught up a little bit before we start talking business. Okay?"

Shell stops to admire the photos of airplanes, "So which one is yours, Uncle T?"

Ty smiles. "All of them, sunshine. Well, they weren't exactly mine, per se, they belong to the navy, or NASA."

Shelly's shoulders drop in shock. "You flew the Space Shuttle? Oh my god!" Her resentment of her father briefly returns as she thinks, *Of course he would never say anything about this, even if they're best friends.*

Ty wistfully smiles. "Almost. Let's go outside and talk about it. I think there are a lot of blanks that need to be filled in, yeah?"

Shelly scowls. "There sure are."

Ty shouts, "Hey, Betty. Don't forget the pie?"

Betty returns the shout with one of her own, "Get it yourself."

Ty hunches his shoulders and grins. "Have a seat, sunshine. I'll be right back."

Shelly settles down at the far end of the deck, which offers a breathtaking view of the hills. She loves the emerald-green winter wheat just starting to turn brown, burned by the sun. She thinks, *There sure is a certain allure to this country.*

Ty and Betty join her; they are holding hands. Shelly thinks it's kind of cute. Ty has the bottle of Jack Daniel's in his other hand. They sit down on either side of Shelly, who watches in astonishment when Ty drains his three fingers in one graceful gulp.

He refills his tumbler but doesn't drink it; he just holds it in his left hand, raises his right hand to his chin, and points upward with his index finger. The gesture causes a flashback in Shelly's mind, but she remains silent, waiting for Uncle T to speak.

Ty begins, "Just to clarify, you may not like everything you hear tonight."

Shelly's mood darkens. She responds with a vicious and impertinent stare and thinks, *Bring it on, old man. You have no idea what I have been through.*

# It's a Brand-New World
# Out There, Uncle T

Ty sips his whiskey and looks out over the hills. Betty takes his hand. Shelly has no idea what's coming. Will he talk about the job opening? Will he talk about how he somehow came to know her when she was a child? Her temperament eases, and she anxiously moves to the front of her chair.

Eventually Ty clears his throat. "The only thing I wanted to do when I grew up was fly airplanes. I mean, I was obsessed. But I grew up in a small mill town, right on the Canadian border. The nearest airport was 150 miles away. My dad worked at the mill, and Mom worked as a cook at the high school. They were older when I was born. Dad was forty-three, and Mom was forty." He winks at Shelly. "I believe I was a mistake between the sheets, as they say." He shifts uncomfortably. "Long story short, the mill closed down, and the town emptied out. Dad lost his job, and Mom did too when enrollments dropped. But we scraped by, you know? Both my folks found work wherever they could, even day jobs, just holding out until they could collect Social Security and Dad's army pension. So the only way I was able to go to college was on a navy ROTC scholarship. And if you know your history, that wasn't a really popular thing to do in 1968. My older brother bolted for Canada to avoid the draft. Nobody blamed him, Vietnam was a fucking mess, pardon my French. So when the folks at NSU offered the full ride, I didn't hesitate to take it. Of course, that's where I met your folks. Well, you remember that story from our fine evening at Lorry's."

Shelly smiles like fire. "You mean Lorraine's, right?"

Ty winks. "Whatever."

Shelly shakes her head and shrugs her shoulders. "Okay, you were a naval pilot. But I don't understand, Ty. I mean, don't most military pilots end up flying for commercial airlines? Why did you quit?" She looks at his cane and studies the faint scars on his face and arms. "I remember. You were in some kind accident. Is that how you came to stay with us? I'm sorry, but none of this makes much sense right now."

Ty smiles warmly at her. "Let us fill in the blanks. Betty's a big part of this too."

Betty explains, "I was the head nurse at the Veterans' Hospital. The one not too far from where you grew up." She pauses and then whispers, "I knew your mother."

Shelly's eyes flare, and she abruptly stands, "I don't want to listen to any of this. I'm sorry, but I'm going to bed . . . where's my room again?"

Ty raises his palm. "Shelly, wait. Please, wait." He tries to stand but stumbles and face-plants on the deck.

Betty screams, "Oh, not again. No!" Both she and Shelly jump to help, but he assures both that he's all right.

"Maybe I should have only had two fingers." He hugs Betty. "I'm sorry I scared you, baby. But really, I'm fine." He looks at Shelly, who is visibly shaken. "Please, Shelly. Let us explain, okay?" He rubs his legs.

Shelly sits back down. "Sure, Ty. Of course." She beams a smile at him, gathers her hair, and tosses it over her shoulder. Her body language is so like Carrie's that Ty winces. "So tell me something, how did I come to call you Uncle T?"

Tyler Eisenhower Keller graduated first in his class at the Pensacola Naval Flight School in 1973. The Vietnam "conflict" was shutting down, but the navy still had a presence in the Philippines, the South China Sea, and the entire southern Pacific Ocean. His first and only deployment was on a bird—an aircraft carrier—the USS *Enterprise*. Although he qualified to fly the F-14 Tomcat, he was rather relieved to be assigned flying reconnaissance missions, searching for boat people. Playing tag with MiGs wasn't all that appealing. He wanted to help people, not hurt people. He was on the fast track for NASA.

Ty, now recovered from the little bit of drama he created, retrieves two small velvet bags from his pocket and hands them to Shelly. "Take a look," he brightly says.

Shelly curiously reaches into the first bag and pulls out a Purple Heart Award. Her eyes grow wide, her mouth agape. She reaches into the second bag and pulls out a Navy Distinguished Service Medal pinned to the Navy Cross Award.

"Are you kidding me?" Shelly says with genuine surprise. "Are these really yours?"

"They are," Ty replies. "I keep 'em in my underwear drawer."

Shelly stares at the medals, suddenly straightens, and narrows her eyes. "Tell me about your Purple Heart."

Betty smiles and rests a hand on her husband's knee. "He'll tell you what he remembers, honey. I'll fill in the rest."

Shelly's eyes turn wide and pleading. She whispers, "Tell me, Uncle T. Please?"

"Of course I'll tell you, it's one of the reasons you're here . . . oops, I probably should have kept that to myself. But here's what happened .

"We were assigned to patrol a quadrant of the South China Sea and took off from Subic Bay in the Philippines, searching for boat people. After about an hour of flying around, I just happen to look out the glass and saw my two starboard engines blowing smoke and then catch fire."

"Oh no!" Shelly exclaims. "What did you do?"

"We sent out distress messages, but I had to ditch the plane in the drink." He pauses and swallows hard. "The crew was fine, all the training they had done worked to perfection . . . but I wasn't that lucky. I was pretty messed up, and when rescue arrived, they thought

I was gone. But they managed to find a pulse and hightailed me to Hawaii. The doctors there figured that I wasn't going to live very long, so I was shipped off to a VA hospital. You know, the one by your home."

Betty begins to speak, her voice just above a whisper. "He was in a coma for almost eight months. Massive head injuries, six broken ribs, a punctured lung, ruptured spleen, lacerated liver, a broken right arm, and a compound fracture of his left and right tibia. Five crushed vertebrae that have caused permanent nerve damage to both his legs. He had burns over 20 percent of his body, on his arms, but mostly his face and scalp. He was all wrapped up, so none of us knew what he looked like except for his identification picture. He was so handsome in his uniform."

Betty continues, distress in her voice, "All we could do is medicate him, and unfortunately, he became hooked on morphine without knowing what was happening. We didn't know what to expect when—if—he regained consciousness."

She looks hard at Shelly. "Your father came to visit him every day without fail. We got to know each other. He pleaded with the staff to wean him off the drugs, which we couldn't do, until the day Ty surprised all of us when he opened his eyes for the first time." Betty begins to cry. "He tried to speak, but he couldn't form any words. I mean, he didn't know who he was, where he was, or how he got there. His eyes frantically moved back and forth, but he couldn't focus on anything. We doubted that therapy would do much for him. He woke up with no memory, none whatsoever."

Ty begins to speak, his voice low and his words staccato. "I do remember, after finally asking how long I'd been there, how shocked I was when I was told eight months." He looked down to the deck. "I wanted to just shut my eyes and never open them again. I figured dying was the best thing that could happen to an invalid with no memory, especially after I was told the extent of my injuries." He cheerlessly smiles at Shelly. "We all have our stories of ruin, sunshine. Maybe yours isn't as bad as you think." It is Shelly's turn to lower her eyes.

"There was this man who showed up to visit. He repeatedly told me his name, Matthew, but that I always called him Mattie. Well, I couldn't remember, but I did come to rely on him. He showed me snapshots, you know, people from my past." Ty laughs. "He used them like flashcards, ya know? And he wouldn't let me move on unless I could recollect the person or persons in the photo, who they were, and what they meant to me. Now that I look back on it, we had a fun time."

He fixes a steady gaze on Shelly. "One day, I heard a different voice, one I'd never heard before, so I closed my eyes for protection." Ty smiles as he recalls the event. "I felt warm, sweet breath wafting over the part of my face that wasn't bandaged up. It was the most wonderful sensation. I thought I had passed into the everlasting. But I keep hearing voices, so I know I'm still alive. I very slowly opened my eyes to find myself nose to nose with the most beautiful little girl I've ever seen. She had dark, midnight-blue eyes and held the most inquisitive look. I slowly crossed my eyes, and she laughed. 'Uncle T made a funny face at me, Daddy.' I wondered, 'Is that who I am? Uncle T?' I don't remember being anybody's uncle. I'd forgotten about my brother and wondered if he'd come to visit after amnesty was offered to draft dodgers. But then I hear the voice of the man who kept saying he was my friend, Mattie."

Ty reaches out and takes Shelly by the hand. "It was you, Shelly. You have that same radiant smile of your mother's, a ray of sunshine. And that's when I started calling you Shelly sunshine or just sunshine for short. And that's also when I became Uncle T. You helped save me, sunshine. You helped bring me back."

Shelly begins to cry, and Betty reaches for her hand. "It's true, Shelly," Betty says. "After that day, his body and mind began to heal with such acceleration, we thought it was perhaps too fast. We hadn't seen anyone quite like Commander Keller before."

"I remember now," Shelly whispers. "I remember you came to live with us and how devastated I was when you decided to leave and come here."

"Well." Ty smiles. "We all have to leave home sometime, yeah? Your mom and dad gave me my life back, the life I now have.

Betty just couldn't help but follow me around, and she agreed to leave her career behind and come here. We both found ourselves in Kinneysville, figuratively and literally." *And remember, you won't be the first person that comes to the prairie to find yourself.*

"I was glad to finally be of use," Ty continues. "You see, Marty was struggling. It was a time when banks weren't lending and prime interest rates were well over 20 percent. He wouldn't take any money from me until I was able to be here, but we had a ringer. It seems Mattie was able to talk the navy into taking over all my affairs, he was charged as my guardian and held power of attorney over my assets, which amounted to two years of back pay plus my sick pay. It was over twenty-five thousand dollars. Your dad was chairman of the Farmers Credit Union, he had all that money transferred to Marty's account in a low interest loan. Now, as you'll find out, Marty is a very savvy businessman, and I know he wondered where the funds came from. He was one of the few ranchers who could read the markets and knew, despite the tight money, that he needed to expand rather than shrink away and sell out to an agribusiness conglomeration somewhere back east that doesn't know a cow from a plow. Well, the plan worked, and Marty and the ranch prospered. He paid off the loan within a year, but we didn't take the interest. And now we're under pressure to either grow and compete or stay the same and go backwards."

"Some plan and some gamble there, Uncle T," Shelly says. "And my dad made all this possible."

"He did, sunshine," Ty replies. "But when your mom got sick, he fell off the deep end. Look, I know you've been hurt. But you owe it to yourself to understand that his condition was not his fault. We always knew he was predisposed to depression, but to watch Carrie suffer and then pass away put him in a dark place that he couldn't understand. I know you and your sister were victims. But he's worked just as hard to recover as I have. Now, I know you well enough that you can put that behind you, but I don't know you well enough to know if you have the gumption to do so. I hope you do, sunshine. Because Matthew Jensen is far and away the finest man I've ever known."

Shelly whispers, "I'll give him that chance, Uncle T. But right now I'm worried about Claire. I think she's sick."

At that moment, Ty's satellite phone rings. Thinking it's just another crisis call from the office, he lets it go to his voice mail. But it rings again. Ty slaps his thigh. "I guess I better answer that, or they'll never stop." As Ty's voice rises with laughter to whomever is on the other end, he shakes his head and hands to phone to Shelly. "It's for you, Shelly sunshine."

"Who could it be?" Shelly eagerly retorts. "I can't think of anybody . . ." She realizes that Claire's test results are back today, and tentatively takes the phone. "Claire? Oh, hi, Dad."

Shelly nods her head and begins to cry. "Yes, great, great news. And Claire is happy? Yes, I guess I'd be ecstatic too. Who, Ty? Yeah he's something else, isn't he? Okay, Dad, I'll say hi to Betty for you. What's that?" She looks at Ty and smiles. "Yes, yes I will." She whispers into the phone, "Thanks for calling, Pops . . . I love you too." She closes out the call, laughs, and then begins to cry. "Claire's tumors are benign. There is no cancer. Wow! What a relief." She grins at Ty. "Dad was by her side the entire time, and he thinks the color in his face has finally returned. Oh wait, there's a postscript. He says I should stay here and help guide you and Marty into the twenty-first century."

"Will you, Shelly sunshine?" Ty asks. "Will you stay here and work for us?"

"Absolutely, Uncle T. Let me introduce you to the brand-new world."

"It's a big job, what we're asking you to do," Ty says. "We have computers, but they're still in boxes. I don't know what kind they are, it's the one that come in cow boxes."

Shelly laughs. "I believe those are Gateways. I can set them up and create the networks. Does Marty have one at the ranch?"

"He does," Ty replies. "And just like us, it's still in the box. I think he uses it as a coffee table in his office. But the first thing we have to do tomorrow is go to the bank and authorize you to sign checks. Then we'll go to the attorney to get you signed up as an officer of the company."

Shelly thinks this is presumptive and way, way premature but says nothing.

Ty continues, "The past few years we've had stiff competition from corporations back east and from conglomerates in Asia who buy up enough acres so they can fix the commodity prices before crops are even harvested. In other words, they're saying, 'This is what we're going to pay, so deal with it.' Well, that's all good if our harvests are sufficient. But if we have a year where our yields are down, our income tumbles too. We can't adjust to fixed prices, our fortunes rely on prices that are market driven. Tax codes have been created, which allow for corporations to just write off any losses and then end up receiving huge tax breaks, but we can't do that. We're always trying new ways to increase our production, and we're diversifying into organic crops. But we need to discover and invest in global markets that will allow us to compete with big corporations. Otherwise, we'll get squeezed out like many others and are forced to sell out at rock-bottom prices. The only other alternative is to scale way back, but as you probably noticed, the entire fortune of Kinneysville is dependent on the TIM, so that's not an option."

He pours himself just a little bit of Jack and notices Shelly's eyelids are growing heavy. He goes into the house and retrieves a blanket and gently places it over her.

"We understand that you specialize in global marketing, and that's just what we've been looking for. But until you came along, we couldn't find anybody with the know-how. Marty and I certainly don't, but we're anxious to learn from you. You come highly recommended, don't ya know?"

"Oh, really," Shelly says, somewhat surprised. "By whom, might I ask?"

Ty smiles at her. "Well, by your dad, of course. Don't you know? He's the chairman of our bank."

Shelly frowns. "No, I didn't know that. He doesn't talk to either me or Claire."

"Well," Ty replies softly, "I believe that's going to change."

"I hope so," Shelly says, and yawns. "We both want our dad back." The rigors of the long day have finally caught up with her. She pulls the blanket around her, curls up, and falls asleep in her chair.

She dreams, or thinks she dreams, that someone is gently stroking her hair. It feels good and sparks a childhood memory. She recognizes a man's scent that she's not sensed since she was six years old. She feels a pleasant smile grow on her face and a warm feeling, long forgotten, flow through her body. With her eyes still closed, she extends her arms like she used to do when she was a little girl, "Will carry me to bed, Uncle T?"

Ty gently laughs. "Well, I'll help you stand up and show you the way."

Shelly stands and wraps her arms around Ty. She snuggles against his shoulder and says, "I loved you, didn't I, Uncle T?"

"Yes, you did, Shelly sunshine. Something we hope to revive."

He releases her to Betty. Shelly leans her head against her as she's led to her bedroom. Uncle T wipes a tear from his eye.

# Cowgirls Don't Cry

Ty bangs on Shelly's bedroom door. "Up and at 'em, Shelly sunshine. It's already six o'clock in the morning. Coffee's on."

Shelly moans, "I thought you were a night owl, not a morning person."

By 7:00 a.m., they have visited and signed papers with the banker and the attorney, both of whom came in early to accommodate Ty. By eight o'clock, they have had a quick breakfast at Hazel's Diner and were heading for the airstrip to get an eagle's-eye view of the Land of Thick and Short Grasses and the canyon that lacerates the prairie's hills like an ugly scar. Ty flies a Beechcraft King Air 100, with room for six, seven, if there's a skinny one. Shelly marvels at the deep and narrow canyon.

"In some places," Ty tells her, "the canyon is over eight thousand feet deep with some of the largest class IV rapids in the country. Legend has it that three members of the Lewis and Clark corps of discovery gave thought that running the rapids might save weeks of walking to the Pacific Ocean. Fortunately, common sense overruled, and they decided on the overland route."

Shelly whispers, "I've never seen anything so spectacular. It's amazing."

Ty brings the plane out of the canyon, revealing the two and half million acres of the land of thick and short grasses. She gazes complacently at the prairie, and in that instant, Shelly Jensen feels the chambers of her soul relieved. Years of anger, chariness, distrust, and cynicism melt away. She feels the country healing her and not only falls in love with this land she's almost decided to call home; she's fallen in love with life.

They fly over a large two-story house on the canyon rim. Large stables are nearby, and stockyards with cattle chutes are about a mile away. "Who lives down there?" Shelly asks.

"It's Marty and Donna's place. We're coming out for dinner tonight. You're the guest of honor . . . unless you have other plans. I mean, I don't want to appear presumptive."

"No, Uncle T." She sighs. "I don't seem to have an active social life . . . anywhere."

Ty smiles. "Well now. That won't do. The world should know the many charms of Shelly Alison Jensen."

"Yeah, right."

Shelly finds herself calling both her sister and her dad every night.

"Dad," she says, "I wish you would have told me how nice Uncle T is."

"That must be a recent development," he replies. "I don't recall him being nice at all. Ever. You must have changed him."

"Nice one, Pops. You wait until I leave, and all of a sudden, you get a sense of humor?"

Her dad clears his throat. "I miss you, Shelly. So much. When is your next trip home?"

"This weekend, I'm picking up some of my stuff. I . . . I miss you too, although I'm leaning toward maybe staying."

"Can we see you while you're home?" Matthew eagerly asks. "Anytime?"

He can sense her smile over the phone, and she taunts him, "So it's *we*, is it?"

"Yes. I think it's safe to say Ginny and I would like to be a couple. But we want to run it by you first . . . Ginny insists. We've already talked to Claire."

"You're a grown man, Pops. You don't need my approval."

"I think we do, Shelly. I mean, it would be nice, wouldn't you agree?"

She warily answers, "Yeah, I suppose."

*　　*　　*

"Did you hear the phone ring at five a.m.?" Ty asks on their way to the airstrip for another tour.

"Nope," Shelly answers. "This country air has turned me into a sound sleeper."

"It was Owen," Ty carries on. "He always calls at five a.m."

"Hmm," Shelly replies. "Wake-up call?"

"No, and since he tends to carry on both sides of the conversation, I didn't catch much. He mentioned a wedding on the canyon rim at Marty's house. I wonder if he's told Marty yet. Probably not."

Shelly thinks, *So that's why dad is so insistent on meeting this weekend. He actually wants to ask my permission.*

Ty notices that Shelly's face is carrying a significant scowl. "You all right there, sunshine?"

"Fine," Shelly replies. "I'm fine. Just fine. Really, I'm fine."

Ty smiles. "You should be fine. I think this wedding is going to be quite the to-do, and I'm sure you're to play a significant role."

"Oh, well that's just fine, isn't it?" Shelly says. The sarcasm does not go unnoticed.

The CB crackles. "Breaker one-nine, breaker one-nine. Are you out there, bean counter?"

Ty picks up. "Yeah, go ahead there, cowboy."

Marty's voice crackles through the airwaves, "Hey, how soon can you get a crew out here? I've got a broken-down fence, and now cows are scattered from here to town. I can use a little help. MJ is the only one here and has more than he can deal with. Over."

"Well, look straight up, and you'll see me and Shelly flying overhead. Looks like a real mess from here. Listen, I can put this plane down on that little strip by your house. Shelly here is quite the cowgirl."

"Hit me with that again, bean counter."

"Shelly, she rides like the wind." He leans over to Shelly and asks, "You do, right?"

"No no no. I've only ridden English-style. I've never ridden western before."

"Well, hell." Ty laughs. "The horse doesn't know that."

"But I'm wearing a dress, Ty. I don't think Marty's going to take that too lightly."

"Oh," Ty assures, "Donna will have something for you. Not to worry."

"Doesn't seem like there's much of choice, is there?"

"Call it baptism by fire. Owen would be proud."

"Yeah, if I survive."

"Oh, don't worry, we'll have your back," Ty assures. "By the way, can you rope?"

"No, but I can tie my shoes. Oh, I can change a lightbulb, you know, by myself."

Ty deadpans, "You'll do just fine."

Ty has to buzz some strays away from the small makeshift air strip before he can land. Donna meets the plane with clothes for Shelly to change into. "We'll put you on old Peasley," she tells her. "He sleeps most of the time. Marty will give you some instructions."

Just then Marty reins up in a cloud of dust. "I was hoping for a larger contingent." He looks Shelly up and down. "But I bet you can hold your own, can't ya?"

Shelly nods uncertainly. "I'll do whatever you need done, Mr. Nevin. So what exactly are we doing here?"

Marty tugged his lower lip with his teeth, sizing up Shelly. "We're missing ninety head, and I think they're between here and the trailer. I need you to take the right flank, Donna will take the left, and I'll go right up the middle. We need to turn them in Donna's direction and then push 'em for that pen over there to the left. I'm afraid you'll be eating some dust, just don't let any get behind you. This isn't like chasing down foxes or whatever you folks do on the coast. Savvy?"

Shelly mounts old Peasley, has Donna slightly adjust the stirrups, and Shelly digs her heels into his side, instantly waking the horse out of a sound sleep. He rears back, and Shelly shouts out, "Let's ride!"

Marty whispers to Ty, "Well, she's got a little of her old man in her, doesn't she?"

"More than she knows, partner. More than she knows. Oh, by the way, have you talked to Owen?"

"Yeah, at four thirty this morning, I forgot he doesn't sleep. Sounds like we're in for a real shindig?"

Ty agrees, "It does at that. About time, I should say."

The three riders start off side by side in a slow trot. Marty wants to make sure Shelly can handle a horse, which she does with practiced elegance. He brings them to a stop just below where the hill tops off. His voice is just above a whisper. "Shelly, if you feel you're in trouble, turn tail for the ranch. If you think you're okay, just wave your hat, no loud or sudden noises, or they'll scatter. I'll find the lead bull and turn him toward Donna, the rest will follow along, I do believe. Just be careful, promise?" Shelly nods.

"Okay, let's dismount and head for the top of this hill and see what there is to see, shall we? And be quiet, they can smell you before they can see you, but fortunately, we're downwind. Ready, cowgirls?"

Shelly struggles to keep Peasley awake and does an admirable job. Marty and Donna are impressed. As soon as they summit the hill, the renegade cattle are spotted spread over the opposite hillside, about two miles away.

Marty tugs on Shelly's sleeve. "See that mean-looking one in the middle? That's Rascal, he's the king of the hill, so to speak. I probably should have castrated him and turned him into hamburger years ago, but he's quite prolific, if you catch my drift. This might be his last roundup." He gently grabs her shoulders and maneuvers her. " So, Shelly, you plant yourself right here. If you see a stray, just saunter on over and nudge 'em back to the herd. Otherwise, stay put. Promise? Just use your lariat to lead them." He winked at her. "No fancy roping."

Shelly nods that she understands, but Marty catches a sparkle in her midnight-blue eyes. Just like her dad whenever he was about to do something unpredictable.

Shelly does as promised and watches in wonder as Marty charges the herd, his lariat high above his head. As soon as he has the herd moving, Donna spurs her horse and, between the two of them, turn the herd back to the pens. All is according to plan until Rascal has a change of heart and decides he rather enjoys his newly found freedom. He breaks from the lead and heads directly toward Shelly.

"Oh boy," Marty says out loud, "this can't be good."

Shelly freezes with fear from her position on top of the hill when she realizes the entire herd is stampeding directly toward her with Rascal snorting out in front. But with a burst of excitement and courage, she takes charge of Peasley, who tries his best to throw her off. Shelly handles him like she's been riding him for years and charges straight toward Rascal, imitating what Marty did, in an ugly game of chicken, which holds no winner. The jarring, head-on collision stuns Rascal into submission, and he trots off toward home, holding his head regally high as the rest of the herd follows. Shelly is not as lucky. The impact throws her off Peasley and, landing on her head, is knocked out cold. Dust settles on her face and forehead; her hair is sticky with blood. Ty is at the stockyard to close the gate and get a count. Once that's done, he climbs on an ATV to search for Shelly, but Marty reaches her first. He pulls smelling salts from his saddlebag and brings her back to the living.

"Don't move, darlin'," he tenderly says. "Don't you dare move. I'm sure Betty's on her way. She'll check you out. You took quite a spill. Tell me where it hurts. I'll take care of you, I promise."

The only word she could manage was "Water?"

Marty pulls out his water bottle but allows her only a sip.

She makes a strained smile. "How's ol' Peasley?"

"Better than you. And I'm thinking we should roast that Rascal for the wedding next week."

Does she hear him right? Are her dad and Ginny getting married so soon? Her eyes roll back into her head, and she passes out again. More smelling salts. Marty takes a sniff himself.

Donna rides up with Ty right behind her. "Well, you found yourself right in the middle of everything. Nobody's gonna call you greenhorn, that's for sure. Wait till they hear about this in town. You'll probably get your picture hung up on Hazel's wall."

Donna scolds, "Why don't you try and give us some help here with Shelly cowgirl. She saved the herd. Do you realize that, Shelly? You saved the herd. I'm gonna turn that Rascal into jerky if it's the last thing I do."

Shelly winces in pain when she tries to sit up. "My shoulder hurts. Any cuts or bruises?"

"Just that walnut-sized bump on your noggin," Ty replies. "And judging by the angle of that left arm, I'd say your shoulder might be dislocated too. I got a hold of Betty on the CB, and she's on her way. She said not to move you and only sips of water until she can check out your lungs. There's a laceration on your forehead that might need a few stiches."

Betty Keller, driving the aid car, made the twenty-five-mile drive in about fifteen minutes. "Let's take a good look at you, sweetie. You're already a hero in town, you know."

"Oh my!" Shelly exclaims. "Your stethoscope is so cold."

Betty laughs and announces, "Bumps and bruises, a few cuts, but no broken bones though, that's quite the miracle." She checks her eyes. "You might have a concussion, so we need to get you to a dark place in a hurry and keep you awake." She looks at Marty. "Let her have a good draw from that water bottle, but just one. I want to get a chest X-ray just in case, although her lungs sound clear. No internal bleeding, just a dislocated shoulder and that nasty bump. Let's get her in the aid car and take her to the trailer, it's closer than the house. I'll have to push her shoulder back into place, so I'm giving her a shot of morphine before we move her."

Marty, Donna, Betty, and Ty each take a six-hour shift, keeping Shelly awake. Only after a full twenty-four hours pass will Betty allow Shelly to fall into heavy sleep. She wakes up in a brightly colored bedroom. Her arm is in a sling with an ice pack on her shoulder and one on her forehead. She wonders who changed her clothes. Ty and Marty are sleeping in chairs at the foot of the bed. She doesn't know they've been there for twelve hours.

Shelly smiles and wakes them with a penetrating shrill, "Hey. I've gotta pee! Which one of you cowpokes is going to help me?"

Marty opens an eye. "You're on a catheter, baby, so just let it fly."

She struggles to sit up and looks around the bedroom. "Where am I anyway?"

"This is the trailer, home for wayward women who have lost their way . . . but find it in the end. It's yours if you want to live here. It even comes with a pickup."

Shelly grins. "I'd kind of like to check out the rest of the place, if you don't mind." She thinks, *And remember, you won't be the first person that comes to the prairie to find yourself.*

"Sorry, sunshine. One more day of bedrest of you, nurse's orders. Besides, there's not much else to see that can't be seen from right here. Except for Marty's collection of *Hereford Journals.* I'll be happy to bring them to you. They're a cure for insomnia."

Shelly sighs. "Well, I'll make it to the wedding anyway, such as I am."

"I wouldn't worry about that, sunshine. She loves you regardless of how you look. Word is that you're a bridesmaid."

Shelly thinks, *Bridesmaid? How is that possible? I mean, I'm a huge fan, but we've barely met.* Both Marty and Ty notice the confusion on her face but choose to ignore it. Rather, Marty holds a cup up to her lips. "Have a sip of juice, Shelly cowgirl. I'm proud of you for not even crying. I know I would have, that's for sure. You rock."

Their heads turn when they hear a car approaching the trailer, gravel crunching under its tires. When it comes to a stop, they hear a single door open and then slam shut, followed by quick little steps.

"Who do you suppose this is?" Ty asks. He struggles to stand and looks out the small window. His eyes narrow, and he scowls, "Oh, for crying out loud. I wish there was another way out of here."

Marty's eyes twinkle with amusement. Shelly is confused.

"It must be Lorry," Marty says.

"Yeah, it's her, all right," Ty muses. "I thought I felt a disturbance in the force."

# The Canyon

Marty glances at his watch. "Medication time, Shelly cowgirl."

Ty offers a sardonic glance toward Lorry as she quick-steps her way to the back of the trailer, where the bedroom is. He says to Shelly, "You're lucky. You'll probably be asleep before you have to deal with her."

Shelly gently lies back into the bed and closes her eyes. She doesn't sleep, but nonetheless, the prescription drug makes her dizzy and drowsy. She doesn't care for whatever Marty has just given her but is grateful, though, when the pain is displaced.

Marty walks out of the bedroom and puts his finger to his lips to caution Lorry. "Quiet, okay? She just fell asleep."

Lorry hisses, "Oh, I just want to look at her. Jeez! Who are you anyway, her guardian angel? Get out of my way and let me through."

Shelly can feel Lorry's hand as she gently caresses the part of her forehead that isn't bandaged. She hears Lorry sigh and whisper, "Oh, she's so lovely. Thank you, boys, for taking care of her. I can't wait to tell her all about the wedding. Claire is coming the day after tomorrow. They're both bridesmaids, you know."

"Yeah," Ty says thoughtfully, "I get the feeling she's a little confused about all that."

Lorry slumps her shoulders. "You haven't told her yet? What is wrong with you two?"

"We just found out yesterday," Ty and Marty say in unison, a talent they've had since college and one they know particularly gets under Lorry's skin. "Give us a break, huh?"

Shelly is confused but about much more than a wedding. She dreams that Marty is at that moment removing his hat and raking his fingers through his hair. It's a familiar gesture. She thinks she hears Ty say that the three of them should go to the living room and leave her alone, which they do, leaving Shelly to her thoughts. There are so many loose ends in her life, so much uncertainty. She has fallen in love with the country but knows enough about this land already that it won't necessarily love her back. And even if an avuncular relationship is now firmly established with Ty and Marty, she's not sure a life in the country, where the only sounds are birds calling, chipmunks scolding, and the incessant howling wind, might be for her after all. She's excited to see her sister.

She asks herself, *What am I doing here? Sitting in a trailer in the middle of nowhere and where my only friends are my dad's age? Ty said it wouldn't do with my lack of a social life. Maybe he's thinking of setting me up with the man responsible for the sinking of Atlantis. Still, there's something about this place that's comforting, even familiar.*

Tired of lying in bed, she swings her feet to the side and, with much effort, stands up. She's instantly dizzy and grabs the top of a dresser to steady herself, knocking over several framed photographs. She gingerly walks to the bathroom, where she splashes cold water on her face and inspects her nasty bumps and bruises. Despite the painkillers, she aches all over, especially her recently dislocated shoulder. She steadies herself once more, waits for the dizziness to clear, and walks to the dresser to straighten up the pictures she knocked over. Picking up the first photo, she looks at it and gasps, covers her mouth, and floats down to the bed. The photo shows her mother in her wedding gown, her head held high in laughter. Surrounding her, with their arms around each other, are Lionel, Ty, Marty, and Owen. She correctly assumes that her father has taken the picture; it would be so like him. Clutching the photo and then inspecting the frayed ends of her cotton nightgown, she cautiously walks through the trailer and wonders where everyone has gone. Still floating from the painkillers, she gets the bizarre sensation of not knowing what's real and what isn't. The picture with her mom's happy face is at the same time comforting and upsetting. She begins the difficult and frustrating struggle to dress herself with the intention of leaving this peculiar place in the middle of the prairie. But there is no one she can call, and there is no place she can go.

*Except,* she thinks. She recalls a place Ty had shown her from the air. A natural rock ledge, a porch, jutting into space just below the canyon rim. It's near the Nevins' house.

"It's where Marty goes sometimes, just to think," Ty had said, and then smiled. "It's a little too Zen for me."

*That's where I'll go,* she thinks, *to the canyon. There certainly aren't any coffee shops around.*

She stumbles outside, careful to keep a hand on the railing. Once on the ground, she looks around and wonders which way to go as everything looks the same. Finally, she notices a faint track leading up a small incline and figures that is probably the best place to start. But then where? She hears someone behind her calling out her name. She screams a disoriented scream.

"Sorry, Shelly. I didn't mean to startle you. But I was just kind of wondering where you're heading."

Shelly carefully turns toward the voice and sees the most beautiful young man she's ever seen. "Who, pray tell, are you?"

"Oh, you don't remember me? I'm MJ. I work here, on the ranch."

Shelly studies the bright red hair and his soft green eyes. "MJ? Is that a code name or something?"

He laughs. "Kind of, its short for Matthew Martin Johannsen. We knew each other when we were kids. I'm Owen and Rachael's son. But in your heighted state of insobriety, you probably can't remember too much."

Indignant at his comment, Shelly retorts, "And what makes you think I'm in a heighted degree of insobriety?"

"Well," MJ observes, "for starters, your pants are on backward. Or is this the latest fashion statement from the coast?"

Shelly looks at her jeans just to confirm MJ wasn't just hitting on her. "Well, I guess you're right about that. Anything else, Mr. MJ?"

MJ looks down the ground. "Your shoes are on the wrong feet. Maybe you could use a little help, Ms. Jensen? I won't look. Promise."

Shelly can't help but giggle. "Well, since you've made such a gentlemanly and chivalrous offer, I'm not sure how I can resist."

"Yeah, well, maybe we should get you inside, for starters." Careful not to cause any more damage to Shelly's injuries, he gently but with ease picks her up and carries her inside the trailer. Shelly buries her head in his broad shoulder.

Easing her down on the living room couch, where she falls fast asleep, MJ pours her a glass of ice water and makes her drink the entire amount. "You really should hydrate, Shelly. Your pupils look like lumps of black coal. Here ya go, down the hatch."

Shelly eagerly drinks two glasses of water and slowly regains her senses.

"So what has Nurse Betty filled you up with?" MJ asks.

Shelly produces a bottle of pills. Percocet. "Hmm," MJ says. "Well, that explains the fashion statement. And you thought you could make it to the canyon?"

"I thought I'd try anyway, you know, just to think. Like Marty. It's his house of Zen, you know."

"For many of us," MJ quickly replies. "Okay, I'll take you there, but you really should change."

"Will you help me, MJ?"

"Of course, that's why I'm here. Ty and Marty figure you might like being around someone your own age. First of all, let's get these shoes off, then we'll work on the pants. You're going to have to keep that shoulder as still as you can. Okay?"

"Okay," Shelly says. "But no peeking."

MJ wrestles off the wrong-fitted shoes and then slips off Shelly's jeans. "Okay," he says, smiling. "I peeked just a little. Unavoidable I'm afraid." He goes behind her and hoists her pants, zips them up, and buttons them. "Nice fit."

"I can put on my own shoes," Shelly says.

"Right, I've seen your work. Allow me, please."

"So," MJ says slowly. "Are you going to wear that nightgown? Don't you have a blouse or a T-shirt?"

"I do," Shelly retorts, "but you're not helping me with that."

MJ waves his hand. "I understand completely. But don't hesitate to call for help. No peeking."

It takes two minutes before Shelly calls for help, "I'm stuck with this stupid sling."

"On my way," MJ says with enthusiasm. He finds her all tangled up, trying to slip a blouse over the sling. "Oh, I see the problem. All your buttons are off. I can fix that, if you want. No peeking."

"Yes, please. Thank you, MJ. And I know you peeked, didn't you?"

MJ sighs. "Once again, an unavoidable circumstance. But with only one eye. Majestic, I must say."

Shelly laughs wholeheartedly this time. She likes this young man. She reaches up and kisses his cheek. "You are quite the gentleman, Mr. Matthew Martin Johannsen. Now, will you take me to Marty's legendary ledge of Zen?"

They drive past Marty and Donna's home, now decked out in wedding regale. Marty emerges from the stables and doffs his hat. Shelly blows him a kiss. The ledge is not an easy descent, even when not injured. MJ takes Shelly's good hand and helps her down. Against his advice, she walks to the very edge and lets the wind spin her hair into tangles. She doesn't mind. Still clutching the wedding photo, she holds it out at arm's length. Cold air rushing deep toward the canyon floor forces warm wind to the canyon's rim. She swears she can hear her mom's voice. "MJ? Can you hear that?"

"No, just the wind. What do you hear, Shelly?"

She turns to him with tears in her eyes, still clutching the photo. "It's my mom's voice. She's begging me to forgive and let love rule my heart. That the only thing vindictiveness brings is a bitter, unforgiving spirit. Forgiveness can never be substituted or disavowed in the human spirit. Do you believe that, MJ?"

"Yes, Shelly, I always have. And your mom just told you this?" He looks at his watch. "We've only been here for five minutes."

"I swear it was Mom, MJ. She comforted me and is leading me down a new pathway. One towards forgiveness and love."

"It wouldn't be the first time, dear Shelly. I've come to this place many times. I didn't hear your mom. But I have heard that someone special would enter my life." He turns and takes her hands. "Someone maybe like you. Is it possible these things can happen so fast?"

Shelly replies, "I believe it's entirely possible." She embraces MJ with her good arm and kisses him tenderly on his lips.

Three days later, Matthew Martin Johannsen asks for the great honor of escorting Shelly to tomorrow's wedding on the canyon rim. He stammers, "Lorraine bought you a bridesmaid dress, but I promise not to help you put it on, although I am sorely tempted. I bought you a corsage. Will you, please? Issac will escort Claire."

"I would be most pleased, MJ. But I will dress myself this time."

"That's fine. I, um, I'm not too good with makeup and such things."

The wedding is no small affair. Guests are bussed in from Kinneysville, most of whom having no idea where in the world they were. Fortunately, the wind cooperates and blows away from the stables and corrals for the ceremony, not that it matters much.

MJ's father, Pastor Owen Johannsen, officiates and proudly announces that the groom may kiss the bride. He then announces that it is his great pleasure and honor to introduce Mr. and Mrs. Lionel Henslaw. Ginny sings the final song, "Listening to Silence." Mattie accompanies with his guitar. The music floats over the gathered crowd and drifts into the canyon. Claire Jensen catches the bouquet. The applause is rumored to reach all the way to Kinneysville. The festivities last well into the early morning hours. Old Rascal makes a fine feast.

Early the next morning, Shelly, Claire, MJ, and his brother Issac are enjoying cups of very strong coffee, sitting on the Adirondack chairs that Ginny had bequeathed to the trailer. Claire is still clutching the bouquet and smiles invitingly at Issac. They spy a couple walking arm in arm down the small incline toward them. The sun shining on their backs makes them appear as if on fire.

"Hey, look," Shelly says quite pleased. "It's Dad and Ginny, best man and maid of honor."

Even from a distance, Shelly recognizes that her dad is a man transformed. Gone are the worry lines in his face. The perpetual frown has given way to a bashful smile. He actually appears taller but she knows that the weight of his illness has been lifted up and away by the woman attached to his right arm.

"Just look at them, Claire, I think they really are on fire. It's as if they were made for each other, predestined and eternal. Ginny is giving him his life back and mending our family." She remembers some words that Owen had spoken to her during the reception. "My dearest Shelly. Always live every day in the reality of God's forgiveness. Otherwise, one's life descends to misery and bitterness without much hope of escape. Promise me you'll try?" Shelly Jensen, with tears streaming down her cheeks, gives Owen her solemn oath that she'll do better than just try. Her soul expands with undeniable freedom. She finally knows how Claire feels.

As she hugs Ginny, Owen's words are deeply embedded in her soul. She whispers to Ginny, "You saved our family, Ginny. How can we ever thank you?"

She hugs her father around his neck. "I love you, Pops. I love you so much. Thanks for being my dad."

# About the Author

Philip Marks was born and raised in Seattle. He is also the author of the novel *Brothers of the Wind*. A member of the Nature Conservancy and the Society for Ecological Restoration, he is active in environmental issues. Philip is a graduate of Washington State University. He lives in Issaquah, Washington, with his wife, Suzanne.

CPSIA information can be obtained
at www.ICGtesting.com
Printed in the USA
LVHW01s0010010518
575513LV00001B/197/P

9 781640 030503